Rise of the Tang Dynasty

Rise of the Tang Dynasty

The Reunification of China and the Military Response to the Steppe Nomads (AD581-626)

Julian Romane

Pen & Sword
MILITARY

First published in Great Britain in 2018 by
Pen & Sword Military
an imprint of
Pen & Sword Books Ltd
47 Church Street
Barnsley
South Yorkshire
S70 2AS

Copyright © Julian Romane 2018

ISBN 978 1 47388 777 0

Printed and bound in England by TJ International Ltd, Padstow, Cornwall

Pen & Sword Books Limited incorporates the imprints of Atlas, Archaeology,
Aviation, Discovery, Family History, Fiction, History, Maritime, Military,
Military Classics, Politics, Select, Transport, True Crime, Air World,
Frontline Publishing, Leo Cooper, Remember When, Seaforth Publishing,
The Praetorian Press, Wharncliffe Local History, Wharncliffe Transport,
Wharncliffe True Crime and White Owl.

For a complete list of Pen & Sword titles please contact
PEN & SWORD BOOKS LIMITED
47 Church Street, Barnsley, South Yorkshire, S70 2AS, England
E-mail: enquiries@pen-and-sword.co.uk
Website: www.pen-and-sword.co.uk

Contents

Acknowledgements

Special Thanks

I need to thank my editor, Philip Sidnell, for his interest and encouragement. I deeply appreciate his handling of my work. I also want to thank Matt Jones, Amy Jordan, and Clive Watson of Pen & Sword for their care and hard work making my manuscript into a book.

I also want to thank two people who are long gone but who directed my attention to the beauty and importance of the Chinese people. Both were teachers at Beloit College in the early Sixties. The first is Professor Gustav Johnson, who spent the Second World War in China. He brought an immediacy and broader vision of current events in China following that war. The second is that prince of historians, Bob Irrmann; always insightful, he spent time discussing the image of Chinese society pictured in Bland and Backhouse's *China under the Empress Dowager* and lent me a copy of Der Ling's *Old Buddha*, another image of Tzu Hsi.

I thank my wife, Judy, for her forbearance and patience that allowed me to write this book.

Any errors in this work are mine alone.

Technical Issues

Dealing with Chinese history, one is faced with numerous technical problems. Firstly, the transliteration of Chinese words into European tongues is not only controversial, but often it represents a political orientation. The older Wade-Giles method was used by the Kuomintang of Chiang Kai-shek (whose name is his personal transliteration) and often stands in opposition to the Zhongguo Gongchandang of Mao Zedong. The Chairman, Mao, instituted an official transliteration format: Pinyin. There are arguments over which method is better, but often the result is more of a political decision than anything else. Those who oppose Red China use Wade-Giles; those who support Red China use Pinyin. Over the years, however, tensions between the People's Republic of China and the Atlantic states have lessened. The scholars in the Peoples' Republic have long been producing high-quality historical works. Clearly, the future of Chinese historical investigation is in their hands. So I use Pinyin.

Secondly, translations of Chinese texts leave a lot to be desired. Many translators use exotic English words to translate Chinese characters; for instance, 'erudite scholar', which could just as accurately be 'accomplished scholar'. I try to use simple English to translate Chinese because, in my experience, Chinese speakers want to be direct and clear. Titles are another issue. The Five Titles of Nobility - *gong*, *hou*, *bo*, *zi*, *nan* - are used from at least the late Shang throughout Chinese history until 1911. Tzu Hsi and her court convinced the British to translate them into English feudal titles: *gong* becomes duke; *hou* becomes marquis; *bo* becomes earl; *zi* becomes viscount; and *nan* becomes baron. This may have been a good idea for diplomatic usage, but it is utterly ridiculous for historical usage. Chinese history has many ins and outs, but there is absolutely nothing like medieval English feudalism in Chinese history. To call the member of the early Zhou Dynasty the Duke of Zhou makes no sense. I translate *gong* as Lord and *Hou* as Master.

As translation aids, I have found the following most useful: Rick Harbaugh, *Chinese Characters a Genealogy and Dictionary* (Yale, 2009); Quanyu Huang et al, *McGraw-Hill's Chinese Dictionary and Guide* (New York, 2010); and Paul Kroll, *A Student's Dictionary of Classical and Medieval Chinese* (Leiden, 2015).

Introduction

China and her Military

In the early twenty-first century, the Peoples' Republic of China is a respected military power. But since the mid-nineteenth century, European commentators have derided and ridiculed Chinese military operations. The Chinese Empire did suffer defeat after defeat at European and then Japanese hands. Yet few looked at the objective factors causing these defeats, because as long as they continued, it didn't matter to anybody. A typical opinion of the Chinese military was: '[I]t was crystal clear to even the most unreconstructed Chinese that firecrackers, gong beating, spears, and generals far to the rear in yellow mandarin coats were not the answer to western arms' (Kemp Tolley, *Yangtze Patrol*, p.9). In actual fact, a close look at the European-Chinese wars in the nineteenth century shows that the Chinese did not do as bad as later accounts assume. We should recall that in 1808, the British decided that they would occupy Macao before the French did, and sent six warships with two companies of 30 Regiment, two companies from the Bengal European Regiment and with 600 sepoys to occupy the place. The local Chinese authorities mobilized their forces and the British saw that they were too strong to attack, but they would also repel the French. If the British in 1842 had brought part of Wellington's army and Nelson's fleet to Canton, the Chinese would have fought them to a stalemate if not outright defeat. Chinese matchlocks were not like those of the Thirty Years' War; they were light, compared to the Brown Bess, mass-produced and cheap. Chinese artillery was as good as most European guns. The Chinese ships, a green water navy to be sure, were manoeuvrable and hardy.

Two main factors lead to the Chinese defeat in 1842: British military improvements and Qing political difficulties. British innovations in weapons and machinery since 1815 stunned the Chinese. Elite European troops were using percussion muskets, and the Europeans also had exploding artillery shells. Then there was the *Nemeses*, a steel (not iron-clad) steam-driven ship with two cannons, shooting explosive shells. It was a weapon unlike anything produced before. It amazed the Chinese, as it did the Europeans. More significant in the long run, the Qing Dynasty was not a 'Chinese' institution but was the instrument of the Manchu ruling nationality dominating and oppressing the Han majority. Chinese men had to shave their forehead and grow the rest of their hair long in a pigtail (the queue). The Manchu favoured certain Han men, making them 'honorary' Manchus, but the vast majority of Chinese – peasants and gentry, merchants and soldiers – were second-class subjects of the Qing Dynasty. As far as the Manchu rulers were concerned, the heart of their empire was Manchuria and northern China. Mongolia and the steppe lands were more important to the dynasty than the lands south of the Yangzi River. The fact that the Western pirates were attacking the south-eastern ocean coast was no more significant to the imperial regime than steppe pirates attacking Tibet.

The Qing had two armed forces: the most important were the Banner Manchu force, elite formations made up of select troops for the most part but also including reservists, retired and sinecure troopers; the other was the Green Standard army, a conscript militia left over from the Ming Dynasty. This army was a constabulary that functioned as a police force, controlling public order. Not particularly well trained or armed, these were the forces the Qing threw against frontier raiders, including the British. The Qing held their elite forces back from the fray in the First Opium War because they did not see themselves as seriously threatened. What really damaged the Qing forces were the massive armed upheavals connected with the Taiping Rebellion (1850-64). Without European and American assistance, the Qing Dynasty may well have gone under. As it was, the struggle seriously weakened the Qing, who managed something of a comeback under the brilliant, unscrupulous and cunning Tz'u Hsi (*pinyin* Cixi), the Manchu Empress Dowager (ruled 1861-1908). Tz'u Hsi played all her opponents against each other in a minuet of astounding virtuosity, but, unfortunately, while she secured her power, the empire ran at cross-purposes.

For the rest of the history of the Qing Dynasty, the contradiction between the interest and concerns of the Manchu regime and the needs and desires of the Chinese peoples, as complex and diverse as they were, distorted the course of military operations. Because of this contradiction, the Chinese military looked particularly inept and archaic. The problem was that lost battles were often more useful to Manchu interests than battles won. And so into the twentieth century, European, American and Japanese commentators described the Chinese military as a joke. When, after many embarrassing defeats, the Qing administrators finally began developing an effective armed force, that force soon removed the dynasty from power.

However, the founding of the Republic of China did not clear up all the questions about what a 'New China' should look like. The interregnum lasted almost forty years, a time full of local warlords' battles, the rise of the *Chunghwa Minkuo* (Chinese Republic) and the great march north, the founding and growth of the *Kuomintang* (Nationalist Party) and the *Zhong Gong* (Communist Party), the Long March, the Japanese invasion and constant wars, three- and four-sided. With the establishment of the *Zhonghua Renmin Gongheguo* (People's Republic of China) in 1949, the leaders of the New China saw themselves as the masters of a modern army, made in a Chinese manner, using tactics designed for a Chinese style of warfare. The New China's army went to Korea.

Field Commander Peng Dehuai's offensives against the UN forces in Korea, starting in November 1950, certainly surprised General MacArthur and President Truman, leading to Truman's firing of the general amidst great consternation. While Chairman Mao's objective of throwing the UN forces off the Korean peninsula was not accomplished, the Red Chinese offensives kept the 38th parallel as the front line. Marshal Peng Dehuai pushed for a Soviet-style armed force, but fell afoul of the Chairman's vision of a Cultural Revolution. He died in prison. After the Chairman's death and the repudiation of the Gang of Four, Deng Xiaoping and his supporters began building an effective modern armed force. Today, the People's Liberation Army, with air and sea forces, is indeed a power to be reckoned with. Offering security to the People's Republic and causing fear to others, the Chinese military represents the results of millennia of successful development.

Problems of Chinese Military History

In order to see this process clearly, we need to understand that 'traditional' China is an illusion. Technological change and resulting economic and social elaboration are always part of Chinese history. There are great literary traditions in China, along with great artistic, philosophical and spiritual traditions, but there has never been a 'traditional' China. This is true especially for the history of the Qing Dynasty through the nineteenth century, when the Western Powers assumed the conditions they found in China had always been there. The Empress Dowager, Tz'u Hsi, readily supported this perception because it furthered her Manchu agenda. In many of the accounts of Chinese history, China often appears singularly isolated from much of the rest of the world, but this too is an illusion. A very different writing system continues to hinder Western scholars' understanding of East Asian literature and history, creating an image of endless cycles of unchanging despotism. In actual fact, East Asian civilization is as changing and voidable as that of Western Europe. Just as European society drew inspiration and ideas from the Mediterranean and Near East, so China constantly received new influences from across the Great Steppe Sea and across the seas of the East Indies.

Another of the main impediments to understanding Chinese history and society is the 'anti-military' attitude of many Western commentators. Chinese is an unfamiliar language to Western historians, and those competent in Chinese studies have long been uninterested and unknowing about military matters. We have many translations of Chinese spiritual and philosophical classics, all well and good, but of Chinese histories, there are very few. I need to mention Burton Watson's valiant efforts of a partial translation of the *Shiji*, along with Nienhauser's attempt of the same (ten volumes long so far, started in 1995, still not complete and expensive). There is also Richard Davis' translation of Ouyang Xiu's *Historical Records of the Five Dynasties* and Michael Rogers, translator of the *Fu Chien Chronicle*. That is all, yet these are no harder to translate than Thucydides or Livy.

When European and American Chinese experts do write about military affairs, they fail to understand the subject. Hans Bielenstein, in his *Restoration of the Han Dynasty* (1953), gives a credible translation of Hou Han Shu's account of the battle of K'un-yang (Pinyin: Kunyang, 7 July AD 23). He concludes the account with the following: 'However, apart from a few main facts, the account is much too vivid not to have been improved by the historian. The description is highly dramatic and therefore highly unreliable' (p.79). As Eisenhower observed, 'War is not a game of chess; it is a drama.' Descriptions of battles in Greco-Roman literature are vivid and dramatic, but certainly seem reliable. Michael Rogers, in his excellent translation of the *Fu Chien Chronicle*, concludes that the celebrated Battle of Fei River never really happened. This ignores basic understandings of military events, as David Graff points out (*Medieval Chinese Warfare*, p.68). Here, I need to note exceptions: David Graff and Peter Lorge have written excellent studies of Chinese military history. Ralph Sawyer's insightful translations and analyses of the classic handbooks are always rewarding. While not as accessible, the superb works of Rafe de Crespigny demonstrate a mastery of the subject. Nor do Chinese scholars themselves ignore the subject. There are current editions of all the *Twenty-Four Histories* and a vast secondary literature on Chinese military history, with multi-volume sets of books describing historical campaigns in great detail.

The Purpose of this Book

There are three purposes to this book: to give a detailed picture of medieval Chinese warfare; to provide background to the structure of Chinese military development; and to illustrate how influences passed across the Eurasian 'world island'. The description of a specific time in the history of Chinese military development is from AD 589-626, an age which saw the rise of a unified imperial institution, modelled on the older Han Empire (206 BC-AD 220) but very different in many ways. The social and political developments of this time gave rise to a dynamic cultural fluorescence which still shines brightly. The result of centuries of upheaval and innovation, the new imperial structure brought together pieces from all parts of the Eurasian world. Building on their accomplishments, creative, able people struggled against each other and constructed a new way of dealing with their human problems. They established institutions which maintained those basic values they favoured, and these institutions preserved and extended the power of their creators and their creators' successors.

The political-military narrative recounts the rise of the Sui Dynasty and its collapse, followed by the emergence and success of the Tang Dynasty. This is a well-trod tale in Chinese history writing. The sources are good; there are material remains, and important and interesting personalities highlight the events. But it is not well known outside East Asia. I support my narrative with appendices that explore significant background aspects of these events. Often appearing far-off, these aspects explain the course of my narrative by recounting important impetuses of these events and how we understand them. I look at the connections of East Asian civilization across the Eurasian 'world island'. Here we see the rise and development of human-horse culture: military forces start as foot soldiers, but the introduction of horses in different ways changed fighting technology and so changed the fighters. Victorious societies had to change their allocation of resources to accommodate successful soldiers. This is the main theme of my narrative.

I want to be clear: this is a tale about power; brutal violent military power that crushes opposition by killing people and destroying property. This is the way of war. People make decisions about how they relate to other people in a stable, efficient order of affairs through some political process. But people often don't agree on just what that order should be or how some people impose it on others. When disagreements are sharp and factions determined, the result is war. The utility of organized violence can easily cut through a whole world of problems. This has always been a part of Chinese political practice: the Chinese way of war.

Part I

THE HOUSE OF YANG

Order out of Chaos

The Central Realm had shattered centuries before. However, the memory of a unified state, at peace and prosperous, remained strong. Nomad tribes occupied the northern lands, while along the great river in the south waves of refugees from the north founded weak regimes which followed each other in succession, each claiming universal dominion over the whole of the realm but most having trouble keeping the peace in their provinces. In the north, historians saw the emergence of the 'Sixteen Kingdoms' (AD 304-439), military states based on the strong cavalry armies of invading nomadic tribes. Haughty horsemen held the peasantry in thrall. Cities contracted into ceremonial centres and supply bases. There remained only a shadow of the mercantile and cultural interests of the Han Dynasty. In the south, along the Yangtze, in the rich rice-producing lands, northerners brought the culture of Han aristocrats, but intermingled and eventually merged with the local elites who remembered the ways of the ancient kingdoms of Chu and Wu.

In the great city of Jiankang (Nanjing), an emperor ruled with the majesty and stature of a Son of Heaven, without, however, the military strength and political force to do anything other than maintaining rituals and ceremonies in lands where the northern horsemen could not go. Here, the imperial court still spoke in the dialect of destroyed Luoyang and wrote proclamations in the most classical of Han styles. Beyond the few great cities and their hinterlands, Chinese farmers pressed forward, pushing aborigines back, settling the land with rice terraces, villages, temples and religious communities. The elegance and luxury of the south clashed against the simplicity and hardness of the north.

The armies in the south remained the legions of foot soldiers that founded the imperial realm under the Qin dynasty (255-206 BC) and maintained it under the Han (206 BC–AD 220). We can see the original of this force in the reconstructed remains of the First Emperor's terracotta army. Here, an infantry legion of some 6,000 foot, divided into battalions of 600 men, stands ready to march. The soldiers carried swords, pole weapons and crossbows. Strong chariot forces supported the foot, sixty two-wheeled carts pulled by four horses. Leather and iron armour protected the elite troops. These powerful striking forces received support from conscripted farmers, whose job it was to carry supplies and dig fortifications. During active operations, the recruits carried spears. The large southern armies built and defended fortifications along the Yangtze and Huai Rivers. Fleets of large riverboats transported and gave support to the southern troops. Never united in one centralized force, the southern armies marched under the command of local land-owning potentates who recruited and commanded their units. They usually recognized the suzerainty of the emperor, but looked to local interests.

In the north, horse soldiers dominated the battlefield. Nomadic tribes had been migrating into the Central Realm for generations. Their light horse archers often swept local infantry forces away. However, from about AD 350, a new technology and weapon came out of Inner Asia, which crashed down on surrounding states. With the development of the stirrup, heavy cavalry produced a powerful energy. Armoured horsemen scattered infantry and horse archers alike. With long lances, shields and new fine curved steel sabres, bearing pennants and plumes, the heavy horse dominated the battlefield. Those who controlled pastures and stud farms became the lords of war. From farming scholar-bureaucrats and nomadic war chiefs, power shifted into the hands of landowners who raised horses and lived in fortified manor houses.

Northern and Southern Dynasties (386–581)
Dynastic Succession in the South

According to later imperial historians, the Wei Dynasty founded by Cao Cao (AD 220) was the legitimate successor of the fallen Han Dynasty. Holding the lands of the Yellow River, Wei was the strongest of the successors to Han, although two other kingdoms held power in other lands once held by Han. Only in 263 did Wei conquer the kingdom of Shu in the Sichuan valley. A successful general of Wei, Sima-Yan, overthrew Wei, founded the Jin Dynasty and conquered the remaining kingdom of Wu. In 280, the Central Realm found unity again. However, the times of chaos had badly damaged the administrative organization of the Han Dynasty. The decades of civil war and upheaval left strong men who controlled fortified settlements in charge of much of the productive lands. Only slowly was the central state reimposing its power in many local areas. Such efforts did not set well with the large imperial family of the Jin Dynasty, and in the early decades of the next century, the princes of the House of Jin joined together to oppose the central authority of their dynasty. Successful, they then fell out over the division of the spoils. As they battled with each other, the weaker princes called on the nomadic tribes living within and beyond the empire to come and aid their cause. Soon these tribes fought for the highest bidder, and then for themselves. They burned cities. They enslaved whole populations. Many people fled south, including Jin princes who founded the Eastern Jin Dynasty (317-419) in the Yangtze area.

The Jin Dynasty fell to a usurping general who founded the Song Dynasty (420-479), called Liu Song by later historians to distinguish it from the centuries-later great Song Dynasty (960-1279). Under powerful leaders, Emperors Wu and Wen, the southern empire advanced to the Yellow River. These rulers united almost all of the Central Realm except the northern lands occupied by the nomadic tribes. While Emperor Song Wen attempted to organize a Confucian civil bureaucracy, power remained in the hands of great families. These families often supported Buddhist temples and monasteries. Since the collapse of the Han Dynasty, Buddhist ideas and institutions came into the Central Realm's lands. Traditional Confucian scholars disagreed with Buddhist values, and the Buddhists saw Confucian ideals as empty. This antipathy was, for the most part, intellectual rather than violent, although such controversy was often a mask for power struggles between different factions in the bureaucracy. Under succeeding emperors, the Liu Song Dynasty weakened; northern forces pushed the southern empire back to the Yangtze and the administration lost focus. The last emperor retired at the request of the leader of another great family.

This family established the Qi Dynasty (479-502). The emperors of Qi sought to identify their rule with the growing Buddhist influences while they struggled to maintain power amid the ongoing intrigues of great families. The dynasty soon fell into weak hands, and the leader of another great family took the name of Emperor Wu and founded the Liang Dynasty (502-57). Emperor Liang Wu spent his long reign (502-49) supporting and spreading the Buddhist faith. While war raged with the northern horsemen regimes, the Liang emperor became a Buddhist monk sometimes, struggled with his sons' revolts and just managed to hold the empire together until a successful rebellion by his sons took away his power, quickly followed by his death. Revolt, pestilence, famine and chaos swept the dynasty away in eight years' time. The rebel Chen Baxian killed the last Liang emperor, who was 16 years old, and founded the Chen Dynasty (557-89). The Chen rulers, some good and some not, could accomplish very little in their ravaged, chaotic lands.

The Northern Dynasties

With the retreat of the Jin Dynasty to the south (316–17), Northern China along the Yellow River fell into anarchy. Within a few years, historians observed that the region was a land of armies but no empire, while Southern China was an empire with no armies. The northern horsemen warlords gathered followings and built states, but as soon as they found defeat or death, a new warlord emerged and started over again. Defeated tribal units simply joined the victor and supported him until the next successful leader appeared. Amidst the chaos, the rulers kept the Chinese masses and the nomadic warriors separated. More importantly, the constant raids, plundering and disorder caused significant depopulation. The northern rulers fought over masses of the population rather than land. The emerging states moved whole populations to the areas of their new capitals as regimes waxed and faded. The numbers of people driven from place to place were in the tens to hundreds of thousands. Chinese populations in defensible areas constructed fortresses and resisted or bargained with the nomadic tribal leaders. These fortresses soon formed leagues and became political-military powers within the chaos.

A successful nomadic warrior captain, Tuoba Gui, organized a new state, the Empire of Northern Wei, and proclaimed himself Emperor Daowu in 398. Tuoba Gui reorganized the tribal forces into a hereditary military-service class bound to the state rather than their commander. The Northern Wei professional hereditary army became the strongest force in Northern China. These armies conquered the Yellow River basin by 450 and sent expeditionary forces to the Yangtze. The dynasty rested on Tuoba military rule, but the administration was simply *ad hoc*. Many at the apex of power saw that a Chinese style of adminis-tration would increase wealth and military power. In 493, the Emperor Xiaowen decreed that the dynasty would become Chinese. The emperor moved the capital to Luoyang. He ordered that all dress in Chinese style and speak only Chinese. The dynasty unified the ranks of both the tribes and the Chinese into one sys-tem and encouraged intermarriage. Those military districts with many Chinese became civil provinces run by Chinese governors. The Wei disbanded the Tuoba professional army, replacing it with Chinese militia for local defence, posting the best soldiers to a field army based in the capital and sending others to garrisons on the northern frontiers.

The reform of the Wei state failed. The Tuoba warriors sent to the frontiers found that their tribal ways, once marks of status and importance, became signs of inferiority and weakness. New recruits sent by the government were simply convicts sentenced to the frontiers. Support in the form of food and goods began to run short. The neglect and abuse developed into a pattern impossible to ignore. In 524, the garrisons rebelled and within a year dominated the countryside north of the Yellow River. The Wei court called on a tribal confederation in Shanxi, the Jie Hu – an Iranian people – to rescue the court. Under their leader, Erzhu Rong, the tribal army marched to Luoyang in 528. The Jie Hu killed any opposition in the court and crushed the rebels. Intending to control the state, Rong installed a puppet emperor. However, the emperor turned on Rong, ambushed him and killed him with his own hand. The result was a return to chaos. In the upheavals of war and confusion, in 534 a large armed force sent to quell disruption in the Wei Valley found itself leaderless and without direction. The army, mostly Xianbei, elected a talented young man, Yuwen Tai, as commander. At the same time, a Wei emperor fled to Chang'an while another appeared at Luoyang. Yuwen Tai killed this Northern Wei emperor and installed a different member of that dynasty.

The result was that the Wei Empire split into two, the Eastern Wei and the Western Wei. In 550, the Eastern Wei fell to the Northern Qi Dynasty. When Yuwen Tai died in 556, a nephew, Yuwen Hu, deposed the Western Wei Emperor Tong and installed Yuwen Tai's son, Yuwen Jue, as the first emperor of the new Zhou Dynasty, later known as the Northern Zhou. Both empires were the holdings of military commanders who directly controlled large armies through dependent subordinate officers. The Northern Qi Dynasty had the upper hand because they could recruit tribal warriors more readily than could Northern Zhou, concentrated as it was in the 'Lands within the Passes'. To increase his strength, the Northern Zhou Emperor Wu accepted the armies of local warlords, making the warlords into officers and inducting the men into the imperial army. The armies had soldiers of both tribal and Chinese background organized into twenty-four major units (the '24 Armies') with officers shifted around so that they did not command troops loyal specifically to them. The new armies proved very loyal to the state. The strong armies led to the emergence of an effective civil administration staffed by local landowners.

Yuwen Hu, a harsh and demanding person, managed the Northern Zhou regime successfully. He maintained control of the military and administration through the reigns of three of Yuwen Tai's sons. The third son, Emperor Wu, killed Yuwen Hu (572) and gathered power into his hands. Emperor Wu (560–578) was capable and energetic; he issued an edict that ordered the closure of both the Daoist and Buddhist establishments. He insisted that his subjects follow the Ruists' teachings and traditional rituals that followed those teachings. At this time, Northern Zhou faced the Northern Qi Dynasty. Their incompetent emperor, Wen Xuan, known as the 'merry monarch', was a child-like stutterer. Emperor Wu's armies seized Luoyang in 578 and pursued the fleeing Qi royalty, capturing and killing Wen Xuan and his son in 577. Sadly for the Northern Zhou, Emperor Wu died in the next year.

References

Introduction: General Histories of China
Sui and Tang China

Materials about Chinese history in English are a very mixed bag. Some material is unusually good, while there is much that is simply pedestrian and some that are badly misconceived. At the top of the good list are a number of multi-volume sets by major scholarly institutions.

The three following are essential:

Cambridge History of China by Denis Twitchett and John Fairbanks (eds) (Cambridge UK, 1979). Specifically vol. 3, Denis C. Twitchett (ed.), *Sui and Tang China, 589-906 AD, part 1, Political History*.

History of Imperial China by Timothy Brook (ed.) (Cambridge US, 2009-10). Especially vol. 2, Mark Lewis, *China between Empires, the Northern and Southern Dynasties*; and vol. 3, Mark Lewis, *China's Cosmopolitan Empire the Tang Dynasty*.

History of Chinese Civilization by Yuan Xingrei, Yan Wenming, Zhang Chuanxi and Lou Yulie (eds) (Chinese original, Peking University Press, Beijing; English translation, Cambridge UK, 2012). Specifically vol. III, Yuan Xingpei (Ed), *Sui and Tang to mid-Ming Dynasties* (Cambridge UK, 2012).

There are numerous single-volume histories of China. Most present pre-modern China as a prologue to accounts of China from the time of the First Opium War. But for the purpose of understanding the different societies that came and went in the development of Chinese civilization, they tend to be superficial. I find the following useful:

John Fairbanks and Edwin Reischauer, *China Tradition and Transformation* (New York, 1978).

C.P. Fitzgerald, *China, a Short Cultural History* (New York, 1954).

Jacques Gernet, *History of Chinese Civilization* (Cambridge UK, 1982).

Richard von Glahn, *The Economic History of China* (Cambridge UK, 2016).

Morris Rossabi, *A History of China* (Wiley Blackwell, 2014).

Military Histories of China

Even a cursory reading of pre-industrial Chinese history finds war was a part of the normal political process. There were vast campaigns, mammoth battles and subtle strategies. There are a series of universally respected handbooks on troop deployment and use, and yet finding detailed descriptions of campaigns and battles in most of the English language literature is very unusual. One might think that the Chinese *literati* ignored such matters, being more interested in the arts of peace rather than the arts of war. But that is just wrong. While discussions of *wen* verses *wu* (civil verses military) is an important dialogue in Chinese political discourse, both Chinese sources and secondary literature cover campaigns and battle in detail. The Beijing Military Museum is a marvel of artifacts and information. The problem is with the English-language writers of academic Chinese history. They pride themselves on their commitment to peace and understanding, and so avoid the difficult questions of war. But we might point out that a major statement of the Chinese point of view is Luo Guanzhong's *Three Kingdoms*. Happy exceptions to this general condition include works by David Graff and Peter Lorge:

David Graff, *Medieval Chinese Warfare* (London, 2002).

David Graff, *Eurasian Way of War* (London, 2016).

Davis Graff and Robin Higham (eds), *A Military History of China* (Lexington, 2012).

Peter Lorge, *War, Politics and Society in Early Modern China* (London, 2005).

Peter Lorge, *The Asian Military Revolution* (Cambridge UK, 2008).

Peter Lorge, *The Reunification of China* (Cambridge UK, 2015).

Accounts of the Steppes of Central Asia

Understandings of Central Asian societies and cultures have developed only slowly. Pre-Islamic times lack any extended local narratives, so historians have stitched together events gathered from Classical, Indian and Chinese sources. The different texts are none too clear and do not readily intersect. The problems are interesting but difficult to resolve. Since the late nineteenth century, investigators on the ground – explorers and archaeologists – have found important remains which clear up a lot, if presenting some more difficult questions. The accounts of these investigators are interesting in their own right, lending local colour to understandings of these areas in history.

Old works of great interest include:

William McGovern, *Early Empires of Central Asia* (Chapel Hill, 1939).

M. Aurel Stein, *Sand-Buried Khotan* (London 1903), two volumes, text and plates (available as eBook, *Internet Achieve*).

M. Aurel Stein, *Ruins of Desert Cathay* (London, 1913), vols 1 and 2, both text and pictures (eBook, *Internet Achieve*).

Henry Yule, *Cathay and the Way Thither*, numerous editions, final edited by Henri Cordier, 1915 (eBook, *Internet Achieve*).

Henry Yule, *The Travels of Marco Polo the Complete Yule-Cordier edition* (Dover, in print).

Current works of interest:

Christopher Baumer, *The History of Central Asia, the Age of the Silk Road* (London, 2014).

Christopher Beckwith, *Empires of the Silk Road* (Princeton NJ, 2009).

H. Dani (ed.), *History of Civilizations of Central Asia,* vol. I, *the Dawn of Civilization*: *Earliest Times to 700 BC*; Janos Harmatta, vol. II, *The Development of Sedentary and Nomadic Civilizations: 700 BC to AD 250*; B.A. Litvinsky, vol. III, *The Crossroads of Civilizations: AD 250 to 750* (Paris, 1996-98).

Rene Grousset, *The Empire of the Steppes* (New Brunswick, NJ, 1970).

Denis Sinor, *The Cambridge History of Early Inner Asia* (Cambridge UK, 1990).

Sources for narrative text:

Rise and Fall of Dynasties

Chinese sources: *Jin Shu*, 4, 56, 101; *Zizhi Tongjian*, 87.

The age of disunion from the fall of Han (220 AD) to the rise of Sui (589) is well described in the following:

Albert Dien, *Six Dynasties Civilization* (New Haven, 2007).

Mark Lewis, *China between Empires* (Cambridge US, 2009).

Specific details of events:

David Graff, *Medieval Chinese Warfare*, pp.35-54.

See also, Albert Dien, 'The Stirrup and its Effect on Chinese Military History', pp.1-21, available online, Silk Road Foundation.

Dynastic Succession in the South

Chinese sources: *Jin Shu*, 62; *Nan Qi Shu*, 1, 26; *Song Shu*, 1, 63, 77; *Zizhi Tongjian*, 113, 115.

Graff, *Medieval*, pp.75-93.

The Northern Dynasties

Chinese sources: *Jin Shu*, 88; 104-07; *Wei Shu*, 24; *Zizhi Tongjian*, 94, 120.

The Chronicle of Fu Chien, A Case of Exemplar History, translated and anointed with prolegomena, by Michael C. Rogers (trans.), pp.111-91. This is an excellent work of scholarship. Unfortunately, Michael Rogers' interpretations of military history demonstrates a confusion between operational records and political spin. For a number of specific military factors, Rogers' assertion that the Battle of Fei River never happened simply makes no sense (see Graff, p.68). That said, the work is both interesting and exceedingly informative.

Graff, *Medieval*, pp.54-73.

Chapter 1

The Establishment of the Sui Dynasty

Wu's son succeeded as Emperor Xuan (578), but Xuan was insecure and paranoid. He had close relatives accused, tried and strangled to death in front of the whole court. He reversed Emperor Wu's support for the Ruists and favoured the Daoists and Buddhists. Xuan, as crown prince Yuwen Yun, had taken Yang Lihua as a wife under the direction of Emperor Wu in 573. Her father was the important commander, Puliuru Jian, Lord of Sui. Her mother was the Xianbei princess, Dugu Qieluo. When Emperor Wu died in 578, Yuwen Yun took the name Xuan and made Yang Lihua empress. As Emperor Xuan's erratic reign continued, his relations with Yang Lihua became difficult. She bore a daughter, but no sons. Imperial Consort Concubine Zhu Manyue did bear a son, Yuwen Chan. In 579, Xuan 'retired' as emperor, placing his infant son on the throne as Emperor Jing. Xuan then elevated three of his concubines as empresses, although Yang Lihua took precedence over them. Empress Yang was an agreeable person who kept good relations with the people with whom she lived. The other empresses and all the imperial consorts appreciated and loved her. When Emperor Xuan became angry with her, she calmly defended herself. This enraged the emperor. He ordered her to kill herself. When her mother, the Lady Dugu, found out, she rushed to the palace and accosted Xuan to his face. Prostrating herself, she shamed him into granting his empress pardon.

Emperor Xuan sent Puliuru Jian as commander of Yang Province to prepare for his war against the southern dynasty, the Chen. However, the emperor became ill during summer 580. Zheng Yi and Liu Fang, confidants of Xuan, recalled Jian as supreme empress's father to attend the emperor. When Xuan suddenly died, Zheng Yi issued an edict in the emperor's name, appointing Puliuru Jian regent and both Supreme Empress Yang and Empress Zhu mother of the heir, as empress dowagers. They acted secretly and swiftly because they feared opposition from Yuchi Jiong, the Lord of Shu. This man, a renowned field commander, was Emperor Xuan's great uncle. His granddaughter, Yuchi Chifan, had married Yuwen Wen, another of the emperor's relatives. This young woman was of great beauty; the Emperor Xuan did not resist his lust, drugging and raping her. Xuan then discovered that a close relative of the woman's husband was plotting to overthrow him. In retaliation, Xuan had executed the man and Yuchi Chifan's husband, and took Yuchi Chifan into the palace, making her the fourth empress.

If Yuchi Jiong could elevate his granddaughter to empress dowager, he could control the empire after he eliminated the Puliuru clan. Puliuru Jian, planning to neutralize this threat, sent Yuchi Jiong's son to Xiang Province to summon Jiong to the capital for Xuan's funeral. To replace Yuchi Jiong as a field commander, Puliuru Jian sent Yuchi Jiong's rival, Wei Xiaokuan. Instead, Yuchi Jiong declared that Puliuru Jian planned to seize the throne and announced that he would protect the Imperial House of Zhou. He elevated to be emperor a son of Xuan's brother. Some regional commanders rallied to Yuchi Jiong, most important of whom was the master of the south along with the commander of the south-west. However, both the commander of Shanxi and the vassal state of Western Liang remained loyal to Chang'an.

When Wei Xiaokuan approached Xiang Province, he found out that Yuchi was planning to arrest him. Without forces to defend himself, he gave out that he was ill and began to return to Luoyang. At each post, he instructed the local officials to give Yuchi's men a friendly welcome. The soldiers saw no threat and did not search for Wei, who found safety in Luoyang. He took charge of the city and prepared the walls for defence. The Xianbei soldiers who garrisoned Luoyang initially supported Yuchi but remained quiet. Regent Puliuru Jian sent reinforcements to Commander Wei with orders to eliminate Yuchi. Wei attacked Yuchi's force in Henan, then crossed the Yellow River to the north and advanced toward Yecheng. Yuchi Dun, son of Yuchi Jiong, massed troops to receive Wei's force, but Wei dispersed them. Yuchi Jiong, in thrall to his secretary and second wife, could think of nothing but to hold out. Wei set up siege lines and prepared to take the city. After some two months, Wei took the city, killing all the defenders. Wei sent Yuchi Jiong's son's father-in-law to tell Yuchi that Wei would grant him the time to commit suicide. This Yuchi did, after strongly condemning Puliuru Jian. Wei had Yuchi's family executed, including his sons. Wei returned to Puliuru Jian in Chang'an, but died a month later.

After the destruction of Yuchi Jiong in late 580, Puliuru Jian found himself in danger. He had gained sufficient power and influence with important local potentates that he controlled the area of Chang'an and the 'Lands within the Passes'. His influence spread along the Yellow River through Luoyang, but only if his primary base in Chang'an held. His power rested, however, on the fact that he was the minister of the child Zhou emperor, Jing. Many members of Jing Di's family, the House of Yuwen, looked to Puliuru Jian's swift elimination. As Puliuru Jian's wife, Wenxian put it, 'When riding a tiger, spur him on rather than try to get off.' Support came to the Yuwen opposition from the Southern Empire under the House of Chen. Jian charged the Yuwen princes with treason and executed all of them. Gathering offices and honours, Puliuru Jian took the name Yang and proclaimed himself Emperor Wen of the Sui Dynasty in 581. The deposed child Emperor Jing received a high title as a great lord but soon perished.

The Sui Administration

Among his first acts, Emperor Wen posthumously elevated his parents – his father now named Yang Zhong and his mother Lady Lu – to emperor and empress. His wife, Lady Dugu, he elevated to empress, and his eldest son, Yang Yong, to the imperial heir. His other sons and his brothers became imperial princes. He appointed his close associates as high administrators and depended on their advice. These three administrators – Su Wei, Yang Su and Gao Jiong – were distinguished men and officials under the Western Wei and Northern Zhou regimes, but at one time or another had fallen out of favour. All three were particularly disliked by Emperor Xuan and so were ready to support their friend, the new emperor. Together, these four reformed and consolidated the new state. They abolished the old system of six departments filled with cronies of the former emperor's families, concubines and eunuchs, and instead set up five main offices: an office of management, of personnel through examination, of law making, of records and of palace administration. There were also independent officers to oversee governmental function and law enforcement. Twelve main commands managed the Twenty Four Armies. Emperor Wen sent out his sons with cadres of advisors to maintain imperial representation in the provinces. The new administration began a reform of criminal law, changing the harsh codes imposed by the nomadic states, decreasing penalties and requiring more rigorous standards of proof for conviction. The resulting code remained in general use through imperial history. Emperor Wen issued orders to mobilize his forces for an attack on the southern empire along the Yangzi, but when he found out that the emperor of Chen had died, he suspended the operation, saying that it was not right to attack a state that had just lost its emperor. Perhaps he saw the Chen Empire falling into his hands without a struggle. In 582, Emperor Wen decided the old and shabby city of Chang'an was not fit to house the new state. He founded a new city, Daxing (Great Prosperity), some miles to the south-west of the ancient Chang'an. The city design was immense, some 30 square miles in area. Ultimately, the city became known as Chang'an, replacing the older site.

The economy of China rested on the farms in the river valleys, notably the Yellow River and its tributaries, the Fen, Wei and Luo. For two millennia, the people of these valleys had fought floods and built irrigation systems. The banks of the Yellow River stood above the level of the plains surrounding them. Floods burst these banks and swept away land plots, villages and even cities. Maintaining control of the river was a constant project. Government organizations built channels that diverted water to safe areas and connected towns and cities. These were very useful but tended to disintegrate with time, particularly when there was no central state to coordinate efforts. Under the new Sui dynasty, the pressing problems with the Yellow River system became a crisis. In 584, the supply route for bulk provision from the Yellow River valley up the Wei River to Daxing failed. Emperor Wen appointed Yuwen Kai to oversee the construction of a canal along the length of the Wei River from Daxing to the Tong Pass. This new Guangtong Canal allowed the transport of large amounts of food and other goods. While the canal remained under construction in the autumn, famine struck Guanzhong. The emperor and court temporarily moved to Luoyang. To connect a water route to the Yangzi, Emperor Wen began the construction of the Shanyang Canal between the Yangzi and Huai Rivers in spring 587. This allowed movement of goods from the Yangzi to Guangtong but also aided the effort to concentrate forces against Chen.

Emperor Wen of Sui, his advisors and administrators merged Ruist theory with Buddhist practices. The result was an effective and efficient administration based on powerful military families of nomad-Chinese descent, controlling herds of horses, along with educated Chinese officials who managed large agrarian populations. Balancing strong cavalry forces with large infantry formations allowed Emperor Wen to protect his holdings and project his power toward both north and south.

The Sui Empire's neighbours

Emperor Sui Wen's north China realm included the Wei and Yellow Rivers, the Sichuan Basin and the Huai River lands. The realm faced three powers that denied Sui supremacy. There was a small enclave, Western Liang, the rump of an old Southern Dynasty, south of Sichuan. There was the current Southern Dynasty, the Chen, along the Yangzi River to the south. To the north stretched the extensive Turkish Khanate. The Western Liang enclave maintained an adroit balance between the Northern and Southern Dynasties. Western Liang Emperor Ming had not supported the efforts of Yuchi Jiong when he tried to remove Yang Jian in 580 and made clear his recognition of Yang Jian as overlord. In recompense, Emperor Wen removed the expensive garrison installed in the Western Liang capital, Jiangling. Moreover, he had his son, Yang Guang, Prince of Jin, marry Emperor Ming's daughter, elevating her to princess.

After the Liang Emperor Ming died (585), his successor, Emperor Jing, maintained his loyalty to the Sui. In 587, Emperor Wen ordered Jing to meet him in Daxing. While Jing was in Daxing, Emperor Wen sent his commander, Cui Hongdu, to secure Jiangling. When the Sui force approached the Liang capital, Jing's uncle, Xiao Yan, Prince of Anping, and his brother, Xiao Huan, Prince of Yixing, believed the Sui were going to take over Western Liang. They evacuated Jiangling and surrendered themselves and their entourages to the Chen commander, Chen Huiji, cousin of the Chen Emperor Shubao. They hoped to induce a war which would break Sui power. Emperor Wen immediately ordered his forces to take over Western

Liang, occupying the country and capital, and reorganized the state into provinces of the Sui Empire. The former Emperor Jing now became Lord of Ju.

From the time of the collapse of the Western Zhou Dynasty (771 BC), nomadic tribes on the northern frontiers had raided, attacked and invaded the Chinese lands. One of the factors leading to the generation of a unified Chinese state was the emergence of a new power on those northern frontiers. As part of the ongoing upheavals in the time of the Western Wei and Northern Zhou, Turkish tribes seized supreme power in the northern steppes. By 552, their power extended from the Manchurian Mountains to Lake Baikal in Central Asia. An official Sui document described the northern nomads: 'The Turks prefer to destroy each other rather than live side by side. They have a thousand, nay, ten thousand clans who are hostile to each other and kill one another. They mourn their dead with much grief and swearing vengeance' (Sinor, p.307). The Turk forces, under their Qaghan's leadership, raided both Northern Zhou and Qi lands. The Northern Zhou Dynasty opened negotiations with the Turks while the Qi built long walls to block Turk attacks. In 555, the Qi constructed 300 miles of tamped earth walls, complete with guard towers, and added 160 miles in 556. Once Northern Zhou seized Qi, the Yuwen family (rulers of Northern Zhou) maintained close relations with the Turks with tribute and daughters as wives for princes. When Yang Jian overthrew the Northern Zhou and founded Sui, he ordered most of the Yuwen family killed. The Turk Shabolue Khan, Ashina Shetu, was married to the Northern Zhou Princess Qianjin of the House of Yuwen. She despised Yang Jian for removing her family from the throne and killing them. In 582, Ashina Shetu ordered his horsemen to raid deep into the new Sui realm. Their raids struck the north and north-west of the Wei River Valley, defeating Sui troops, plundering six commanderies and seizing vast numbers of livestock. Ashina Shetu also allied with Gao Baoning, a former Qi commander who still held Ying province (in modern Liaoning) and continued to raid the eastern frontier. The Emperor Wen decided to undermine the Shabolue Khans' hold on his subordinate commanders.

By spring 583, Emperor Wen's plans reached fulfilment. His gifts reached many of Ashina Shetu's subordinates, including the Khan's uncle, cousin and brother. The Shabolue Khan soon faced dissension within his dominion. Disagreements about policy and distribution of wealth led to conflict within the Turkish territory, and this ended the war against the Sui. In spring 583, Emperor Wen appointed his brother, Yang Shuang Prince of Wei, commander of a large cavalry army and ordered him to attack Ashina Shetu's forces. Yang Shuang routed the Qaghan's forces. Yang then detached a force under Yin Shou to attack Gao Baoning. After a resounding Sui victory, Gao tried to flee but was killed by his officers. This ended Qi resistance. In 584, Ashina Shetu recognized Emperor Wen as suzerain and Princess Qianjin referred to the emperor as 'father'. In return, he acknowledged her as Princess Dayi.

Ten years later, in 593, after Ashina Shetu had died, Emperor Wen recognized that the Princess Dayi still worked for his downfall. He sent his agent, Pei Ju, to the Tuli Khan, Ashina Rangan, subordinate to the Dulan Khan, Ashina Yongyulu, with the proposition that if he had Princess Dayi killed, Emperor Wen would reward him with a Sui princess for a wife. Ashina Rangan accused Princess Dayi of adultery; Ashina Yongyulu had her executed, and both expected Sui princesses as a reward. But Emperor Wen only allowed Ashina Rangan to marry into the Sui Dynasty. After four years of procrastination, Emperor Wen finally agreed to hold the wedding. Ashina Rangan arrived at Chang'an with his retinue. The emperor created the daughter of a rather distant clansman to be Princess Anyi, and saw her married to Ashina Rangan. As part of the wedding, Emperor Wen awarded Ashina Rangan great riches, thus tying his loyalty to the Sui more than to the head Dulan Khan, Ashina Yongyulu. Ashina Rangan maintained his commitment to the Sui in 599 when he reported Ashina Yongyulu's preparations for a great raid into the Sui dominions. The emperor decided to strike pre-emptively at the Dulan Khan's forces. Under the command of Fifth Son Yang Liang, led by his three senior advisors – Gao Jiong, Yang Su and Yan Rong – the emperor launched a three-pronged attack against Ashina Yongyulu. When he found his plans disrupted, Ashina Yongyulu called on Ashina Dianjue and other subordinate Khans to attack Ashina Rangan. Their assault broke Rangan's tribe apart, and he fled to Sui territory. Emperor Wen welcomed him, treating him as an honoured guest. Gao Jiong and Yang Su maintained pressure on Ashina Yongyulu, eventually pushing his forces away from the imperial frontiers.

In winter 599, Emperor Wen elevated Ashina Rangan to Qimin Khan. The Sui built a walled city at Hohhot to be the Qimin Khan's base and refuge. Sending a small army of crack Sui horse troopers, the emperor made sure that Ashina Rangan and his people were a power on the frontier. At this time, the Princess Anyi died. The emperor awarded Ashina Rangan another wife from a clan family, whom he elevated to be the Princess Yicheng. Intrigue continued in the Supreme Khan's court. Ashina Yongyulu soon fell to an assassin. Ashina Dianjue assumed the title Bujia Khan. Organizing the Turkish forces, he attacked Ashina Rangan, whose Sui forces repelled them. By 603, rebellions among his subjects discouraged Ashina Dianjue, who surrendered to Ashina Rangan, who now became Supreme Khan of the Turkic Empire.

Sui Conquest of Chen

The Chen Dynasty, the fourth and last of the Southern Dynasties, was a ramshackle structure from its beginning (557 AD). The powerful armies of the Northern Dynasties failed to conquer the south because the southern complex of watercourses stymied the cavalry that formed the northern striking force. Emperor Wen gave Gao Jiong the task of planning the campaign to conquer Chen. Chinese military thought always emphasized detailed planning for any large-scale action. Logistics was the first and foremost consideration. No matter how many men were to attack the enemy, if supplies ran out, they would fail. Information was also most valuable: this includes all sorts of things about his forces, the peculiar qualities of commanders, the strength and weakness of different units, quantity and quality of weaponry and so forth. But besides his understanding of his army, the commander needs to understand his enemy, including personalities, organizations, deployments and favoured tactics. Only after knowing his own and his enemy's troops can the commander begin planning his campaign. Moreover, campaign plans are never straightforward. Deceptions, trickery and treachery are all useful and necessary to the successful commander.

Gao set up a long-range war plan. While Sui collected troops and materials, units on exercise would approach Chen lands but not enter them. The Chen would evacuate their borderlands and then Sui agents could burn the farms, causing disruption. Besides disruption, these manoeuvres made sure that the Chen forces became accustomed to seeing Sui forces near the frontier, so when the attack came, Chen commanders would not be alarmed. Gao began raising and training Sui forces in late 585. In two years, he was ready. In spring 588, Emperor Wen announced the war to conquer Chen. He appointed second son Yang Guang as supreme commander, with third son Yang Jun subordinate commander. The emperor appointed Gao Jiong as Yang Guang's chief of staff.

Defending behind the Yangzi River, the Chen dynasty forces believed they could stop any Sui offensive. They fortified possible crossing sites on the Yangzi with palisade encampments held by strong infantry garrisons. These fortified sites ran from the Sichuan gorges to the sea. The Chen navy consisted of a few hundred war junks, each carrying about 100 men armed with crossbows and throwing machines. The army numbered tens of thousands of soldiers. Since the Northern Zhou, Sui's predecessor, had seized the Huai River valley and the Sichuan Basin, the crux of the problem that faced the Sui military was crossing the Yangzi. They had clearly seen this and decided what they needed were warships.

Shipbuilding had been an industry along the Yangzi, its tributaries and connecting lakes since before the Han Dynasty. Major battles had occurred between fleets of purpose-built warships during the fall of the Han Dynasty and after. Yangzi boat builders had developed different types of warships. The ships were junk-built: they had solidly constructed flat bottoms, from which rose the hulls and gunwales, secured by transverse bulkheads set on the bottom structure (Turnbull, pp. 11–12). They were rectangular in shape and had upper works of wood covered by ox hides, giving protection for oarsmen. The soldiers shot crossbows from openings in the walls and operated throwing machines of different types from the tops. Combat between ships was by missile barrages, boarding and fire rather than ramming.

The Sui commanders had been constructing ships for some time. They built two types of battle craft. The Five Banner warship was a large barge with a five-storey superstructure holding 800 men. Rowed from inside the hull, with an armoured rudder, the ship's primary weapons were crossbows shooting out of windows in the towering superstructure. Along each side of the hull, three 50ft poles held large grapples on their ends. These 'striking arms' would fall on enemy ships, holding them to the Five Banner Warship's side, while the soldiers in the warship destroyed them by shooting bolts and then boarding. The Yellow Dragon ship was a smaller barge with a single-storey superstructure holding some 100 men. There were also many other smaller boats that served many functions.

In late autumn 588, the Sui high command had mobilized eight armies with a total of 518,000 men to conquer the Chen regime. After thorough reconnaissance, the commanders had identified weak spots in the Chen deployment and organized their forces accordingly. Their troops concentrated in main bases along the Yangzi; the high command made sure that the Chen leaders had no idea where they would strike. In the west, at Yong'an in Sichuan, Yang Su controlled a strong army backed up by a powerful flotilla of warships. At Xiangyang on the Han River, third son Yang Jun was in overall command of a flotilla with supporting infantry. At Qichun, second son Yang Guang commanded another large flotilla and four strong cavalry armies with strong infantry support. On the coast at Donghai, Yan Rong commissioned a large flotilla, facing the coastal area near Lake Tai.

The decentralized government in Jiankang, under Chen Shubao, a weak and childish emperor, depended on local potentates to provide weapons and men to defend the regime. The Chen administration's main concern was to protect their capital, Jiankang. Other fortified positions sat along the Yangzi, with the strongest position in the far west, where the Yangzi emerges from Sichuan. Their total forces were some 100,000 men. The Sui high command saw their battlefield as double-pronged: Yang Su's powerful army and third son Jun's flotilla would attack in the west, destroying or at least holding the western concentration of Chen troops, while second son Guang's forces would cross the Yangzi and assault the capital. Should the Chen's western army manage to disengage and retreat toward the capital, the Sui forces would pursue.

In late 588, Yang Su's flotilla rode downstream from Sichuan through the gorges. Below the gorges, the Chen had prepared blocking positions along a 50-mile stretch where the Yangzi flowed through rapids. Their first position was based on the Wolf's Tail rapids. Along the river banks, the Chen had built palisades on both sides, armed with throwing machines and heavy crossbows. These backed up a flotilla of some 100 Green Dragon warships that would contest the river passage. Yang Su saw a robust and threatening defence. Waiting until a dark night, Yang Su directed his forces in a massive attack: strong infantry columns advanced along each bank of the river as a powerful select flotilla silently floated downstream. Everyone on the ships had to bite on sticks to prove they would stay silent. The attack was overwhelming; the Chen forces surrendered. Yang Su regrouped his forces and proceeded down the Yangzi.

About 20 miles downstream, there was another Chen fortified length of river. Commander Lu Zhongsu had stretched three great iron chains across the Yangzi and secured them to forts on the banks. Yang Su saw the tactical problem as similar to the previous river block. The key to breaking the chains was the forts that protected their moorings. Among his tens of thousands of troops, the Sui commander had a large contingent of Man tribesmen. These were armed with their traditional weapons, fierce fighters but not subject to military discipline. Rather than expend his regular infantry in attacking the forts, Yang Su launched his Man fighters against them. The soldiers attacked in surges, but arrows and bolts from crossbows cut them down. The defenders killed almost 5,000 of the combatants. The Chen soldiers ran out of the forts to recover expended arrows and bolts, and also to cut off the noses of the dead in order to collect rewards from their commander. But the many attacks consumed most of the missiles for bows and crossbows. In the night following the last attack, Yang Su launched his skilled regular soldiers against the forts in a sneak attack. The forts on both sides of the river quickly fell. As Yang Su's men dismantled the chains, Lu Zhongsu sailed his flotilla downstream to escape the Sui forces. The Chen fleet reached an anchorage at Yan Island beneath Mount Jingmen.

Yang Su's flotilla rode the current downstream, reorganizing their formation. The Sui flotilla approached Lu Zhongsu's ships with four of their great Five Banner warships leading the attack, each ship carrying a large contingent of the fierce Man tribesmen. The river boats collided. The Five Banner warships' striking arms crushed and held many Chen Yellow Dragon boats, allowing the crossbowmen to slaughter their soldiers and the Man fighters to finish off those who escaped the arrows and bolts. The Chen forces collapsed. More than 2,000 men surrendered, along with the boats that did not escape. As the Sui forces mopped up the remaining forces which stayed near Yan Island, the Chen defences along the Yangzi quickly surrendered, all the way down to their base at the mouth of Dongting Lake. The Chen garrison commander at Gong'an, Chen Huiji, regrouped 30,000 men and more than 1,000 warships to reinforce the capital. But third son Jun's command had descended the Han River and blocked the Chen's retreat. By that time, the Chen capital, Jiankang, had already fallen.

Second son Guang's powerful force concentrated at Guangling (Yangzhou) on the Yangzi. Commander Heruo Bi managed the base for the initial assault across the Yangzi. Through the autumn and into winter, Heruo ordered the guard units along the river shore to march into Guangling with flying flags and beating drums and set up new camps, so it appeared that new forces were coming in every day. As new ships arrived, Heruo had them hidden while ensuring a fleet of old damaged junks remained visible along the shore. The Chen scouts reported the arrival of many units. The damaged ships were obviously a ruse. The Sui were hiding the real assault boats. The Chen brought in reinforcements and heightened vigilance. After weeks of waiting, the Chen command decided that they were being duped. They assumed the attack would come elsewhere. Heruo supervised his soldiers in massive hunting exercises. The Chen authorities became used to large troop movements across the river and assumed it was part of the same deception plan.

Heruo Bi launched his assault on New Year's Day, 22 January, 589. In the early morning, his flotilla brought across thousands of Sui soldiers against the Chen positions. The Chen forces fled. The main Chen fleet, concentrated near Jiankang, could not react in time. By 27 January, Heruo took a central Chen base, Jingkuo. While Heruo advanced along the south shore of the Yangzi toward Jiankang, another Sui commander, Han Qinhu, had crossed the Yangzi with 500 heavy cavalry, just upstream from Jiankang. His forces found their Chen opponents drunk and undisciplined. He quickly took the town of Caishi. Soon, 20,000 light cavalry arrived to reinforce Han Qinhu. With his 500-strong striking force leading, Han Qinhu advanced against Jiankang from the south. At the same time, Heruo's army approached Jiankang from the north-east.

The Chen Emperor, Chen Shubao, received a strategic battle plan from his military advisor. The military commander's suggestion was to defend the city and send the fleet out to cut the Sui forces' supply lines. This strategy had worked before, but the problem with it were the Sui flotillas. These were large, well-managed and had already defeated the Chen fleets. Instead, Chen Shubao ordered his whole force, including his crack Guard soldiers, to march out of the city and attack Heruo's forces. If the Chen armies defeated the Sui armies, they might discourage the Sui sufficiently to reach a compromise. If the Chen experienced failure, at least Jiankang would not suffer siege. On 10 February, the Chen forces deployed on high ground some miles east of the capital. Divided into five main sections, the Chen force covered a front of more than 6 miles. The whole force consisted of spearmen with a few crossbowmen, most dragooned from the city and lightly armed. Only the southern section contained crack troops. The army contained a large number of men but only a few soldiers.

Heruo deployed his 8,000 soldiers in compact columns, cavalry protecting infantry and infantry shielding cavalry. The Chen commanders sounded the attack. Of the five sections, only the southern contingent charged forward. Striking Heruo's southern flank, they pushed the Sui forces back, killing over 200. Setting the fields on fire, Heruo withdrew behind the smoke. Turning his cavalry around, Heruo drove an attack against another of the Chen sections. That section broke and ran. When the other sections saw this, they also ran. The southern section surrendered, news of the defeat quickly spreading.

When Han Qinhu's cavalry striking force approached Jiankang, they found routed troops of the Chen main force. A Chen commander willingly surrendered to Han Qinhu and ordered the garrison of the great South Gate to open the gates to him. The Sui forces went to the palace but could not find the Chen Emperor, Chen Shubao. Finally, a palace attendant told the Sui officers that the emperor and his three favorite concubines were lowered down a well to hide. The Sui officials quickly drew them up, to the derision of the populace and soldiers of Jiankang. Han Qinhu took command of Jiankang, sending his troops to garrison the walls and gates of the city. A few hours later, Heruo led his forces to the Great Northern Gate, only to find Han's soldiers holding the gate. They opened the gates to admit Heruo's troops. Han Qinhu had the honour of capturing the enemy capital, but Heruo claimed that his victory over the Chen actually captured the city. The two commanders accused each other of stealing military honours. Their quarrel continued for years. Two days later, Gao Jiong, the Army Commander, arrived and encamped his forces outside the city. Gao took charge of the city and started to make an inventory of Chen Dynasty holdings. The most important captives were Chen Shubao and his two favourite concubines, Consort Zhang Lihua and Consort Kong. Second son Guang had ordered Gao to take special care that Zhang Lihua came to no harm, but Gao saw her as a threat to the Sui Dynasty. Concerned that her obvious talents at intrigue would ensnare Guang, he had her executed. Guang was not pleased; he saw Gao Jiong as an enemy.

After the surrender of Jiankang and the Chen emperor, the rest of the southern realm fell into Sui hands. At the request of second son Guang, Chen Shubao issued orders for all of his forces to lay down their arms. The eastern force under Wang Shili had defeated a Chen force at the mouth of the Qi River and continued to occupy the areas in what is now Jiangxi province. A core of resistance remained near Lake Tai, but a force from Guang's army, supported by Yan Rong's fleet, made short work of it. The Sui leaders accepted the acknowledgment of suzerainty from tribal leaders, and so pacified the South. Emperor Wen had directed his forces to deal lightly with the people of the Chen state. His commanders prohibited looting and released captured soldiers. Instead of killing aristocrats and enslaving the populace, the Sui did not upset the existing social structure. Even the former emperor, Chen Shubao, found his retirement near Chang'an pleasant. The conquest was surprisingly easy.

The Sui officials were therefore surprised when a sudden revolt erupted around Lake Tai, spread toward the coast and then south along the coast to northern Indo-China. Mobs quickly formed. They killed Sui officials, disemboweling, cutting up and eating many. The problem was that the sophisticated descendants of ancient Han aristocrats had no problem surrendering to a Northern Chinese dynasty so long as they retained their positions, but they didn't control much of the area of the Chen Empire. Local potentates of non-Chinese settlements found the Sui imposition of bureaucratic order irksome. Then a rumour spread that the Sui official was going to round up the local population and make them march to the north of the Yellow River. Rather than try to deal with the Sui officials, the local powers killed them. When he heard of the massacres, Emperor Wen appointed Yang Su as commander of an expeditionary force to restore order. Crossing the Yangzi near Jingkou, Yang delivered defeat after defeat to rebel forces, who lacked efficient crossbows and swords and had no discipline. They either melted away before the Sui force or they died. Once he cleared what is now Zhejiang, Yang Su sent his assistant, Shi Wansui, with 2,000 men to sweep the mountains and coasts in the south. Shi marched over 300 miles and was out of communication for more than 100 days. He fought some 700 battles. Using a mixture of force and amnesty, Shi settled the southern tribes. Yang Su ended the revolt by coming to terms with one rebel faction and having them help eliminate the others. The Sui re-established their bureaucracy, but this time took care not to upset the local power-holders. However, to make sure that Chen was gone, Emperor Wen ordered the city of Jiankang destroyed.

In 589, the Sui Dynasty united the Yellow River lands with the lands of the Yangzi, extending a central administration over the whole. Production of food and goods immediately began increasing as personal and regional security became normal.

References

The Establishment of the Sui Dynasty

Chinese sources: *Sui Shu*, 24, 28, 48; *Wei Shu*, 74; *Zhou Shu*, 1, 2, 5, 6, 16, 18, 23, 33, 35, 43; *Zizhi Tongjian*, 149, 152, 155, 157, 158, 169, 172

Woodbridge Bingham, *The Founding of the T'ang Dynasty: the Fall of Sui and the Rise of T'ang, a Preliminary Survey* (Baltimore, 1941), pp.1–10.

David Graff, *Medieval Chinese Warfare*, pp.121–22.

Mark Lewis, *China between Empires, the Northern and Southern Dynasties* (Cambridge MA, 2009).

Arthur Wright, 'Sixth Century China', in Twitchett, pp.47–58.

Arthur Wright, *The Sui Dynasty* (New York, 1978), pp.21–54.

Sui Administration

Arthur Wright, 'Sixth Century China', in Twitchett, pp.77–106.

Arthur Wright, *The Sui Dynasty*, pp.108–38.

The Sui Empire's Neighbours

Christopher Baumer, *The History of Central Asia, the Age of the Silk Road* (London, 2014), pp.255–70.

Christopher Beckwith, *Empires of the Silk Road* (Princeton, NJ, 2009), pp.112–18, 123–25.

David Graff, *Medieval Chinese Warfare* (London, 2004), pp.142–44, 188–89.

Rene Grousset, *The Empire of the Steppes* (New Brunswick, NJ, 1970), pp.80–90.

Dennis Sinor, 'The Establishment and Dissolution of the Turk Empire', in Denis Sinor, *The Cambridge History of Early Inner Asia* (Cambridge UK, 1990), pp.285–316.

Dennis Sinor, 'The First Turk Empire (553–682)', in Litvinsky (ed.), *History of Civilizations of Central Asia, Crossroads of Civilizations: AD 250 to 750*, vol. III (Paris, 1996), pp.322–30.

Sui Conquest of Chen

Chinese sources: *Zizhi Tongjian*, 176–77; *Sui Shu*, 48.

David Graff, *Medieval Chinese Warfare*, pp.131–35.

Stephen Turnbull, *Fighting Ships of the Far East (1) China and Southeast Asia 202 BC–AD 1419* (Osprey, 2002). Information spread throughout the text regarding construction, appearance and use.

Chapter 2

Imperial Consolidation

Emperor Wen Organizes his State

Sui officials escorted the former Chen emperor, Chen Shubao, to the new capital, Daxing. Elite army units, victorious commanders and high officials joined with the imperial family for a thanksgiving ceremony in the Hall of Ancestors. Emperor Wen announced to his ancestors his victories that reunited the realm: since the collapse of the Western Jin some three centuries before, the great realm had split into competing states; now the Sui Emperor had succeeded in drawing all the realm's lands together. As witness, the emperor paraded Chen Shubao in front of the assembled notables. The former emperor reverently recognized the Sui emperor as his superior. After the former Chen ruler played his part, Emperor Wen called forth his two commanders who had captured Chen capital Jiankang, Heruo Bi and Han Qinhu. Heruo Bi spoke first:

'I met the armies that opposed me on the way to Jiankang and not only did I defeat them but I made prisoner one of the very distinguished and brave Chen commanders. It was really through me that the victory over Jiankang was gained, because of the courage of my men, the enemy was so terror struck that resistance was abandoned. And so your greatness rules the whole of the Great Realm.'

Han Qinhu responded that his was the decisive blow that had brought the campaign to a victorious conclusion: 'With but a handful of men, I moved rapidly on Jiankang. I took possession of the city and seized the emperor. I was there when Heruo Bi arrived in the afternoon of the same day to open the city gates to let him in.' Emperor Wen awarded the distinction of capturing Jiankang to both commanders. Heruo Bi, he created Lord of Sung; Han Qinhu, he established as Supreme Supporter of the State, with holdings to support the dignity. Emperor Wen then called on his friend and advisor, Gao Jiong. The emperor announced that it was Gao Jiong's brilliant plans and skillful execution that made the conquest of Chen possible. His should be the greatest award. Gao replied: 'The army commanders risked their lives along with their soldiers while I was but a scholar. Such men always deserve the highest honours.' The emperor expressed his approval of Gao's response and made him Lord of Chi.

The Sui celebration of victory and unity in 589 led to difficult questions of peace and economic development. The administration would release large numbers of soldiers into civilian life. They needed to repair and upgrade irrigation and flood control infrastructure, neglected as a whole for centuries. They needed improved transportation. As with military campaigns, such problems required deep study and correct execution. Emperor Wen joined together with his three main advisors and their staffs to prepare a unified plan for reform of the empire. On 16 June 590, Emperor Wen issued an edict that changed the basic military structure of the empire and began a reform of land use. The edict began:

> 'At the end of Wei there was chaos and loss and the empire's territory was divided like a melon. Mobilization for military service occurred every year and there was no time for rest.' (Graff, *Medieval*, p.138)

After the conquest of Qi in 578 and the need to hold Qi lands, and then the conquest of Chen in 589, soldiers of the empire moved from their homes in Guanzhong to the eastern plains. Because of the constant deployments, soldiers depended on their commanders rather than on civil authority. These commanders kept registers of soldier families, so they were separated from the civilians with fixed residences who were under civil authority. The emperor decreed that henceforth soldiers and their families were to join the whole population and settle in specific locations. The result was the establishment of a new *fubing* system. The appointed soldiers were member of the horse aristocracy. They managed estates, farmed by peasants using the equal field farming methods in which each family received a homestead and civil officials registered them along with everyone else. Their officers, appointed by the emperor, came from the north-western horse aristocracy, most families having nomad antecedents. Each *fubing* headquarters was known as a Soaring Hawk command, a manoeuvre unit of some 1,000 horsemen. The result was that the central authority controlled armed forces, not local commanders. The soldiers, given long-term tenure and professional training, were more than a simple militia. Placed in settlements at strategic areas, the *fubing* formed the bulk of the imperial forces. There were four main garrison commands, but the Guanzhong commander was the emperor. This was because Emperor Wen saw the need for a strong permanent military force at the emperor's hand. To ensure this, he expanded the Imperial Guard in the capital from the four regiments under Northern Zhou to twelve. These regiments represented different groupings of the Sui military: some were the old regiments of Xianbei, others came from *fubing* units near the capital and still others from a distance. The emperor's personal guards were paid professionals. Guards of gates and walls were *fubing*. Officers were often military cadets from important families; that way, no officer clique could hope to unify the guards to effect a coup.

The Imperial Border Lands

The most important external threat to the Sui Empire lay beyond the long northern frontier: the massive nomadic tribal confederations. The people of the Yellow River Valley had lived with this threat for a millennia. Different rulers had tried many different solutions. The Warring States and their successor, the Qin Empire, built extensive barriers to channel attacks into certain areas. The Han Dynasty counter-attacked, marching large armies deep into Central Asia. At the end of the Later Han era, efforts at amalgamation of certain tribes began, attempting to build a unified state of nomadic tribes and farmers that could satisfy both herdsman and settler. With the collapse of central control, the nomads swept into the Yellow River Valley, setting up their own regimes. The Chinese who found this unacceptable migrated south to the Yangzi, vowing to return. This was, of course, the Age of the Northern and Southern Dynasties that preceded the Sui Dynasty. The Chinese elite families who remained in the north remained proud of their connections back to the time of the Han Dynasty and before. But these northern houses also had to deal with the nomad tribal leaders. Strong forceful nomad khans made good partners in maintaining elite status and its prerequisites, but in order to do that, these aristocrats had to recognize the tribal leaders as aristocrats. In essence, the two groups merged. Given the infinite variety of individual human experience, such a social development happened in many ways and had many results. But by the time of the Sui Dynasty, a Chinese aristocrat could ride a magnificent horse, dress in nomad fashion and inspect his herds and his farmers during the day, and in the evening dress as a Chinese scholar in high fashion and discuss poetry. The great houses intermarried and generated genealogies as necessary.

Buddhist religious practices connected China with Central Asia and India, and became an important factor that bred common ground between different backgrounds. Buddhist text and worship entered China during the Han Dynasty. Many Buddhist practices and beliefs interacted with traditional Daoist and Ruist thought, all translated into the Chinese script. While some Buddhists read non-Chinese language text, those who did read the Chinese were also open to the world of Chinese literature. Understanding Chinese thought and processes became part of the nomad world and Central Asia, because of the use of the Chinese script. Some modern commentators make an issue out of whether the Sui Dynasty and the northern aristocracy were 'Chinese' or not. While this is of interest to some nowadays, it was of no concern to the Sui and Tang aristocracies, who saw themselves as the epitome of 'Chinese'. The great northern houses also had close economic connections with the nomad tribes. The Turks mined and processed iron and steel, raised horses and manufactured weapons. The northern houses supplied silk, different weapons, agricultural goods and finished products. These goods did not just circulate between the Turks and northern houses but continued on the one hand throughout China, and on the other west through the deserts to Central Asia and beyond. The Sui Dynasty under Emperor Wen managed the different Turk factions maintaining peace.

Struggles with Neighbours

The Kingdom of Koguryo (Goguryeo) held northern Korea and much of Manchuria down to the Liao River. (There is a dispute about the ethnic nature of this polity. Those supporting the answer given by Chinese scholars use Koguryo; those supporting the Korean scholars' answers speak of Goguryeo. I am using Koguryo because this narrative is from a Chinese perspective.) Emerging during the upheavals during Later Han era, the kingdom was a strong and successful military power. The King of Koguryo, Yeongyang, was appointed crown prince in 566 and ascended the throne upon the death of his father in 590. He was an energetic and popular ruler. Sui Emperor Wen recognized and approved Yeongyang on his accession. At the same time, the Koguryo monarch understood that the new unified China was just a recent development and might not last. The collapse of the new regime would allow Yeongyang to expand his kingdom to the south. His father had planned to attack the emerging Sui Empire and Yeongyang saw no reason not to pick up the pieces if Sui fell apart. He made alliances with the Malgal Tungusic tribes in eastern Manchuria, supporting their raids into the lands to the west of the Liao River (*Samguk Sagi, Annals of Goguryeo, vol. 19*, Graff, p.145). After Sui envoys to the court of the Eastern Turks found Yeongyang's representatives hiding in a yurt, Emperor Wen sent a strongly worded message to the Koguryo Court: the emperor demanded that Yeongyang halt all military activity with the Turks, that the raids stop and that Yeongyang recognize Sui suzerainty. Yeongyang readily agreed to the demands, but scouts still reported Koguryo men in Turkish camps and the raids did not stop. In spring 598, Emperor Wen and his advisors had had enough of what they saw as Yeongyang's double dealing and decided to give him a forceful lesson. Orders went out to mobilize in the Linyuguan region (north of the Yellow River, on the Bohai Sea, south of the Liaodong Gulf). Command went to fifth son Liang, with Gao Jiong as advisor and supported by the fleet under Commander on Water Zhou Luohou. The force reached a total of 300,000 men. On 4 August, the advance began with a sizeable cavalry force backed up by infantry marching toward the Liao River valley, while the fleet carrying strong infantry forces sailed along the coast. The turn of the seasons brought unusually heavy rains. Rivers flooded and supplies failed to arrive. The army, particularly the horses, suffered. The fleet, too, was hit with stormy weather. The barge-like boats did not stand up to the heavy swells and some were lost. Fifth son Liang decided to load the strongest part of his land army on the ships and continue by sea into the Liaodong Gulf. As they proceeded into the gulf, they found that the Koguryo troops held the landing spots. A Koguryo fleet appeared with some 50,000 men. The Sui fleet was repulsed with significant loss. With the coming of October, the commanders saw that they could do nothing before winter set in. They cut their losses and withdrew. Planning not being sufficient and the weather not cooperating, it was best not to lose more. The effort, though, was sufficient to remind Yeongyang of his vulnerability, and he complied with Emperor Wen's demands.

For years, the court of Daxing had heard rumours of great wealth in the lands beyond the southern frontiers. Information followed that the local forces in those rich lands were weak and the land open to easy conquest. In 602, Emperor Wen sent an infantry army by sea to seize Jiaozhou (modern Hanoi). The commander, Liu Fang, easily succeeded but did not find the great wealth. The local elite claimed descent from Chinese refugees who had fled the disruptions that had convulsed China. Their ruler, Ly Nam De II, quickly surrendered and the Sui occupied the main fortified towns. Liu Fang understood that just to the south, the Cham Kingdom of Lam Ap (Lin Yi) was that site of wealth for which he was sent. While Chinese culture was a great influence in Jiaozhou, the Cham peoples followed Sanskrit Hindu traditions. King Sambhuvarman (Pham Phan in Vietnamese, Fan Che in Chinese) ruled a strong domain along the Cham coast. As an important nexus of sea routes from what is now the Philippines and Indonesia with south China in one direction, and India in the other, the Kingdom of Lam Ap was indeed fabulously rich. In 605, Liu Fang sailed his infantry force south, landing near Indrapura (Da Nang). Marshalling his troops, he crossed the Duli River (Song Cai?) and marched toward Sambhuvarman's capital. The king's forces, mounted on war elephants, suddenly attacked Liu Fang's army, pushing them back. Liu Fang drew his army into a defensive position and ordered his men to dig pits across his front, which they then camouflaged.

The Champa commander ordered his elephant corps to attack Liu Fang's lines. The charging elephants hit the pits, which caused significant disruption. At that point, Liu Fang ordered his massed crossbowmen to fire, aiming for the elephants' eyes. The wounded elephants recoiled against the Champa army's own lines and sent them into retreat. The Sui spearmen followed and completed the victory. Liu Fang took the Champs capital, seizing a vast plunder, including over 1,000 Buddhist books and golden tablets which commemorated the ruling Cham dynasty. Liu Fang understood that while Jiaozhou might receive a Sui garrison, the Cham kingdoms were too different to become part of the Sui Empire. He loaded his plunder on his fleet and sailed north. Sickness overtook the expeditionary force and many died, including Liu Fang. King Sambhuvarman returned to his capital and continued his long and successful reign. However, he did not neglect to regularly send proper tribute to the Chinese court.

Along the southern and western imperial frontiers, small garrisons of local militia maintained the peace and allowed the Chinese farmers to slowly expand their lands. At times local tribes rebelled, attempting to eliminate some objectionable imperial settlement or profit from plundering the Chinese. In 597, the Nanning tribe in Yunnan attacked the nearby settlements when their king, Cuan Wan, decided to expand his domain. Emperor Wen, receiving reports about the incursions and considering the Nanning tribe as subject to his universal rule, sent a small expeditionary force to restore order. The commander, Lord Shi Wansui, forced a mutually agreed settlement. At the same time, a group of tribes in the mountains of Guilin began attacking settlements. Emperor Wen sent a number of commanders to pacify the region. Such small-scale squabbles with local non-Chinese tribes continued, with some damage to Chinese settlements and bloody destruction of the offending forces.

Internal Threats to the Sui Dynasty

Emperor Wen was concerned with the expansion of his realm into the fullness of the Han Empire. He was also concerned with external threats to the imperial frontiers, but he was most concerned with the greatest threat to the unity and efficiency of his rule: those people close to him who could disrupt the regime from the inside and allow the empire to break apart into warring factions. Having achieved pre-eminence, the emperor was the target of every ambitious unscrupulous potentate. Even if a plot merely destabilized the state, clever and cunning men would profit. And to some in the second or third tier of power, a regime collapse was not undesirable. The road to power and disruption runs through those who loyally serve the state. They are the ones who hold the actual levers of power. The secret to regime destruction is to influence those loyal servants to act unwisely and then force them to act against the others in the regime. This creates chaos and, with intelligent management, will cause the state to collapse. Emperor Wen, who had played the game himself, understood this only too well. Every person who helped him to power, every person who had a strong claim on him, was his worst potential enemy. Emperor Wen was not paranoid, but the game had high stakes and the emperor preferred that others than he should pay them. In 586, three friends who had helped him formed a clique because they felt themselves slighted. They were executed. His friend, Li Dekin, a key strategist in the Sui assumption of power and in the conquest of Chen, seemed to know too much. The emperor removed him from his high post in the central government and sent him off to be a provincial governor. In 592, Prime Minister Su Wei lost his position when charges of factionalism raged back and forth between high officials. Yang Su and Gao Jiong became co-prime ministers, but Heruo Bi complained that he should be sole prime minister. The emperor stripped both Su Wei and Heruo Bi of their honours, but relented a little later.

If his companions and servants presented problems, his own family was an even greater difficulty. His sons were the future of the empire, but they could also fatally damage the dynasty by squabbling among themselves. Emperor Wen could slap down, even kill his companions; he would always find people to replace them. However, he could not eliminate his own family because that would make all his work futile. This was a delicate difficulty. Unlike many similar dynamic leaders, Wen had a partner and perceptive advisor in his formidable wife, the Empress Dugu Qieluo. The seventh daughter of a prominent Western Wei commander, Dugu Qieluo was in part a descendant of the steppes. Married early in a love match long before the throne had called, she and the emperor worked together for the good of the empire and the Chinese people. Like many prominent powerful families, their children had problems. In 597, third son Yang Jun, Prince of Qin, Commander of Bing Province, was taken ill and transported to Chang'an for treatment. Emperor Wen checked the accounts of the province and decided that Yang Jun had spent a significant amount of state funds on favourites. The emperor stripped the prince of all of his offices. Then, after accusations that Yang Jun's wife, Princes Cui, had poisoned him, the emperor ordered Yang Jun to divorce her and then saw to it that the woman killed herself. The emperor's advisors remonstrated against the harsh punishment. Wen replied:

> I am the father of five sons. I am not the father of all the people in the lands. If I should agree with you, would I not have to issue a separate criminal code just for the sons of emperors? Even a man as caring as the Lord of Zhou executed his brothers for crimes. I am not at all as able as the Lord of Zhou. Can I break my own laws?

Disagreements did erupt between the emperor and empress. Dugu made very clear when they married that she expected her husband take no other woman. When she discovered that Wen was intimate with Yuchi Jiong's granddaughter, she had the woman killed. Wen became very angry. He left the palace to live elsewhere. Gao Jiong and Yang Su, long-term trusted advisors, convinced the emperor to return to the palace, but Dugu heard Gao Jiong refer to her as 'only a woman' and decided that he had to go. Another family quarrel arose about the imperial succession. The imperial successor from the beginning was the first son, Yong. But second son Guang lusted after power. Evidence came to Emperor Wen that Crown Prince Yong gave a great deal of wealth to his friends, and Empress Dugu heard that he had hundreds of concubines. Both began to consider appointing second son Guang as a more appropriate crown prince. Advisor Gao Jiang saw a nasty plot building against Yong and opposed any move to replace him. Accusations appeared in 599 that Gao Jiang had associated with traitors, and the emperor stripped him of office. Further accusation surfaced that Gao cursed the emperor. Wen refused to execute Gao, as many wished him to do, and merely reduced him to commoner rank. The next year, second son Yang Guang allied with Yang Su after receiving support from Empress Dugu. They convinced first son Yong's assistant to bring accusations of treason against him. The emperor deposed Yong and appointed Guang to be Crown Prince. Many of Yong's supporters were executed.

Empress Dugu died in 602, removing a valuable and beloved advisor. Emperor Wen soon took up with two young concubines, Consorts Chen and Cai. That year, second son Guang allied again with Yang Su and accused fourth son Xiu, administrator of Sichuan, of attempting to be emperor in his domains. Yang Su submitted the evidence to Emperor Wen, who recalled Xiu to the capital, stripped him of office and reduced him to commoner. Two years later, the emperor travelled to the Summer Palace in spring. He soon fell ill and remained in the palace through the summer. Second son Guang found consort Chen attractive and attempted to force his attentions on her. She went to Emperor Wen and complained about Guang's attitude and behaviour. The emperor suddenly saw Guang as a danger. He ordered his trusted officials, son-in-law Liu Shu and Yuan Yan, to recall first son Yong, intending to restore him. Panic hit Guang, who followed Yang Su's advice. They sent soldiers to arrest Liu Shu and Yuan Yan, then sent a trusted retainer to kill Emperor Wen. Guang took over the Summer Palace, had Yong killed and took Consorts Chen and Cai as his own. Finally, he announced the death of Emperor Wen and proclaimed himself as Emperor Yang.

References

Imperial Organization

Chinese Sources: *Sui Shi*, 2, 64, 84; *Zizhi Tongjian*, 166, 175, 180.
Woodbridge Bingham, *Founding of T'ang Dynasty*, pp.11-14.
David Graff, *Medieval Chinese Warfare*, p.138.
Arthur Wright, *The Sui Dynasty*, pp.82-107

Military Reform

Chinese sources: *Suishi* 2.
David Graff, *Medieval*, pp.138–40.
Edwin Pulleyblank, *The Background of the Rebellion of An Lu-Shan*, pp. 61-63.

The Imperial Border Lands

Christopher Baumer, *The History of Central Asia*, vol. 2, pp.173-97.
Christopher Beckwith, *Empires of the Silk Road*, pp.112-18, 123-27.
Carter Findley, *The Turks in History*, pp.37-54.
David Graff, *Medieval*, pp.142-44.
Rene Grousset, *The Empire of the Steppes*, pp.80-90.
Dennis Sinor, 'The Establishment and Dissolution of the Turk Empire', in Sinor (Ed), *The Cambridge History of Inner Asia*, pp.285-316.
Dennis Sinor, 'The First Turk Empire', in Litvinsky (Ed.), *History of the Civilizations of Central Asia,* vol. III, pp.322-30.
Jonathan Skaff, *Sui-Tang China and its Turko-Mongol Neighbors*, pp.33-35, 39-50.

Internal Threats to Sui Dynasty

Chinese sources: *Suishi* 64, 84; *Zizhi Tongjian*, 166, 175, 180.
Bingham, *Founding of the T'ang Dynasty*, pp.1-10.
Graff, *Medieval Chinese Warfare*, pp.140-44.
Arthur Wright, 'The Sui Dynasty', in *Cambridge History of China*, vol. 3, part 1, pp.115-28.
Arthur Wright, *Sui*, pp.157-81.
Victor Cunrui Xiong, *Emperor Yang of the Sui Dynasty*, pp.29-49.

Chapter 3

The Imperial State Weakens

The Reign of Emperor Yang

T he reign of Emperor Yang is complex and confused. Chinese historical tradition masks the nature of the second Sui emperor with the well-known story of the 'bad last emperor', vilified by the succeeding dynasty as justification for his overthrow. Modern commentators have made much of this tradition because the history of the Sui Dynasty was written by Tang Dynasty historians during the reigns of the early Tang emperors. Therefore, commentators say, accounts of Emperor Yang's reign are biased against him to glorify the Tang. This neglects the facts that Emperor Yang lost control of many areas before the Tang leaders decided to assume imperial trappings. For numerous reasons, as this narrative will describe, Emperor Yang's regime failed in holding together major parts of the empire. The Tang historians had no need to exaggerate the extent of these failings: they speak for themselves. Emperor Yang seized power, but he did not handle it well. Emperor Wen, his father, ruled with a firm if harsh hand. Depending on a group of experienced advisors, Emperor Wen dealt with local leaders in a way that allowed imperial interests success without unduly harming local power bases. Local interests may not have liked working for the central authority, but the bottom line was always that any alternative to the Sui Dynasty was far more expensive than submission. Emperor Yang did not understand these limits to 'unlimited' power. His visions for improving the empire were phenomenal. His energy to accomplish his goals was spectacular. His efforts ran roughshod over poor and rich, peasant and lord. Whatever value the emperor placed on his numerous projects, too many people found them far too expensive.

Emperor Yang was born in 569, originally named Puliuru Ying. His father had just ascended to the lordship of Sui under the Zhou Dynasty, and renamed him Guang, believing that name more auspicious. His father then changed the family name to Yang in 580, about a year before he ascended the throne as Emperor Wen. At the age of 19, Yang Guang was overall commander of the Sui offensive against Chen. He acquitted himself well, impressing and making friendships with many commanders. Two years later, he participated in plots that removed the first son from the succession, and he ascended the throne after the death of his father in 604.

As soon as news of Yang Guang's assumption of power spread, fifth son Liang, governor of Bing Province, proclaimed himself emperor. His support came from the officers and men of the frontier forces. Army units in nineteen provinces pledged support to Liang; few people trusted Emperor Yang. The frontier force commanders dithered about whether to consolidate their rule north of the Yellow River or attempt to extend their efforts to seize the whole empire. Emperor Yang moved quickly and appointed Yang Su to suppress the rebellion. With a special force, Yang Su went to Liang's command post in Bing Province. Repelling all efforts by Liang's army to stop him, he captured Liang's commanders and outbid Liang's offers to his army. The rebellion collapsed; Yang Su executed many of Liang's supporters. Liang surrendered and Emperor Yang was the unquestioned ruler. The emperor stripped Liang of office and rank, imprisoning him indefinitely.

Later that year, Emperor Yang began to remake the empire following his visions of how China should be. Prosperity and plenty flourished in the central plains along the Yellow River after more than twenty years of peace. Grain and goods poured into the imperial coffers. Emperor Wen had built his new capital at Daxing near the abandoned Han Chang'an in the 'Land within the Passes'. Easy to defend, the city was isolated from the central plain and the south by mountains. Yang saw the future of China in the central plain. He saw China drawn together by a transportation nexus, this becoming a rich and flourishing land. The emperor's first action was to move his residence and administration from Daxing to the central plain. The official reason was a prediction that Daxing's site was not good for the emperor's health. Yang decided that the ancient capital of Luoyang was the most appropriate site for his new residence. Victorious commanders and bandit chieftains had looted and plundered the old city since the Han Dynasty tottered. Many hundreds of thousands of conscripts cleared the land, dug moats and raised an immense city wall enclosing a wide space.

The next year, 605, the emperor sent his engineers, labour organizers and logistics staffs to repair and strengthen the Yellow River's banks. Because the silt brought by the river always kept raising the flow, the Yellow River flowed higher than the surrounding countryside. Generation after generation of farmers had channelled the river, but periodic floods devastated vast tracts of land. Centuries of invasion and war had replaced the central planning of the Han Dynasty with a myriad of local fixes. Now Yang intended to unify the whole system. The basic solution to problems caused by an excess of water was the construction of secondary channels to drain the water off in a controlled manner. Such a channel took water to a lower point than that from which it came. Since the Yellow River is broad and deep, these channels were massive; they could carry significant traffic as long as they were properly maintained with banks and locks. The key to maintaining the canal as water relief and transportation system were the locks, that allowed sufficient water to keep the water level but also allowed the excess to drain off. Previous flood control and transportation channels built during the Han Dynasty did not have the efficient locks available to the Sui Dynasty. The older flash locks could not handle large changes in elevation, but Yang's engineers developed canal lock gates that allowed transport through wherever drainage channels led.

Emperor Yang had a staff of experienced designers and constructors at hand. Back in 584, Emperor Wen's new capital, Daxing, needed the delivery of vast amounts of grain and other goods. The Wei River proved too troubled a route to ensure regular shipments of large amounts. The emperor commissioned engineer Yuwen Kai to design and oversee the construction of a canal from Daxing to the Tong Pass on the Yellow River. Yuwen Kai built the Guangtong Canal running parallel to the Wei River. Emperor Wen even moved his court to Luoyang in order to relieve the supply situation in Daxing, but once Yuwen Kai had finished the canal, the court remained in Daxing. The new canal impressed Emperor Wen. In 587, the emperor appointed engineer Liang Rui to oversee a project to construct dykes along the Yellow River. Here, Liang Rui designed a channel along the Yellow River that maintained water levels using a sophisticated system of locks. These locks also allowed traffic to move along the channel safely, without the dangers of the Yellow River itself. Where the water levels were too high for flash locks, the engineers installed double slipways that let operators haul barges from one level to the next. Emperor Yang was fascinated with both the techniques for moving massive amounts of earth and the efficiency of the finished design.

The projects convinced the emperor to extend the whole system. In early 605, he presented plans to the imperial court that would change the structure of the empire. He had enjoyed directing the construction of the new capital at Luoyang, including miles of defensive ditches and walls, new markets, streets and administrative buildings, and, of course, a whole new spectacular palace. While this work continued, he ordered the construction of large canals connecting Luoyang with the Yellow River, and then more canals connecting the Yellow River with the Huai River and beyond, south to the Yangzi. All the canals provided flood relief from excess water and transportation routes for goods. These projects required millions of workers moving earth. Completed in five months, the Tongji Canal, which connected Luoyang and the Yellow River with the Huai River, and the rebuilt Han Canal, which connected the Huai River with the Yangzi River, permanently changed the landscape of the empire. The line of the Tongji Canal started west of Luoyang at Xiyuan, taking water from the Luoshui River to the Yellow River, then ran from Banzhu to take water to Daliang (Kaifeng) and on to the Huai River. Then another 100,000 men excavated a canal from the Huai River to Shanyang, to Jiangdu and then to the Yangzi River. All these canals were 40ft wide with roads on either side. There were willow trees planted on both sides. Emperor Yang built Dragon boats to sail in his canal system. Dragon boats were 200ft long, 45ft high and some 35ft wide to fit into the 40ft-wide canal. The lowest deck was the servants' quarters, the next deck was for water and food supplies, the next had 120 rooms with spectacular decorations, and the top deck held two large royal courts. The boat for the empress was just a little less long. Several thousand smaller boats followed. Some 80,000 people were pulling the boats; the line of boats occupied 500 miles of canals.

Much of the Yangzi's length was now interconnected with the Yellow River valley, the central plain and the 'Land within the Passes'. What were independent regions become interdependent. To ensure proper administration of the river and canal system, Emperor Yang had forty administration building complexes constructed throughout the area to keep an eye on the system. In autumn 605, the emperor started out on an inspection trip through the empire on his fleet of Dragon boats, from which he ran the empire, from floating administrative offices, entertainment spaces and residential quarters. Once the emperor saw the transportation system in operation, he ordered the construction of two huge food storage facilities near Luoyang.

The New China

Emperor Yang had a grand vision for the future of China. He began a long-term and well-planned series of operations to further develop the empire. Firstly, he decided to put his house in order. In the summer of 606, Crown Prince Yang Zhao, died. Yang did not elevate a new crown prince but made Yang Zhao's sons imperial princes. His second son, Yang Jian, became the master of Luoyang when Yang was elsewhere. The next year, 607, the emperor ordered the eight sons of former Crown Prince Yang Yong executed. With the succession secured but without a single person who could challenge him, Yang was ready to continue his restructuring of the empire. Secondly, the new canal system changed the economic relations between sections of the empire. Governors of provinces brought complaints to the imperial court. Clearly, they might become a nexus of opposition. Emperor Yang abolished all provinces, so the imperial government dealt directly with commanderies (or prefectures). This removed a whole tier of administrators and displaced many local power brokers. He also eliminated the lower orders of nobilities, thus reducing many local leaders to commoners. Thirdly, he reorganized the central administration by founding a series of independent agencies through which he could impose his orders without reference to high administrators. Emperor Yang also reorganized the military forces. He eliminated all high commands and subordinated all units directly to his personal oversight. He reduced all military commanders' rank by a full grade and under-officers by a partial grade. All these actions did not sit well with many aristocratic families and others.

Late in the summer of 607, the emperor ordered the construction of a highway from Daxing to Jinyang, near the northern frontier. Personally inspecting the road, Yang travelled beyond the frontier to the imperial tent of the Eastern Turk Khan, Ashina Rangan. The khan respectfully greeted the emperor as his overlord. In return, Yang granted powers over the frontier districts and the right to draw on revenue in the frontier area. While the emperor was with Ashina Rangan, an agent from King Yeongyang of Koguryo was introduced to him. The defeat of Emperor Wen's army by Koguryo still rankled. Yang demanded that King Yeongyang come and present his respect to him. If he came, he would have a reward; if he failed to come, he would be punished. Yeongyang did not accept the invitation. Since the Turks supplied excellent horses, along with iron for tools and weapons, the emperor believed that his concessions to the Turks would allow the empire to become stronger, help settle the frontier areas and isolate Koguryo. Imperial senior officials Gao Jiong, Yuwen Bi and Heruo Bi began talking about the need for better, more settled policies. When Emperor Yang heard about this, he had them executed and removed their friends from all official posts. Yang then began to pursue new expansive projects.

With his usual careful planning, in spring 608, Emperor Yang issued orders to build a canal from the Yellow River to Zhuo Commandery (near modern Beijing). This would become the supply route for an attack on Koguryo. He called for the conscription of a million men from all over the empire, and had them brought to the canal system. Officials could not produce enough men, so the emperor ordered the conscription of women as well. Any objections which may have arisen were quickly quashed when the emperor opened investigations into the actions of his son and assumed heir, Yang Jian. Blaming Yang Jian for wanting the deaths of his late elder brother's three sons, Emperor Yang left Yang Jian in his positions but executed his son's close associates. Yang Jian thus lost any political influence he might have had. Minor campaigns and concessions cleared any possible trouble on other fronts: in 608-09, frontier forces upset the Tibetan Tuyuhun regime in the north-west, while in 609, the emperor received Ashina Rangan and solidified their trade agreements. With the vast upheaval caused by the mobilization of so many people, the emperor ordered an empire-wide redistribution of farmland and imposed a special tax on wealthy families to pay the Turks for horses. Finally, to extend imperial control over all parts of the empire, he founded the third capital in Jiangdu, near where the emperor's new canal flowed into the Yangzi. With the new massive transportation system, direct control of all commanderies, huge conscriptions, redistribution of land and three capitals from which administrators could enforce Yang's orders, the Sui Empire had become something very different from the Han Empire and its successors. Some people were no doubt happy with the new order of things; many were not.

The great construction project of the Yongji Canal from the Yellow River to Zhuo Commandery was finished in the 'Seventh Year of the Great Enterprise, in the reign of Emperor Yang', that is, 611. Emperor Yang announced an expedition against Koguryo on 14 April. He ordered the construction of 300 sea-going warships capable of troop transport at Donglae on the north side of the Shandong peninsula. To man the ships, he conscripted 10,000 boatmen from the Yangzi and Huai Rivers.

By 1 June, he established a forward base in the Zhuo Commandery as a concentration point for the armies. He brought 30,000 infantry crossbowmen and 30,000 aborigine spearmen to secure the area. The whole transport system Yang had spent years constructing now served as a logistical support structure for the Koguryo expedition. Troops, horses, grain and equipment came up the Yongji Canal to Zhuo Commandery. In Henan and the lower Yangzi, craftsmen built 50,000 deer carts – one-wheeled, two-man transport carts – to carry armour, clothing and tents. The emperor conscripted all the larger boats on the Yangzi, sending them north to the Yellow River to haul grain from the imperial granaries to Zhuo. He enlisted 600,000 men to load the grain on the carts, each carrying about 400lb of grain, and take them to advanced army bases at Luhe Garrison (near Jinzhou) and Huaiyuan Garrison (near the Liao River), some 250 miles north-east of Zhuo Commandery.

Emperor Wen had considered one of his most important accomplishments his disbanding of the Zhuo Dynasty mobile armies and settling their soldiers in farming communities. This had certainly contributed to the rise in productivity in the Central Plain. Emperor Yang decided to conscript large numbers of men from these families, along with those from many other families, and organize new mobile armies. On top of the massive mobilization of labour to construct water projects, the result of the emperor's actions upset the security and settled life of millions of families on the Yellow, Huai and Yangzi Rivers and their tributaries. Emperor Wen followed Buddhist and Ruist thought. He understood that, in the end, the central realm existed to benefit the lives of its hard-working productive members. As long as their lives were their own, at least to some degree, the society would prosper. Emperor Yang failed to understand this basic concept. He clearly viewed the subjects of his empire as his personal servants. He ordered them about in vast numbers, without regard for their interests or safety. A stern and brutal military enforced the emperor's orders without question. Still, the soldiers faced the same problem as the general subjects. The massive mobilization for the war against Koguryo was successful, but if the war was a failure, the whole imperial structure Emperor Wen built to unify and organize the realm would collapse. Vast numbers of conscripts deserted and migrated to areas far from the major river systems. Mountains, dense forests and swamps, already populated by people uninterested in the settled imperial realm, received migrants who would rather be outlaws than abused slaves.

Emperor Yang was good at organization, if not human relations. The great army took shape in Zhuo Commandery. The emperor set up a military headquarters, the Soaring Hawk administrative staff, to oversee collection and supply of the arriving units. He re-established the twenty-four armies of the old northern regimes, appointing a senior commander of each army. The core of each army was heavy cavalry, organized into manoeuvre units of 100 men called *dui*. Ten *dui* made a *turan*. Each army had four heavy cavalry *turan*. Infantry backed up the cavalry. Eighty *dui* of infantry, or eight *turan*, completed the fighting part of the military units. Each army also had four *turan* of labour and supply troops. There were 12,000 fighting troops for each army, with another 4,000 supply troops. The twenty-four armies totalled some 354,000 troopers. However, each heavy cavalryman needed at least three horses, a warhorse and backup, along with a riding horse, and probably had more. He needed an assistant, a groom and a general maintenance person; so each cavalryman should count as at least three. The infantry, with special clothes, crossbow and other weapons, also needed at least one assistant. So the twenty-four armies actually had a total of around 672,000 men. These were only the troops sent to the Koguryo front. There remained garrisons and policing troops throughout the empire. The total military force of the Sui Dynasty was 1,133,800 men. There were also another two million people moving supplies, maintaining the transport systems and processing goods for the army and court.

The Sui Dynasty military wore yellow clothing underneath all their trappings. Over the basic yellow clothes, each of the twenty-four armies had distinctive banners and colours. The first cavalry *turan* of each army carried lion banners, wore burnished silver armour joined by dark green cords, and armour with dark green tassels covered their horses. The second cavalry *turan* of each army carried panther banners, wore vermillion leather armour joined by deep red cords, and their horses had armour with animal patterns and red tassels. The third and fourth *turan* carried their own banners with their own colour combination. Each infantry *dui* had its own banner; each infantry *turan* had their own colour scheme. Each army had two bands: one had ninety-four drums of different types; the second had thirty-seven instruments, including bells, flutes, whistles and horns.

Many modern commentators suggest that these numbers and details are exaggerations, inflated or invented by the early Tang historians who wrote the 'official' histories of the Sui Dynasty and the rise of the Tang Dynasty. They point to the literary convention of the 'evil last emperor' as the reason for the intentional smirching of Emperor Yang's actions. I cannot agree. The examples nearest Emperor Yang were the dynamic dynasty founders, the First Emperor of Qin, or Cao Cao. Later examples would be Zhu Yuanzang, founder of the Ming Dynasty, or perhaps Chairman Mao. Yang's problem was that he never considered the human element with which he worked. The Qin emperor and Zhu probably generated as much disruption, but they always kept an eye on levers of power. Yang appeared to think that he merely needed to make an order and all would fall into place. What is amazing about his reign is the loyalty demonstrated by many influential and powerful people who tried to hold the dynasty together and did not give up until the situation was hopeless.

In 608, the Western Turkish Khan, the Heshana Khan, Ashina Daman – son of a Chinese mother – recognized Emperor Yang as suzerain. As a rival to Ashina Rangan, the Eastern Turkish Khan, he wanted to receive similar imperial largesse. The next year, Ashina Rangan died. His son, the Shibi Khan, Ashina Duojishi, succeeded as Grand Khan of the East. He requested that the emperor grant him permission to marry Ashina Rangan's widow, Princess Yicheng, whom Emperor Wen had awarded to Rangan. Such approval carried imperial recognition of Ashina Duojishi's status. This was granted. Later, in 611, the Western Khan, Ashina Daman, failed to visit Emperor Yang's court. This displeased the emperor, who gave support to subordinate khan Ashina Shegui to rebel against Ashina Daman. Daman fled to the imperial court, where Emperor Yang received him. The emperor split the Western Turk realm into three sub-realms, with Ashina Daman as over-lord. But Ashina Daman never again left imperial lands.

References

Reign of the Emperor Yang Begins

Chinese sources: *Shishu*, 64, 84; *Zizhi Tongjian*, 166, 175, 180.
Woodbridge Bingham, *Founding of the T'ang Dynasty*, pp.1–10.
David Graff, *Medieval*, pp.140–44.
Arthur Wright, *The Sui Dynasty*, pp.115–28.
Arthur Wright, *The Sui Dynasty*, pp.157–81.
Victor Cunrui Xiong, pp.29–49.

Emperor Yang's Public Works

Woodbridge Bingham, *Founding of the T'ang Dynasty*, pp.11–21.
Victor Cunrui Xiong, pp.75–93.

The New China

Chinese sources (narrative): *Zizhi Tongjian*, 181; (numbers), *Suishi*, 4; (appear-ances), *Shushi*, 4, 8.
Woodbridge Bingham, *Founding of the T'ang Dynasty*, pp.11–21.
David Graff, *Medieval*, pp.146–47.
Victor Cunrui Xiong, pp.75–93.

Chapter 4

The Reign Fails

War with Koguryo

Feeling satisfied with his management of the northern frontier, Emperor Yang moved to begin his chastisement of Koguryo. On 8 February 612, the emperor held a grand review of his main forces, presenting himself to his army as Son of Heaven. He then ordered his vanguard forces to advance east from Zhuo Commandery. King Yeongyang had pulled back from the lands he had occupied after the war with Emperor Wen. Assuming that the Sui would return, the Koguryo forces retired behind the line of the Liao River, where they built a series of strong fortresses. The Sui military wanted to start the offensive against the Liao as soon in the spring as possible, remembering the failed 598 campaign. They hoped to pierce the Koguryo fortress line before the summer wet season. The Sui army advanced eastward, through the mountains and plains of southern Manchuria to the Liao River, the line of which they reached on 18 April. Because of an early spring, the river was in full flood. The emperor had decreed that he must approve any significant operation, so the armies concentrated along the Liao and Yang received some different plans. The Koguryo troops were clearly in position along the eastern side of the river, but the Sui commanders were unsure about both the quality and number of soldiers. The emperor listened to the commanders' plans and approved them.

The Sui forces threw three pontoon bridges across the Liao, extending about three-quarters of the distance to the far bank. Crack Sui troops conducted a reconnaissance, crossed the bridges and advanced through the water. Not knowing quite what to expect, if the Koguryo troops attacked in great strength, the Sui soldiers could withdraw through the water while they also drew back the bridges. The Koguryo troops proved to be good, but nothing that the Sui could not face. Several days after the reconnaissance in force, the Sui army assaulted and carried the river line. Once across the Liao, the emperor reorganized his troops, setting up battle groups to besiege the Koguryo forts along the frontier. The emperor's main objective was the walled city of Ryotongsong (modern Liaodongcheng near Liaoyang City). Emperor Yang did not press the sieges, but masked and isolated each one, thinking that they would all surrender without trouble once the Koguryo capital fell. He even ignored a request from his commanders to accept the surrender of Fort Yodong, thinking that it was better that the Koguryo troops were trapped in their fortresses than having surrendered and potentially causing trouble.

The key to victory, according to Emperor Yang's operational scheme, was the sea striking force sailing from Donglai on the Shangdong coast. Hundreds of ships transported 40,000 troops to the estuary of the Taedong River and up the river to about 20 miles from the Koguryo capital, Pyongyang. Under the command of Lai Huer, they reached their landing in mid-July. Lai Huer's staff suggested that they camp in place until the Sui land forces arrived. Lai Huer decided differently. He mobilized his 40,000 troops and marched toward Pyongyang. The Koguryo forces faded from his route as the Sui army reached the walled city. The rich farmland around the city offered an opportunity for plunder, and the Sui army took advantage of the situation. Suddenly, a mass attack by crack Koguryo troops emerged from a Buddhist temple complex and cut into the disorganized Sui force. Lai Huer managed to draw his soldiers together and retreated to his river base. The Sui army was not badly hurt, but their opponents had proved to be more formidable than they thought. Lai Huer fortified his base and waited for the Sui land forces to arrive.

Along the Liao River, the Emperor Yang maintained his investment of Koguryo border fortresses, arraying his army in a way that would repulse any relief attempt coming from Pyongyang. No relief came. The Koguryo command put their trust in the strength of their fortresses and hoped that the Sui would break their teeth trying to capture them. Emperor Yang had no intention of assaulting the fortresses. He formed a striking force of nine separate armies to march on Pyongyang and join with his sea landed force. The emperor issued 100 days' worth of provisions drawn from the depots at Luhe and Huaiyuan to the striking force. Here, the weakness of Emperor Yang's methods of doing things became apparent. The provisions were ordered, but the delivery was beyond human endeavour and physical fact. The crews moving the provisions from the depots to the Liao had to eat, and they ate much of what they carried. Moreover, each soldier of the striking force had to carry heavy provisions, and they found this difficult; they often buried their loads beneath their tents as they march forward. Once the striking force reached the Yalu, the commanders, considering their supply situation, discussed their future moves. Yuwen Shu suggested they withdraw and preserve their men. The commander-in-chief, Yu Zhongsheng, decided that they would strip down their forces and advance swiftly toward Pyongyang. The nine armies, if full, numbered about 100,000 fighting men. By separating out the heavy cavalry and building a force around them, Yu generated a mobile army of some 30,000-plus. Since horse fodder was the primary supply concern, infantry forces and some horse remounts would help transport necessary fodder. Excess manpower could march back toward the Liao.

The Sui force advanced toward Pyongyang, and King Yeongyang ordered his field commander, Eulji Mundeok, to open negotiations with Yu Zhongsheng. The Sui commanders received the Koguryo commander with the intention of detaining him, but Eulji managed to talk his way out. The war would continue.

The Sui force drove deep into the Koguryo hinterland. Still the Koguryo forces never appeared in force but, using 'panther' tactics, hit and ran. The Sui force managed to collect some supplies and continued to march toward Pyongyang. Around the capital, supplies were very short, especially after Lai Huer's depredations. The Sui land forces came within 10 miles of Pyongyang's walls. Lack of supplies, hitting at the enemy but finding only air, plus constant harassment, brought desperation. Yu's army never connected with Lai's, where large magazines on ships held grain and fodder. Yu's problem was that if he did connect with Lai's base, he would improve his supply situation, but for how long? Obviously, the Koguryo king was not going to surrender or even come to terms, so the only option was a long drawn-out siege of Pyongyang. Even if he carried the city, Yu would not end the war. Seeing the Sui commanders' difficulty, Eulji Mundeok sent a poem to Commander Yu:

> Your brilliant plans expose reality.
> Your subtle understandings encompass the world
> You win all the battles; you are invincible.
> Why not accept victory and end this war?

Sending a spokesman, Eulji offered that King Yeongyang would recognize Emperor Yang as his overlord if Yu, as representative of the emperor, would accept and withdraw. Yu agreed because he saw that the best answer to his situation was to withdraw, just as Yuwen Shu had advised. Yu formed his force into a great square, with infantry masking the horse but with openings for the horse to charge out. He marched north. Even though the Koguryo forces continually harassed the Sui army, the withdrawal proceeded successfully until they reached the Salsu River (Ch'ong Ch'on River) in the second half of August.

Eulji had sent forces ahead of the Sui army. The Salsu River was low, but Eulji's men constructed a dam far above the Sui crossing point, cutting the flow even more. When Yu's soldiers reached the river, they saw an easy task in front of themselves. The army broke formation to cross the river. Koguryo scouts immediately sent messengers to the force that had built the dam, who quickly breached the dam, and a massive wave of water swept down the Salsu River. The flood overwhelmed the Sui army, causing disruption and panic. Just then, strong Koguryo forces suddenly appeared and attacked. The Sui army collapsed. The cavalry reached the Yalu in a single day and night; the infantry routed and disappeared. Word of the collapse reached Emperor Yang on 27 August. The emperor immediately ordered the withdrawal from the Liao River, back to the Yellow River valley.

The Collapse Begins

The summer rains of 611 brought flooding on the lower reaches of the Yellow River. Because of the massive mobilizations, there was little labour to repair the drainage irrigation system. The next year, drought and plague arrived. The price of grain went up as much of it went to the imperial granaries. The disruption led to desertion. Many people simply went elsewhere, away from direct Sui control. So long as they avoided the waterways and fled to the hills, the Sui forces did not follow. The refugees and deserters joined with local hill people and set up independent settlements. The imperial authorities saw these communities as fugitives, outlaws and bandits. In mountains and marshes, along backwaters and in isolated settlements on the coasts, local leaders, both ancient aristocratic houses and newly minted strongmen, organized their own little regimes, united only in their desire to escape the Sui state. By spring 613, disorder had spread to most of the eastern parts of the empire that were not directly connected with the waterways.

Sui security forces kept the waterways open and supply flowing, even if the hinterlands fell away. Emperor Yang decided that the most efficient way of re-establishing authority was to complete the conquest of Koguryo. On 28 January 613, the emperor issued orders to again concentrate troops at Zhuo Commandery. The security forces collected all the supplies that they could force out of the communities under their control and sent them to the emperor. He sent them to new depots set up on the west side of the Liao River. The emperor's troops collected more grain from the granaries near Luoyang and shipped the supplies down the river and out into the Gulf of Bohai and on to the port of Wanghaidun on the Manchurian coast. The emperor, discussing the previous campaigns with his military staff, decided to relinquish more authority to local commanders. Emperor Yang also reorganized the structure of the imperial army. He abandoned the conscript army, establishing the Xiaoguo (brave and determined) warriors. These forces restored the old Western Wei-Northern Zhuo army of local leaders and their personal following of 'volunteers'. The emperor's imperial headquarters directly oversaw the Koguryo troops.

On 30 March 613, the emperor arrived at his advance base on the west side of the Liao River. He supervised his forces as they concentrated and stockpiled supplies. He ordered the army to cross the Liao River on 21 May. With his advisors, the emperor planned a new campaign to overthrow the Koguryo kingdom. First they would besiege the frontier fortresses, especially Ryotongsong, and take them, not simply mask them. Once the fortresses fell, an elite force of Xiaoguo under

Yuwen Shu and Yang Yichen would advance against Pyongyang from the north. Lai Huer would then sail his force from Donglai and link up with Yuwen and Yichen. The Sui invested Ryotongsong, surrounding the fortress with siege works, complete with wheeled siege towers that held telescoping ladders. Massive throwing machines cleared the wall tops with stones and arrows. The assaults hit all four sides but were repulsed. Not to be undone, the Sui military staff began building a massive earth ramp leading up to the wall's top. Batteries of throwing machines were ready to clear the walls of defenders and eight siege towers on wheels were ready to advance up the ramp when it was completed.

On 2 July news came of a massive rebellion centred on Luoyang. Emperor Yang was so upset that he immediately ordered the siege abandoned and ordered his army to march west. Under cover of night, the Sui force withdrew from Ryotongsong, leaving equipment and supplies. The Koguryo soldiers, suspicious of a trap, waited two days before they set out in pursuit of the Sui army. When Emperor Yang's men were crossing the Liao River, the Koguryo light troops attacked and cut off several thousand Sui supply troops, striking them down. The emperor also sent orders to Lai Huer, who was waiting to sail to Koguryo, to come to Luoyang instead.

The rebellion had started on 25 June. A Sui official, Yang Xuangan, controlled the town of Liyang on the Yongli canal. He was a son of Yang Su, one of Emperor Wen's original compatriots before he became emperor. He was important in Wen's elevation, was a successful high administrator in Wen's government and held high honours. Yang Su also helped Emperor Yang gain the throne. Nevertheless, Emperor Yang was very suspicious of Yang Su. When Yang Su became ill, he understood that the emperor wanted him to die. Saying, 'Why should I live?', he refused treatment and soon died in 606. Yang Xuangan believed that Emperor Yang was responsible for his father's death and intended revenge. His headquarters were the centre for the canal maintenance crews and traffic control. All supplies and reinforcements for the Koguryo campaign had to move up this canal past Liyang. The failure of the 612 campaign opened an opportunity for Yang Xuangan. He spent months placing trusted supporters in important positions. Once the emperor was away, beyond the Liao River, Yang Xuangan began slowly allowing a supply backlog to develop. Then he announced that bandits were blocking the supplies. Finally, he raised the banner of rebellion.

Gathering 8,000 troops, he marched to Luoyang. The eastern capital was under the command of the King of Yue, Yang Tong, a grandson of Emperor Yang. The king put the walls in a position of defence. Yang Xuangan's force now numbered 50,000. They pushed the defenders into the city, but the walls held. Chang'an was under the command of the King of Dai, Yang You, another grandson of Emperor Yang. Yang You sent Commander Wei Wensheng with 40,000 men to relieve the eastern capital. Emperor Yang sent Yuwen Shu and Qutu Tong to attack Yang Xuangan. Yang Xuangan, seeing the powers gathering against him, abandoned the siege of Luoyang. Instead, he marched his army west, toward the 'Land within the Passes', heading toward Tongguan pass. The commanders of Emperor Yang pursued him. Yang Xuangan planned to seize Hongnong (Lingbao in Henan), but the city was defended by another member of the Sui Dynasty, Yang Zhiji, King of Cai. For three days, Yang Xuangan assaulted the walls but, being repulsed, he decided to bypass the city and continued toward the west. His forces reached Wenxiang (to the west of Lingbao Henan), but the forces under Emperor Yang's commanders still followed. They brought Yang Xuangan's forces to bay at Huangtianyuan. Yang Xuangan put his army in battle formation to meet the Sui troops. The Sui forces launched three assaults against Yang Xuangan's men, one after another. Each one pushed the rebels further back. Finally, at day's end, the Sui commander launched an all-out assault and broke Yang Xuangan's army. Yang Xuangan and his brother Yang Jishan fled to Jialushu. Yang Xuangan told his brother to kill him, so he would not face disgrace at Emperor Yang's hands. Yang Jishan killed his brother with a sword and then stabbed himself, but his suicide attempt failed. Sui forces captured him. Emperor Yang started a massive purge to eliminate anyone who had supported Yang Xuangan. Very many died. As part of his New Year's celebration of 614, the emperor had Yang Xuangan's brother and his main strategist executed. A large number of officials shot them in a barrage of arrows; their bodies were torn apart and burnt. Their ashes were scattered. The emperor had sent Wang Shichong to put down the rebellions along the Yangzi. The officials could confiscate the property of any rebel. Resistance soon stopped as a large amount of property changed hands.

The rebellions lasted a little less than three months but shattered the power structure of the Sui Dynasty. The failure of the second Koguryo campaign was bad enough, but the imperial forces now depended on local leaders and their loyalties. Moreover, the most powerful families in the realm, the old Wei-Zhuo northwest clans, wavered in their support of the dynasty. Many other local powers also saw the regime as vulnerable to a little blackmail if not outright independence. The lower Yangzi, the Huai valley and even the western part of Guanzhong fell out of imperial control. Emperor Yang was a remarkable person: his power was seriously eroded, but his personal connections and charismatic approach maintained his personal ascendency over whichever local leaders were nearby him. He often travelled around the realm, yet was not assassinated. The emperor's solution to his empire's collapse was simple: conquer Koguryo.

On 4 April 614, Emperor Yang ordered troops to concentration in Zhuo Commandery for another campaign. Soldiers came slowly. Not until 27 August did the emperor receive his forces on the Liao River, after a four-month wait. This was too late in the season to besiege the Liao fortresses. Lai Huer, on the other hand, had good weather crossing the Gulf of Bohai and sailed up the river toward Pyongyang. King Yeongyang, who had faced Emperor Wen's invasion and two of Emperor Yang's, had enough of the yearly disruption of his capital and farmlands. After pulling his armies back from Lai Huer, he asked for terms. Knowing about the widespread disruption of Yang's realm, Yeongyang saw that he could agree to anything and deliver nothing. The king decided to recognize Emperor Yang's supremacy and promised to go to the emperor's court with many valuable gifts. The king also surrendered a former Sui commander who had led Yang Xuangan's army. Emperor Yang proclaimed victory and withdrew his troops from the Liao River, marching back into the realm. But King Yeongyang never showed up at the emperor's court. The emperor ordered preparations for another campaign against Koguryo, marching to Yanmen to collect fresh troops.

References

Chinese sources: *Sui shi*, 8, 24; *Zizhi Tongjian*, 181–82.
Graff, *Medieval*, pp.149–54.

Chapter 5

Rise of the House of Li

Li Yuan's Career during the Sui Dynasty

The family of Li Yuan traced their line back seven generations to Li Gao, founder of the kingdom of Western Liang, part of the chaotic Sixteen Kingdoms. Successive ancestors were military officers. Li Yuan's grandfather, Li Hu, was a commander for Yuwen Tai, the military leader of Western Wei. Yuwen Tai rewarded Li Hu with the title Lord of Longxi, along with the Xianbei surname Daye. After Li Hu had died, Yuwen Tai's son became Emperor Xiamin, founder of Northern Zhou. He posthumously made Li Hu the Lord of Tang and Li Hu's son, Li Bing, received the title. Li Bing married a daughter of the distinguished commander Dugu Xin. He died in 572. His son, Li Yuan, received the title Lord of Tang and maintained the title when the Northern Zhou fell to the rising Sui in 581. Emperor Sui Wen's wife was Empress Dugu, who was Li Yuan's aunt. Li Yuan married Lady Dou, daughter of Dou Yi, Lord of Shenwu, and Yuwen Tai's daughter, Princess Xiangyang.

Emperor Wen appointed Li Yuan a provincial governor three times. Li Yuan was governor of Xingyang Commandery (Xingyang Henan) and Loufan Commandery (Jingle Shanxi) when Emperor Yang had gained the throne. Emperor Yang appointed Li Yuan as commandery commander, having abolished provinces. Li Yuan also served as under-minister and logistics manager. In 613, the Emperor appointed Li Yuan commander of the palace guards in Daxing. When Yang Xuangan rebelled, Emperor Yang sent Li Yuan to Honghua Commandery (Qingyang Gansu) as supreme commander. In 616, Wei Daoer, rebel commander of 100,000 men, attacked Taiyuan (Shanxi), captured the town and killed the Sui commander. The emperor then appointed Li Yuan military governor of Taiyuan, commissioning him to retake the town and deal with Wei Daoer. As Li Yuan marched his vanguard of some 5,000 men toward Taiyuan, they encountered Wei and his forces in an engagement in Queshugu valley (near Jiexiu Shanxi). Wei Daoer surrounded Li Yuan's force. When the main force commander, advancing behind the advanced force with Li Yuan's elder sons, received this news, they swiftly organized a relief force to rescue him. With a body of select soldiers, the relief force hit Wei and broke the encirclement, followed by the main army. Attacking Wei from many sides, they defeated him.

As he moved from post to post, Li Yuan built a staff of able and loyal people. When Emperor Yang's emotional instability began to appear threatening, Li Yuan and his companions drew closer and began planning how to survive Yang. The emperor ordered Li Yuan to come to court, but fearing for his life he pleaded ill-health. Becoming publicly drunk and openly receiving bribes, Li Yuan appeared to the emperor as someone without great ambition. In 615, the emperor appointed Li Yuan commander in Hedong to suppress bandits, but removed him the next year, only to reappoint him commander of the important town of Taiyuan (Shaanxi).

Li Yuan had four sons by Lady Dou: the eldest was Li Jiancheng, followed by Li Shimin, Li Xuanba (who died as a child) and Li Yuanji. The brothers had at least one sister. The most important for this narrative is Li Shimin, who was born in 598 at Wugong (Xianyang Shaanxi). Li Yuan named his son Shimin, a short form for 'Save the earth; pacify the people'. The young Shimin excelled in the classical curriculum of the time, Chinese literature and calligraphy. His calligraphy was impressive and has remained a model for Chinese script ever since. He also demonstrated great skill in the Tartar martial arts, horsemanship and archery. When he was a teenager, Shimin's father received an appointment as commander in Shanxi province (615), and he spent his youth at the frontier post of Taiyuan, high in the mountains bordering the steppe. There, besides studying literature and calligraphy, Shimin hunted in the hills and battled frontier raiders.

The first major event that erupted into his life came when he was about 16, in the summer that his father first received an appointment as commandery commander. Emperor Yang travelled north to escape the heat and inspect the imperial frontiers, establishing a base of operations near Taiyuan and advancing beyond the frontier fortifications into the steppe. Emperor Yang believed that the dominant power in this part of the steppe, Shibi Khan, Ashina Duojishi, Chief of the Eastern Turks, was a close ally of his administration. The Chinese Princess Yicheng, the widow of the previous khan, had married Shibi Khan as a token of the close relations between the Turkish chief and the Sui Dynasty. However, at the same time, Emperor Yang was trying to weaken Shibi Khan's power by subverting some of his lesser chiefs into opposing the khan's rule. The Chief Khan knew about these efforts and decided to teach the emperor a lesson in manners. When Shibi Khan heard that Emperor Yang's entourage had passed beyond the imperial frontier fortifications, he organized a force of some thousands of light horse and set out to capture the Sui emperor. The Princess Yicheng, ever loyal to her Chinese origin, sent a secret message to the emperor, warning him of the impending attack. Yang only had time to redeploy his forces to a modest frontier town, Yen Men, before the Turks swept around the imperial party.

The fortifications of Yen Men provided temporary safety. However, while the Chinese soldiers held the Turks at bay, the large number of people trapped in the town – including local settlers, the imperial entourage and the soldiers guarding the emperor – were without sufficient supplies. Reportedly, the emperor panicked and hugged his youngest son, 'weeping till his eyes were swollen'. Emperor Yang, after his death, was always a good target for an embarrassing story, but he was clearly emotionally unstable and did many of the things attributed to him. The emperor was certainly upset. Offered alternative courses of action by his advisors, he could not make up his mind. The commanders pointed out that by forming a force of elite troops, the emperor could cut his way out of Yen Men in the dark of night. The ministers, not included in the commanders' plan, suggested that the emperor issue a decree abandoning the current war in Korea to reinvigorate his soldiers. More to the point, the empress's younger brother, Xiao Yu, gave a practical piece of advice. They were members of the former southern ruling house, the Liang, and understood the twisted loyalties of those placed in positions of conflicting interests. Xiao Yu suggested sending a secret message to Princess Yicheng, wife of Shibi Khan, informing her that the Turkish army had trapped the emperor and asking her to find a way to help the emperor. The emperor finally decided to act. He approved sending the message to the princess; he announced that he was giving up the war in Korea and awarded noble ranks to all who fought at Yen Men.

Li Yuan quickly responded to the news that the Turks had trapped the emperor. Rounding up a motley collection of troops, he sent them toward Yen Men to rescue the emperor. Led by one of his commanders, Li Yuan included his son, Shimin, who was then about 16, with the expedition. This demonstrated Li Yuan's loyalty and provided his son with practical experience. When the force set out, the whole situation was very unclear. The officers were always unsure of the emperor's moods: he had a nasty habit of beheading people for errors. If Emperor Yang did not survive, the Turkish force might find their existence inconvenient. Therefore, they put their plan of operations in Li Shimin's mouth.

The official histories of the Tang Dynasty describe Li Shimin as an extraordinary leader. Many modern commentators assume that much of the credit given to Shimin was simple flattery given him by the scholars working under his ultimate direction. That may be, but Li Shimin was a remarkable man. He ended up emperor of a united China and ran a very effective administration. That he needed to be flattered, that he cared about such things, is unlikely. These stories are probable, if not quite in the way their writers present them.

The young man was bright and well informed. By taking the credit for the officers' plan, he assumed the main responsibility for failure. As a youth, the chance for great retribution was minimal, yet was still there. This way Shimin gained the loyalty of these officers. The plan was common enough: make a small scratch force appear to be a great army. Deception was always a part of war, and was emphasized by the military handbooks. The relief army spread its forces along miles of road, raised clouds of dust and carried a multitude of banners. At night, the soldiers lit many fires, beat drums and made a commotion. The idea was that the Turkish scouts would think that a large relief army was on the way, and the Turks would abandon the siege of Yen Men. As the army approached Yen Men from the south, news came to Shibi Khan from Princess Yicheng that Tartar tribes in the north were collecting to attack the Turkish pastures. On the other hand, perhaps Shibi Khan judged that Emperor Yang understood his lesson in manners. The Turks withdrew. Emperor Yang quickly left Yen Men, travelling to Taiyuan and then to the Yangzi.

The House of Tang Becomes a Power

While Emperor Yang's rule was tottering in the south, the Lord of Tang, Li Yuan, continued the war with the Turks, who were raiding and plundering settlements within their reach. Orders soon came from the emperor directing Li Yuan to cooperate with the other northern administrators to suppress the rising tide of rebellion that had erupted when the imperial government had published the new orders for conscription in 616. There had arisen a widespread prophecy, as was common in the Central Realm during troubled times, that a new dynasty would come forth. This vision specified that the new ruler would have the name of Li. Emperor Yang knew of this prophecy. He had executed a family of official status because he thought they were the ones meant. The potential for trouble was not lost on Commander Li Yuan. Moreover, as the year turned (616-617), the forces of disruption became greater. Sui authority remained strong around the emperor's southern palace at Jiangdu. At Luoyang, Yang Tong, the King of Yue, a grandson of Emperor Yang, still upheld Sui authority as the figurehead of a group of administrators. At Daxing, Yang You, the King of Dai, another of Emperor Yang's grandsons, also remained a figurehead, and in the distant province of Sichuan, unaffected by the tyranny of Emperor Yang, a loyal government remained at peace. Elsewhere, chaos reigned.

In April 617, a district administrator, Liu Wenjing, was arrested and held in confinement because he was married to the sister of the notorious rebel, Li Mi. It was clear to all that the empire was descending into chaos. Liu Wenjing was a friend of Li Yuan's son, Li Shimin. Liu was closely connected to the powerful local landlords. With full granaries at hand and danger facing the area, Liu Wenjing believed he could raise 100,000 men. Li Yuan, Soaring Hawk Commander and administrator of the region, commanded several tens of thousands of men. With a capable leader, they could gather together an imposing army, march south and capture the Guanzhong area along with the imperial capital, Chang'an. Liu Wenjing was close friends with the eunuch superintendent of the imperial residence near

Taiyuan, one Pei Ji. This eunuch was also friends with Li Shimin. They put pressure on Li Shimin to take up the issue with his father, Li Yuan.

In the April, the Turks attacked Mayi (Shuozhou Shanxi). Li Yuan sent Gao Junya with a force to deal with the Turks, but he was defeated. Li Yuan feared that Emperor Yang would consider this as treason. Emperor Yang sent an order for Li Yuan's recall and ordered him to Jiangdu. Instead, Li Yuan and his officers reinforced their armies and recalled his sons. Gao Junya and a fellow officer saw the military preparations and decided to halt what they saw as treason. But Li Yuan was warned. In May 617, he allowed Li Shimin to handle the situation. The next morning, Li Shimin led the officer in charge of espionage into the government quarters where Li Yuan, Gao Junya and the other officer were working. The official spy said that he had information for Li Yuan alone. He then handed a paper to Li Yuan, who immediately announced that Gao Junya and his fellow officer were conspiring with the Turks. They vigorously denied this but were thrown into jail. Li Yuan ordered their immediate execution.

The Lord of Tang, Li Yuan, faced a serious quandary. His legal authority and noble title came from the Sui emperor. An elder of the House of Li, any action he might take reflected on the whole clan. If he repudiated the Sui Dynasty, he not only undermined his own authority but also, should the Sui Dynasty recover, put himself and his clan at risk. His heir, the first-born son, was equally vulnerable. However, a wild second son could explore options closed to his elders. That way, Li Yuan remained the loyal servant of the ruling dynasty as commander at Taiyuan, while Li Shimin, a 16 or 17-year-old young buck, rode with the soldiers and fought with the Turks. If Shimin was at times indiscreet, that was only a natural result of youthful passions. The official histories reflect conventional roles expected from the traditional status structure. Older, more prominent men deal with problems slowly and carefully. Impetuosity is the privilege of the young. Therefore, the Lord of Tang appears as indecisive, perhaps even weak, while Li Shimin seems to be the driving force. Moreover, since the course of action was successful, the scheme of responsibility never changed. In reality, reading between the lines of the official accounts, the members of the House of Li sought to advance their collective interests by operating in different directions at one time. That way, they could pursue whatever was successful and ignore blocked paths. That the histories say one thing and mean another is not surprising. This is part of the meaning of the title of the work by the great Sung historian, Sima Guang, *Zizhi Tongjian* (*Mirror for the Perceptive*).

The moment of decision came when a representative of Emperor Yang appeared at Taiyuan with an order directing Li Yuan to travel to Jiangdu and explain why he had not yet suppressed the rebellions in the north. If Li Yuan went, he would never return. Given the state of the Sui administration, no one could suppress the rebellions, but to say so to the emperor was an insult. Emperor Yang also had a deserved reputation of swiftly beheading those who displeased him. Li Yuan would not go. However, that was rebellion. How could the ever loyal and honourable head of the House of Tang become a common bandit? Here is where the stories fit in: Li Shimin had wanted to set up an independent state for some time, but his noble father had stopped him. The eunuch superintendent of the imperial residence near Taiyuan, Pei Ji (eunuchs are all untrustworthy!), presented Commander Li Yuan with some attractive young women and, not knowing that they came from the imperial harem, Li Yuan accepted them. These actions of Li Shimin, Liu Wenjing and Pei Ji, so it was said, entrapped the noble but naïve Li Yuan. Perhaps this was not the most believable of stories, but the tale allowed a great deal of plausible deniability. To be clear, what started as propaganda later became hagiography. However, Li Shimin was a bright, bold, impetuous young man; as an adult, he was extremely successful, cunning and brave. To imagine the youth as any different would not be accurate. On the other hand, such a youth, in the hands of other much more experienced men, became a willing and useful tool.

References

Chinese sources: *Jiu Tangshu* (Old Book of Tang), 1; *Xin Tangshu* (New Book of Tang), 55–56; *Zizhi Tongjian*, 175.

Bingham, *The Founding of the T'ang Dynasty*, pp.75–76, 138–39.

C.P. Fitzgerald, *Son of Heaven, a Biography of Li Shih–Min, Founder of the T'ang Dynasty* (Cambridge, 1933), pp.13–30.

Graff, *Medieval*, pp.160–63.

Hung, pp.23–24.

Chapter 6

War for Guanzhong

Battle Begins

Once Li Yuan decided that he must act, the decision still had to be secret for some time. The advisors of the child princes of Sui at Daxing and Luoyang held strong forces. By striking between the two capitals, the army of the Lord of Tang would separate the armies of Sui and be able to destroy them in detail. The initial objective was the city of Hedong (Puzhou Shanxi). However, both the eldest son, Li Jiancheng, and youngest son, Li Yuanji, were in the city of Hedong, and under the eye of the local military commander. Without attracting attention, both brothers made their way to Taiyuan. His family safe, the Lord of Tang called together his military officers, local officials and important people in the area and announced his intention to rectify the disturbed political conditions. Of course, he was working in the interests of the Sui Dynasty. He would take his army to Daxing. Once there, the Lord of Tang would expel bad advisors and support the child King of Dai. While, to the rank and file, this may have sounded straightforward, to those with knowledge of history, it was clearly an attempt at founding a new dynasty. The lands around Daxing, 'Within the Passes', were a natural fortress out of which came great military conquerors. From this area, the ancient Zhou Dynasty swept away the Shang Dynasty; the Qin Dynasty founded the dominion of the First Emperor; the founder of the Han Dynasty battled his way to supreme power; and the Sui Dynasty had taken the same route. The House of Li aimed high.

The Lord of Tang met no organized opposition to his assumption of authority. Those who opposed him disappeared; the only forces to attack Taiyuan were a band of marauding Turks, who were easily repelled. Perhaps this was part of a process through which the Lord of Tang made an alliance with Shibi Khan, the Turkish suzerain. Liu Wenjing suggested an alliance with the Turks in order to gain strong soldiers and, more importantly, their horses. Li Yuan sent a message to Shibi Khan of the Eastern Turks. He made up a tale that he would take control of Emperor Yang and bring him to Daxing so that the administration could be rectified. He asked for armed assistance and forbearance. In return, he offered money and goods. To show the Turks that the government had changed, Li Yuan ordered the flags be changed from red to red and white: 'This is as good as plugging your ears while stealing a bell.' But it was necessary. They understood that Shibi Khan was not really going to support their efforts, but what they needed were horses.

When the order to change flags was issued, Gao Deru, the administrator of Xihe Commandery (Jiexiu Shanxi), refused to obey. Li Yuan sent first son Jiancheng and second son Shimin to the area with a strong force. Accompanying them, Wen Dayou was to give them advice. 'My sons are young. You will offer good military advice. Our future depends on this action,' said Li Yuan. Jiancheng and Shimin recruited experienced soldiers and shared in their lives and exercises. They did not allow looting. When they discovered looting, they returned the goods but did not unduly punish the soldier; so both locals and soldier were happy. When the brothers Li reached the city of Xihe, they made ready to attack but did not disrupt the lives of the civilians. Gao Deru defended his position resolutely but without much effect. In just a few days, the city fell. Shimin had Gao Deru dragged to the gate of his camp, saying: 'I have raised an army to punish toadies like you.' Shimin ordered Gao Deru executed. No one else, however, was punished. The city returned to normal and there was no plundering. The brothers Li marched their army back to Jinyang. Only nine days had passed from the start of the expedition when they returned to Li Yuan, who was pleased.

In June 617, Shibi Khan of the Eastern Turks sent envoys to Jinyang with 1,000 horses. The khan requested permission to sell horses in China. In return, they offered a powerful army to support Li Yuan's march to Guanzhong. Li Yuan received the emissaries with honour. He bought 500 horses and sent the rest back. Some of Li Yuan's followers complained that they wanted to buy horses for themselves with their own money. Li Yuan pointed out that the Turks had a lot of horses. If they sold them now, they would ask a higher price in the future, but if Li Yuan's men only bought some and showed that they had no immediate need for them, the price would be much cheaper. After the emissaries had left, Li Yuan sent Liu Wenjing to the court of the Eastern Turks. Li Yuan told him that allowing the Turkish cavalry into China was dangerous. Li Yuan made clear that his intention was to forestall the northern rebel, Liu Wuzhou, from calling on them for help. If the Turks had troops with Li Yuan, they would not sent men to Liu Wuzhou. Li Yuan did not need a large Turkish force. He explained that the Turks did not need much in the way of supplies because they grazed in the fields: 'So, with only a few hundred Turkish soldiers, I show how powerful my army is.' Liu Wenjing reached the camp of Shibi Khan, and he made an agreement that if the Turks would send a small army to Li Yuan for the march on Daxing, Li Yuan would keep the land and people, and he would give the Turks gold, jade and other treasures. Shibi Khan agreed, and sent envoys to tell Li Yuan that an army was coming.

Satisfied with the development of his military power, Li and his advisors organized the march to Daxing. He order the granaries open to supply the army and relieve distress. Many people came to join Li Yuan's forces. Li Yuan was supreme commander, with Pei Ji head of the general staff. Liu Wenjing was head of military personnel and training. Tang Jian and Wen Daya handled the secretariat, while Wen Daya and Wen Dayou collected and analyzed intelligence. Wu Shiyue ran the weapon and armour manufacture and supply. Cui Shanwei and Zhang Daoyuan handled finance and taxes, and Jiang Mo handled any other problems. Yin Kai Shan was the chief propagandist. There were two armies: the Army of the Right and the Army of the Left. First son Jiancheng was made Lord of Longxi and commanded the Army of the Left, with second son Shimin appointed Lord of Dunhuang and given command of the Army of the Right.

Li Yuan held a great ceremony on 5 July 617. He entrusted the defence of Taiyuan to fourth son Li Yuanji. Li Yuan proclaimed to all commanderies under his rule that he recognized Prince Yang You, King of Dai, as Emperor of the Sui Dynasty. He officially began the expedition to Guanzhong. The Tang army set out, accompanied by the Western Turk Khan, Ashina Danai. The way from Taiyuan to Daxing follows the valley of the Fen River down to the Yellow River; the Luliang Mountains separate the Fen River from the Yellow River for much of the way. Not particularly high or formidable, they are nevertheless an obstacle to the movement of large groups of men. Using the Luliang Mountains as a screen, an army can move down the length of the Fen valley without being seen. The Lord of Tang and his military advisors carefully considered this fact while planning the coming campaign.

The Tang Offensive Begins

In early summer 617, the army of the Lord of Tang marched west, toward the Luliang Mountains. Comprising some 30,000 men, the force consisted of a strong infantry armed with spears, swords and shields, and a force of skilled archers. Accompanying them were a small but well-trained heavy cavalry unit along with a mass of Turkish light cavalry. Perhaps a little more than half of the 30,000 were peasants armed with light weapons, who were used for logistic operations and digging fortifications. The Lord of Tang, his sons and advisors led the soldiers. Marching south along the mountains, screened by light cavalry, the army moved toward Squirrel Pass, a major route through the valley of the Fen River, outflanking some towns to the north and opening a way to the fortress town of Huoyi, a major base on the way to the Yellow River. As the army threaded its way through the mountains, the weather turned and constant rain pelted the soldiers. Coming to the head of the pass which overlooked the Fen River valley, the army made camp while the rains continued.

Li Yuan and his forces reached Guhubao, near Huoyi (Huozhou Shanxi), on 14 July. Li Yuan's enemies hurried to Daxing and reported that the Tang were on the march and approaching Huoyi. The court of Yang You, King of Dai, sent commander Song Laosheng with 20,000 select troops to defend Huoyi. They also sent Commander Qutu Tong to garrison Hedong (Yongji Shanxi), to block Li Yuan's advance. The bad weather continued; rain fell for days. Li Yuan encamped to wait out the storms. He sent Shen Shu An with older and weaker soldiers back to Taiyuan to collect the supplies needed to maintain Li Yuan's force for a month.

The rains continued. While his advance stalled near Guhubao, Li Yuan sent an offer of alliance to Li Mi at Luokou. Li Mi was one of the many rebels who had seized local power with the collapse of Sui administration. He thought his army was stronger than Li Yuan's, and while not rejecting an alliance, demanded the leadership of the alliance and ordered Li Yuan to come to Henei (Qinyang Henan). Li Yuan and his advisors agreed that Li Mi was much too impressed with his position; but if they simply refused him, he would see them as enemies. Rather, they should placate him. Li Yuan's advisors agreed that they should let Li Mi attack the Sui forces in Luoyang, pinning them in place and so keeping his own forces busy. Then Li Yuan could continue his advance on Daxing without worrying about his rear. Li Yuan wrote to Li Mi to the effect that Li Yuan was only a minor official who was thrust into an important position. He was merely attempting to keep suffering to a minimum. If Li Mi could bring peace to the empire, Li Yuan would only be pleased and requested just the title, Lord of Tang. Li Mi was very pleased and saw himself already as emperor.

The situation suddenly shifted. Supplies and food failed to arrive and news came that Liu Wuzhou, in the north, was allied with the Turks. They were about to attack Jinyang. This threatened the Tang base at Taiyuan. Some of Li Yuan's advisors recommended that they give up the expedition and return to Taiyuan to protect their base, which held their families, relatives and treasure. However, Li Shimin and his supporters pointed out that the crops were ripe, and in their front Song Laosheng was not a great military leader. Li Mi would cause no trouble, and Liu Wuzhou was not really in agreement with the Turks. If they gave up their march to Daxing, what were they trying to do? Be bandits like the rest? If so, would their men follow them? Rather, he argued, they should continue with their expedition and pick up the pieces later. After much travail, back and forth, Li Yuan agreed on continuing the expedition. Then the supply train finally arrived.

On 1 August 617, the rains stopped and the weather cleared to become bright and sunny. The Tang army laid out their equipment, weapons and trapping to dry in the sun. On the morning of 3 August, Li Yuan resumed the march on Daxing. Taking a mountain road, they headed toward Huoyi, a town held by Song Laosheng. The problem for the Tang was that if Song Laosheng simply stayed put and defended the town, then the Tang advance would again be blocked. Li Shimin pointed out that Song was brave but none too bright. They should have light cavalry demonstrate before the town walls and spread the rumour that if Song did not come out, the Tang would claim he had joined them, and so he would lose whatever credibility he may have had.

Li Yuan led his personal guard and some *dui* of light cavalry to about a mile from the town and waited. First son Li Jiancheng and second son Li Shimin, with about fifty cavalry, rode up to the walls. They pointed with their whips this way and that, pretending to lay out a siege deployment. They saw Song standing on the wall, and they yelled insults at him. Song returned the insults and ordered his army of some 30,000 men to deploy out of the town by the east and south gates. As Song's army began marching out, Li Yuan sent Yin Kaishan to his main force, ordering them to come quickly. They soon arrived, and rather than wait while the troops deployed, Li Shimin led the attack while Song's force was still deploying.

The attack launched, Li Yuan and Li Jiancheng led their heavy cavalry to the east gate, Li Shimin leading his force of heavy cavalry to the south gate. Li Yuan led the primary force against Song's main body while Li Shimin attacked with the secondary force and his personal guards against Song's secondary force. Song's men pushed back Li Yuan and Li Jiancheng, but Li Shimin tore into the force facing him, breaking through their lines and swirling around. He fought with two broadswords, killing some thirty men, blood covering his sleeves, which he shook off. He is said to have fought until his swords were blunted. While Li Shimin ripped apart the support force, Li Yuan and Li Jiancheng's men beginning yelling that they had captured Song Laosheng. The detritus of the support force sweeping through the area and hearing that their commander was captured unsettled Song's army. The men began to withdraw into the town. Seeing this, Li Yuan and Li Jiancheng threw their army at Song's forces, which broke and ran toward the gates. As the Tang advanced up to the east gate, the guards closed it. Song Laosheng was left outside. His men on the wall top, seeing him, threw him a rope to climb into the town. Song began climbing, but an under officer, Lu June, and his squad ran to the rope and caught and killed Song.

Lu brought the head of Song to Li Yuan at dusk. Li Yuan ordered his army to assault the walls and carry the town by escalade. Without scaling equipment, the Tang soldiers formed up in human ladders, climbing on each other's backs to get to the wall top and capturing the town. Li Yuan announced, 'In the rain of arrows and stones in the battlefield, both noblemen and humbled servants are equally exposed to death. Why should there be any difference then when they are rewarded? So they should be justly rewarded if they render the same service.' On 4 August, Li Yuan accepted the allegiance of the officials and people of Huoyi and gave food to the poor. The Tang conscripted able-bodied men into the army.

The Tang leaders turned the captured town into a new base for their campaign. Regrouping their army and resupplying their logistical column, the Lord of Tang and his generals saw that the route down the Fen River valley to the Yellow River was open. Li Yuan and his army soon resumed the expedition to Guanzhong. On 8 August, they took Linfan and its hinterland. On the 13th, they took Jiang (Xinjiang, Shanxi), and on the 15th, they reached Longmen (Yumenkou) on the east bank of the Yellow River. Before them, beyond the great Yellow River, was their objective.

Battle for Guanzhong

The military geography facing the Lord of Tang was complicated: the military history of the Central Realm contained accounts of many campaigns in this area, with both crushing victories and shattering defeats. The Yellow River is already some 1,000 miles long by the time it reaches this vicinity. It wanders and twists around in vast loops and curves, heading north, then east, then south. Flowing along the line of the Luliang Mountains, the river heads south. Then the great flow of the river turns at a 90° angle to the east and proceeds for another 500 miles. At this change of direction, the 'Great Bend' of the Yellow River, mountains enclose the river's swift flow. Here the Wei River, a much smaller but substantial tributary, flows from the west directly into the angle of the 'Great Bend'. The valley of the Wei extends west into a series of hills and mountains. This is the 'Land within the Passes' and here is the great city of Daxing (renamed Chang'an in 618). The objective of the Tang army, coming south along the Fen River, was to cross the Yellow River and advance up the valley of the Wei River to Daxing. However, strong fortresses and the swift deadly flow of the Yellow River were in the way.

Liu Wenjing arrived at Li Yuan's camp near the Yellow River, bringing 500 Turkish cavalry and 2,000 horses. Li Yuan was very pleased that the Turks came only after he reached the Yellow River. He complimented Liu on bringing few Turkish soldiers but many horses. At Longmen, Li Yuan and his staff had to consider their next move. They directed a small select force to cross the Yellow River at Longmen and take Yongfengcang, the site of an imperial granary. Then, the proponents asserted, they would advance their main force across the Yellow River near Hedong. With a proper pronouncement, Guanzhong would recognize Tang supremacy. They may not have Daxing fall into their hands, but the province would be theirs.

Much of the Sui administration in Guanzhong had fallen apart. The strongest local potentate-warlord was Sun Hua. Li Yuan had asked him to join the Tang cause. While the Tang were collecting forces to move into Guanzhong, they had sent an army north to Hukou (Jixian Shanxi). Here Tang agents began collecting boats and rafts to transport troops and supplies across the Yellow River at Longmen to the north of the main crossing site. On 24 August, Sun Hua brought a force to the river bank opposite Longmen. He crossed over to meet Li Yuan, bringing just a few cavalrymen. Li Yuan received him with honour, appointing him Lord of Wuqinqxian and governor of Pingyi Commandery (Dali Shaanxi). Li Yuan appointed Sun Hua as leader of the Tang forces in his lands on the Shaanxi side of the Yellow River. Sun Hua's force provided protection while 6,000 Tang infantry with a small force of cavalry crossed the Yellow River. Here they built a camp awaiting the arrival of the main Tang forces. Li Yuan appointed Ren Gui as extraordinary envoy and sent him to the governors of Guanzhong commanderies. He first sought out the governor of Hancheng, persuading him to recognize Li Yuan as legitimate.

Li Yuan and his council discussed their next operation. The commander of the Tang field army, Wang Changxie, received his orders: take a mixed force of heavy infantry and cavalry and cross the Yellow River at Longmen, advance south along the western bank and take up position opposite Hedong, on the east side of the Yellow River near where the Wei River enters the Yellow River and the Yellow Rivers turns from flowing south to flowing to the east. Li Yuan pointed out that the Sui commander of Hedong, Qutu Tong, had a strong force of elite troops. He made no move to attack the Tang forces, even though some of his soldiers were within 10 miles of them. When Wang encamped, Li Yuan would attack Hedong. Qutu Tong could either stay and defend Hedong or leave the city and march his army west toward Daxing. If he remained in the city, the Tang would capture it and him. If he attempted to leave, then Wang's army would defeat him and the city would fall.

Qutu Tong decided to try to both defend Hedong and defeat Wang's field force. Besides maintaining the walls of the town, Qutu Tong organized a special strike force under Sang Xianhe of several thousand heavy cavalry. On the night of 7 September, the Sui forces threw a pontoon bridge across the Yellow River and Sang led the heavy cavalry onto the west bank. Sang's attack surprised Wang's camp. Wang's force mobilized and fell back under strong pressure, but the infantry held off the attack long enough for Wang to organize his cavalry force. They escaped from their camp, swung around and attacked Sang's army in the rear. Sang's force broke and fled back across the bridge into Hedong.

Now Tang had Sang Xianhe blockaded in Hedong. Thousands had come from Guanzhong to join with the Tang. Li Yuan and his staff had to consider their next move. Should they besiege Hedong and finish with Qutu Tong or mask Hedong and advance on Daxing? Pei Ji supported the case for ending with Hedong. His argument was that if the Tang left Hedong uncaptured in their rear while they advanced against Daxing and failed to carry the city, they would be caught between two enemies, the force in Daxing and the powerful army in Hedong. But if they took Hedong, then Daxing would fall of its own accord. Li Shimin countered: they had won victories. If they pushed on to Daxing, they would not be ready for them. Speed would conquer. Their strategist would not have plans; the fighters would not have organized their tactics. But if they spend time in an extended siege, many of their new-found allies would leave them, bad morale would strike their army and their enemies will perfect their preparations. Qutu Tong had enough to do to defend Hedong. Li Yuan agreed with those who wanted an immediate offensive.

Li Yuan marches into Guanzhong

On 12 September 617, Li Yuan crossed the Yellow River on the pontoon bridge between Hedong and Pujin. On 16 September, the Tang forces reached Zhaoyi (east of Dali, Shaanxi). Li Yuan took up residence in the Changchun Palace and received the support of thousands of local militia and many officials. Many people high in the Sui administration came, and Li Yuan confirmed their positions. Seeing that no force would immediately challenge him, Li Yuan began to consolidate his position. On 18 September, he organized an army of 30,000 men, led by first son Li Jiancheng, with an experienced staff, to go to Yongfengcang (near Huayin, Shaanxi), a critical food depository. Once they secured the warehouse, Li Jiancheng's troops were to block the Tongguan Pass to cover the Tang position from a Sui attack from the east. Li Yuan also organized another force of 30,000 under second son Li Shimin, again with an experienced staff, to hold the area north of the Weishui River.

When Qutu Tong found out that Li Yuan was advancing toward Daxing, he appointed commander Rao Jun Su as defender of Hedong. Qutu broke out of Hedong with 30,000 men and marched toward the Daxing. First son Li Jiancheng's force blocked the way. The Sui commander, Liu Gang, held the Tongguan Pass. After avoiding the Tang force, Qutu Tong marched to join Sui troops in the Tongguan Pass. But Jiancheng launched a surprise attack and swept through the pass, taking the town of Tongguan, killing Liu Gang. Qutu Tong quickly counter-attacked Tongguan, but Jiancheng's force repelled him. Qutu Tong then encamped some miles north of the town. Li Yuan sent reinforcement to keep Hedong blockaded.

Upheaval in Guanzhong

As the Tang forces fought through Shanxi, the Guanzhong area devolved into chaos. Li Yuan's daughter, Lady Li, was married to Chai Shao; they lived in Daxing. When news of uprisings came, Chai Shao decided to go to Li Yuan, but Lady Li stayed in Guanzhong to work for her father's success. She went to Huxian

(Shaanxi), where she joined up with a cousin, Li Shen Tong, who was involved with a group of rebels. Under her directions and with their group, they raised money and soldiers, attacking and taking towns, kidnapping officials and attracting numerous groups of bandit rebels. Lady Li soon led an army of 70,000 men, taking towns and gathering recruits. Another son-in-law, Duan Lun, raised 10,000 men. When Li Yuan crossed the Yellow River, these leaders came to him. He accepted their submission, rewarding many with offices and others with gifts. The newly raised forces were placed under the command of second son Shimin.

The head of the Sui administration in Daxing was Wei Wensheng, Minister of Justice and head of capital defence. News arrived that Li Yuan and his army was marching toward Daxing. Wei Wensheng suddenly became ill. The Sui prince, Yang You, King of Dai, appointed as governor of the capital Gu Yi and commander Yin Shishi to organize its defence. On 21 September, Li Yuan reached Pujin on the west bank of the Yellow River. On 22 September, he crossed the Wuishui River from Linjin (Zhaoyi in Dali Shaanxi) and moved on to Yongfengcang. On 23 September, Li Yuan returned to Zhaoyi and Changchun Palace, then the next day, Li Yuan moved to Pingyi (Dali Shaanxi).

As second son Li Shimin marched toward Daxing, numerous officials came and pledged allegiance to Li Yuan. Shimin occupied Jingyang and organized his army, now of about 90,000 men. Lady Li met Shimin to the north of the Wei River with 10,000 professional soldiers. Chai Shao also brought his force. The three armies camped separately under separate commands. Li Shimin took the allegiance of numerous bands that came to offer their services.

Li Yuan Takes Daxing

Li Yuan sent a force of 60,000 men toward Daxing. They arrived at Fufeng (Fufeng Shaanxi) and crossed the Wei River to the south side, near Daxing, moving to the site of old Chang'an. Sui forces emerged to test the strength of the Tang army. They then returned to the city. As this force approached, Li Shimin led the main force of 130,000 men to Sizhuyuan (Zhouzhi Shaanxi), proceeding to Echeng, where the old Epang Palaces were located (near Xian). The Tang forces were strictly disciplined; they neither pillaged nor abused the people.

Li Shimin sent a messenger to Li Yuan, telling him that the area was secure and Daxing was vulnerable. Li Yuan told Li Shimin that Qutu Tong was well contained, and his force was coming. Li Yuan ordered a selection of his best troops to march through Xinfeng to the Changle Palace in old Chang'an. Li Shimin brought his troops to the north of old Chang'an. On 28 September, Li Yuan took command of the whole army and advanced on Daxing, setting up camp to the north-west of the Chunming Gate. He gathered his army and surrounded the city, deploying some 200,000 men. Li Yuan then commanded that his army not interfere with the civilian population and stay within their camps. He sent spokesmen to the wall, announcing that the Tang force was there only to support the Sui Dynasty. The spokesmen addressed his message to Wei Wensheng: they received no answer. On 13 October, Li Yuan ordered the investment of Daxing. On 26 October, he ordered his troops to prepare visibly for an assault. His orders included that the seven ancestral temples of the House of Sui not be damaged. He also ordered that the King of Dai and his family receive proper respect. On 8 November, the Tang force set ladders against the walls and began the assault. Resistance was minimal. Under-officer Lei Yongji was first to scale the walls. Troops followed and opened the gates, and Li Yuan marched into the city.

Yang You, King of Dai, was staying in the East Palace, the Crown Prince's Palace. All his attendants fled. Only his personal attendant, Yao Si Lian, stayed. When the Tang soldiers arrived in the king's court, Yao Si Lian ordered them to stop. He announced that if the Lord of Tang's army was law-abiding and supported the imperial house of the Sui Dynasty, then they must show proper respect. The troops withdrew from the court. When Li Yuan arrived, the King of Dai received him well. Li Yuan accompanied the imperial prince to the Daxing Palace, the official seat of the Sui Dynasty. Yao Si Lian organized the King of Dai's residence, and the king sat upon the throne in the Hall of Shunyangge.

Li Yuan took up residence in the Changle Palace. His advisors rewrote the Sui law code, making twelve sections, which abrogated the harsh legislation of the Sui emperors. Wei Wensheng had died by the time Li Yuan entered Daxing. Li Yuan arrested ten chief officers and executed them; everyone else was pardoned.

Li Yuan Elevates the King of Dai as Sui Emperor

On 15 November, Li Yuan organized an imperial procession to install the 13-year-old Yang You as emperor. The imperial carriage carried him to Tianxing Hall, where Li Yuan placed the young man on the imperial throne as Emperor Gong. Emperor Yang, far away in Jiangdu, now became Father Emperor. Emperor Gong soon appointed Li Yuan as prime minister. He awarded Li Yuan with the Golden Ax, symbol of military and civil power, and granted Li Yuan the authority to formulate and issue decrees. Li Yuan established an administration in the Wudi Hall of the imperial palace that would re-establish order in those parts of the realm controlled by Tang. He appointed first son Jiancheng as heir apparent, with second son Shimin as Lord of Qin and third son Yuanji becoming Lord of Qi. In January 618, Emperor Gong elevated Li Yuan to King of Tang. All the area under Tang military occupation accepted the prime minister's administration.

Li Yuan Accepts Qutu Tong's Surrender

For a month, Liu Wenjing, supported by Li Yuan, confronted Qutu Tong in the Tongguan area. Qutu Tong sent Sang Xianhe in a surprise night attack against Liu Wenjing's camp. Liu's soldiers responded quickly, repelling Sang's attack. Liu counter-attacked, capturing most of Sang's men. Qutu Tong's soldiers deserted in large numbers. His advisors told Qutu Tong that he should surrender to Li Yuan. But Qutu Tong believed his loyalty should remain with Emperor Yang, and he killed an envoy sent by Li Yuan to request his surrender. Qutu soon heard that Daxing had fallen to Li Yuan and his family was held by the Tang. He gave the command of Tongguan to Sang Xianhe and took his main force on the road to Luoyang. Sang immediately surrendered Tongguan to Liu Wenjing, who sent his lieutenant, Dou Cong, and Sang Xianhe with light cavalry to capture Qutu. They caught up with him at Chousang (Lingbao Henan), where Qutu Tong deployed his army in battle formation. Sang Xianhe appealed first to Qutu and then to his army, telling them that the Tang now controlled Guanzhong, their homes. Qutu's army put down their weapons and Sang enrolled them in Tang service. Qutu dismounted and surrendered. Taken to Daxing, Li Yuan received Qutu Tong and appointed him a minister of war and Lord of Jiang. Li Shimin took him into service.

References

Chinese sources: *Jiu Tangshu* (*Old Book of Tang*), 1, 2, 57–59, 64; *Xin Tangshu* (*New Book of Tang*), 79, 88; *Zizhi Tongjian*, 175, 184; Wen Daya, *Da Tang Chuangye Qiju Zhu* (*Court Diary of the Founding of the Great Tang*) (used by *Zizhi Tongjian*).
Bingham, pp.83–104.
C.P. Fitzgerald, pp.31–36, 41–47.
Graff, *Medieval*, pp.164–65.
Hung, pp.24–28, 40–45.

Part II

The House of Li

The Splintered Realm

From 614 through to 618, the Sui administration crumbled. Because Emperor Yang could still control the areas near his waterway systems, rebel-held lands were small and unconnected, even though extensive. A number of rebel leaders raised themselves into potentates by forming alliances with local powers, but these political units were unstable. In order to see the political setting facing the House of Li, I include here a basic overview of the splintered realm. This anticipates some of the events in the following narrative but should help to clarify the complex setting from which the House of Li rose.

By mid-summer 618, nine potentates had divided the Sui realm, each scheming to find ways to supreme power. Centred in Hebei, Dou Jiande took the title King of Changle in 617, then advanced south to the Yellow River. Originally a well-off peasant in Qinghe Commandery (Xingtai Hebei), Dou was made commander of 200 men conscripted for Emperor Yang's war with Koguryo in 611. Because of floods followed by famine, caused in part by the massive conscriptions taking most of the men away, Dou allowed his men to collect several hundred more conscripts and flee from imperial control. The Sui officials suspected Dou of conspiring with the deserters, raided his farm and killed his family. Dou fled to the deserters' camps and eventually became a leader of some 10,000 men. Many local rebel leaders had made it a point to kill educated men and landowners. Dou respected former officials and the educated. He employed them in office and reconstructed an administration. Former Sui officials recognized his regime and brought whole commanderies under his power.

In Henan, south of the Yellow River, Li Mi now held power. He had come from the same old north-west nomad-Chinese background as the Sui and Tang. He had supported Yang Xuangan in 613, and fled to the bandit chief, Zhai Rang. Zhai set up Li Mi as the respected figurehead leader of his band, but Li Mi turned the tables and eliminated Zhai Rang. He assiduously recruited former Sui troops and peasants. Li Mi's grasp of power rested on his control of the great Sui granary at the confluence of the Luo River with the Yellow River. This surplus of food allowed him to feed his followers and attract new followers in Henan and Shangdong. He received the title Lord of Wei from the Sui Emperor in Luoyang. However, everyone understood that he was looking at the imperial throne.

A rival to Li Mi, Wang Shichong, held Luoyang. Emperor Yang had sent him north after he crushed a revolt in Jiangdu. Wang came from a Sogdian family connected to the old nomad regimes of the north. If not a member of the Chinese aristocracy, he certainly was a great Iranian horse lord. The Sui Emperor in Luoyang was 14 and was managed by a regency council. Wang controlled the council as prime minister, and so ran the regime in Luoyang. Li Mi hated Wang for trouncing his efforts to become Sui prime minister. He blockaded Luoyang and kept threatening to cut supplies.

Between the Huai River and Yangzi River, Du Fuwei, a poor peasant and brigand, held control. He had become a bandit during the upheavals of Emperor Yang's reign in the Long White Mountain of Qi Commandery, which was south of the Yellow River in Shandong. Du led his band south across the Huai River to escape Sui soldiers. When the Sui regime collapsed in the south, Du extended control over the south side of the Yangzi.

Xiao Xian, who ruled in northern Hunan, was a former Sui rural official and descendant of the Liang Dynasty. The Soaring Hawk Command appointed him military commander. But with the death of Emperor Yang, Xiao Xian proclaimed the Liang Dynasty restored, with himself as emperor. He established his capital in Jiangling and controlled most of the ancient kingdom of Chu south of the Yangzi.

In the north, in Jincheng Commandery (Lanzhou), the local Soaring Hawk commander, Xue Ju, sent troops to arrest the local Sui officials, opened the public granaries to feed the population and proclaimed himself King of Western Qin. He expanded his power across eastern Gansu and proclaimed himself emperor. On the southern edge of the Ordos, Liang Shidu, a military commander at Shuofang Commandery, took over the area and proclaimed himself emperor in spring 617. At the same time, the local commander at Mayi Commandery (south of Datong Shanxi), Liu Wuzhou, killed the governor, opened the granaries and proclaimed himself emperor. Shibi Khan of the Eastern Turks supported both Liang and Liu, putting his finger in the rotten Sui pie to pull out a couple of juicy morsels.

In autumn 618, there were three major regional powers: Li Mi in Henan, Dou Jiande's Xia Dynasty in Hebei and Li Yuan's Tang Dynasty in Guanzhong and Shanxi. In this mix, there were two large-scale wars testing the viability of major powers: Li Mi had to eliminate Wang Shichong and seize Luoyang if his regime was ever going to expand. Wang, as representative of the Sui Dynasty, just might be able to turn the table on Li Mi. Li Yuan and the Tang faced a strong threat from the Xue forces in Gansu, who fought with Turkish assistance and were expanding into the Western Wei Valley. While needing to at least check the Xue, Li Yuan sent small forces west to meddle in the major war on the central plains.

References

Chinese sources: *Suishi*, 4, 24, 70, 83; *Jiu Tangshu* (*Old Book of Tang*), 53, 56; *Xin Tangshu* (*New Book of Tang*), 84; *Zizhi Tongjian*, 183.

Woodbridge Bingham, *The Founding of the T'ang Dynasty*, pp.51-72, gives the most complete account in English of the collapse of the Sui Dynasty.

Chapter 7

Battles for the Heart of China

Fall of Emperor Yang

After Shibi Khan and his Turks withdrew from Yen Men, Emperor Yang also left. He went to Taiyuan and began preparations to travel south. The emperor revoked all of the promises he had made when he and his entourage were trapped by Shibi Khan. He was unaware of the widespread upheavals, rebellions and banditries which racked the Sui Empire. His ministers and attendants told the emperor that there were only minor disturbances that could be easily handled. When the emperor reissued the orders for the Koguryo conscription, resentment and rebellion boiled up, but Emperor Yang remained oblivious. He decreed that he would now direct the realm from his southern palace at Yangzhou near the Yangzi. The emperor loved the complex and luxurious life in the south. He easily spoke the 'tongue of Wu'. His administrators feared that if he took the administrative centre south, the northern part of the realm along the Yellow River would establish independent regimes. Since they feared to tell the emperor about the severity of disturbances, they tried to argue that such upheavals would arise if the emperor went south. The emperor ended the discussions when he ordered the officials who presented these arguments to be executed immediately.

Once at the eastern capital, Luoyang, Emperor Yang organized his river fleet flotilla, imperial guards and labour gangs. He set off in the great decorated barges carrying his large court down the Yellow River toward the canals connecting with the Yangzi, on the way to Yangzhou. When the flotilla reached the canal, imperial cavalry rode along both sides as labourers pulled the barges along. When the emperor began moving along the canal, many people gathered, demonstrating their displeasure with him for leaving them. He ordered the troops to kill the protestors: that stopped all demonstrations. Once in the south, Emperor Yang settled in his palace and large gardens, ignoring the developing chaos in the north. Any official unwise enough to bring up the subject was lucky if he survived the experience.

By 617, Emperor Yang's personal authority only extended around Yangzhou, modern Jiangxi and Jiangsu. Strongmen supported by local landowning families set themselves up as rulers of independent states. The only other areas firmly recognizing the Sui Dynasty were the western and eastern capitals, Chang'an and Luoyang, along with Sichuan up the Yangzi rapids. The emperor's hold on the south was none too strong. A rebellion led by Liu Yuanjin had swept through the Yangzi delta region in Jianqnan to the south-west of the river. Emperor Yang appointed Wang Shichong commander of Jiangdu in 613, assigning him some 30,000 men, and ordered him to suppress the rebels. Wang attacked Liu Yuanjin's forces, scattered them in battle and killed Liu. But most of the rebels, who were escaped conscripts, bandits, peasants and displaced people, hid rather than surrender, keeping up a desultory campaign against local officials. Wang chased here and there but got nowhere. He published a notification that he would pardon any rebel who surrendered. Within a month, tens of thousands of rebel soldiers surrendered; Wang had them all killed in a single day. While some who were sceptical of the offer stayed away from Wang's reach, the rebels' numbers were much reduced. Wang Shichong then became a favorite of the emperor.

The imperial court knew that the dynasty's future rested with the emperor's grandson, Crown Prince Yang Tung, who resided in Luoyang. Yang Tung was the son of Emperor Yang's son, former Crown Prince Yang Zhao, who had been grossly overweight and died in 606. A rebel army led by Li Mi threatened Luoyang. This Li Mi had been chief strategist for the rebel Yang Xuangan, leader of rebellion against Emperor Yang during the Koguryo war. After Yang Xuangan's defeat and death, Li Mi went into hiding. Once Emperor Yang went south, Li Mi reassembled the old rebel army and began to build a new regime in the north. His first major objective was Luoyang. He defeated forces of Crown Prince Tung and seized the imperial granaries, distributing the grain to local people. With local reinforcements, he put Luoyang under siege. Emperor Yang sent Wang Shichong north with an army and supplies to succour Luoyang. Li Mi attacked Wang's force and pushed him into Luoyang. The men and supplies strengthened Luoyang, but could not defeat Li Mi.

Beyond sending Wang Shichong to Luoyang, Emperor Yang did nothing but stay in the recesses of his great palace and gardens. Surrounded by troops of beautiful women, the emperor enjoyed the entertainments they provided. However, news of the disturbances in the north bothered his officials and commanders, who did not like the south anyway. Their families and properties were in the north, and they wanted to go back. Many of the officers and men of the Imperial Guard left and returned to their homes on their own. Emperor Yang ordered the execution of all deserters, but understood the desires of his men. In the spring of 618, he organized a massive marriage ceremony of all his soldiers with new southern women so that they would start new families. Despite this effort of imperial compassion, Emperor Yang's administration disintegrated. Soldiers, commanders, officials and ministers disappeared as they returned to the north and the ongoing upheaval. The emperor was aware of the collapse continuing around him. His empress related the story: Emperor Yang looked into a mirror while combing his hair and remarked, 'Such a beautiful head! Who would dare to cut it off?'

Commander Sima Dekan was in charge of the elite cavalry troops in the eastern part of Jiangdu. He and his subordinate commanders decided to march north to their homes. One of the subordinate commanders informed a high official in the civil engineering department, Yuwen Zhiji. This man, part of the old imperial dynasty of Zhou, welcomed the news. However, he told the conspirators that Emperor Yang still had strong support among the troops, and if they tried to escape from the south, they would be caught and killed. However, together, the officers commanded tens of thousands of powerful troops. They thought it better that they should rebel here and now and overthrow Emperor Yang. Then they would be masters of China. Sima Dekan agreed. The conspirators chose Yuwen Huaji, elder brother of Yuwen Zhiji, as their leader. Sima had the rumour spread that Emperor Yang had learned that the elite cavalry was going to flee, that he prepared a lot of poisoned wine and intended to kill them all. This rumour spread fear throughout the armed forces. The conspirators repeated the story that the emperor intended to stay in the south, and he would deal harshly with any opposition.

On 12 March 618, a windy and clouded day, Sima gathered all his officers in Yangzhou and explained the new plan of action. They all pledged to support Sima. As the day waned, Sima stole horses from the imperial stable and ordered his elite cavalrymen to ready their accoutrements. When night fell, Pei Yutong, who was a conspirator, commanded the Imperial Guard of the inner palace. Tang Feng, also in the conspiracy, commanded the guards of the city gates. He ordered the guards to close the gates, as they did every night, but this time to leave them unsecured. Sima sent orders to his cavalry to mobilize their 30,000 troopers in the eastern section of Jiangdu. Sima then fired a small building, so the flames were visible from quite a distance. This was the signal to his compatriots outside the city that all was ready.

Emperor Yang saw the flames and commotion outside the palace and became alarmed. He demanded to know from Pei Yutong what was going on. Pei answered that a straw shed was on fire, and everyone was doing their best to extinguish it. The emperor was somewhat relieved. At that time, Yuwen Zhiji gathered 1,000 infantry outside the city. Yang Tan, a grandson of the emperor, learned of the rebellion and hurried to the palace to tell Emperor Yang, but Pei intercepted him and locked him away. Before dawn the next day, Sima ordered all guards at the city gates replaced with troops loyal to Pei. Then Pei brought a squad of heavy cavalry to the great audience hall, the Chengxiang. The guards in the hall began yelling that rebels were coming. Pei Yutong had his troopers close the great doors of Chengxiang Hall, except the east door. The troopers then pushed the guardsmen out of the east door. The guards obeyed the order to leave their arms by the door as they left. The guard commander, Gudu Sheng, heard this disturbance and came from his office without his armour, followed by ten of his officers. Gudu accosted Pie, demanding to know the purpose of this bizarre military action. Pie informed Gudu that a rebellion was in progress and that he should best stay out of it. Gudu responded that Pie was an old rebel, and he and his men attacked Pie. Pie's troopers quickly cut them down.

Meanwhile, Sima Dekan led a large contingent of heavy cavalry through the Xuanwu Gate up the main street to the palace. Emperor Yang now realized things were going badly. He dumped his imperial robes and dressed in the clothes of a palace servant, hiding in a utility room in the waiting rooms to the west of Chengxiang Hall. Pei Yutong needed to find the emperor, but could not do so. Pei and Yuan Li looked for the emperor in the suite of rooms on the east but found nothing. Pei assembled the palace women and demanded to know where the emperor had gone. A beauty pointed to the suite on the west side. Officer Linghu Xingda went into the suite and found Emperor Yang behind a curtain. Linghu assured the emperor that he was not going to kill him. Indeed, they were going to escort him back to the north. He brought the emperor into the great room. Seeing Pei Yutong, an old friend, the emperor wanted to know why they were in rebellion. Pei informed the emperor that they were not rebelling but were going to take him back to the north. The emperor agreed, adding that he always intended to return to the north. Pei assigned an honour guard for the emperor.

In the morning, Yuwen Huaji, recognized as the prime minister by the insurgents, arrived at the palace gate. Sima Dekan met him and welcomed him into the great open court in front of Chengxiang Hall. Inside the hall, Pei had Emperor Yang dressed in the imperial robe and told him that the ministers were in the court ready to receive him. A courtier brought a horse, and the emperor mounted. When the emperor rode out into the court, the soldiers cheered. Yuwen Huaji was not pleased. He told Pei, 'Don't show the emperor. Take him back. Kill him.'

Sima and Pei, as personal guards with drawn swords, turned the emperor around and led him back into the hall. The emperor saw what was going to happen and began whining about his innocence. His youngest son, 12-year-old Yang Gao, King of Zhao, stood by the emperor crying. Pei Yutong took his sword and killed the child, the blood splattering on the emperor's imperial robes. Pei raised his sword to kill the emperor, but Yang cried out that an emperor had his way to die and ordered poison brought. Instead, Linghu Xingda placed the emperor in a chair. The emperor handed his silk neck scarf to Linghu, who draped a loop about the emperor's neck and strangled him. The insurgents then spread out in the city, plundering and killing. They killed all the emperor's sons and his ministers, except Yang Hao, King of Qin and friend of Yuwen Zhiji. Yuwen Huaji made Yang Hao emperor to give legitimacy to his rule.

The Sui regime in the south collapsed. Yuwen Huaji assumed command and organized a march north. With some 100,000 men and Empress Xiao, along with Emperor Yang's concubines, they travelled by boat to Pengcheng (Xuzhou Jiangsu). Here the waterway was blocked. Yuwen Huaji commandeered some 2,000 wagons for transport of the women and supplies, but the soldiers had to march with all their arms and armour. Discontent led to plots, but Yuwen found and executed dissidents. Yuwen decided to march to Luoyang. Because he was related to the old Northern Zhou Dynasty, Yuwen Huaji saw himself as successor to the Sui Dynasty.

War for Luoyang

In Luoyang on 25 May 618, Yang Tong proclaimed himself Sui Emperor Tong when confirmation came that Emperor Yang was dead. A little later, word came that Emperor Yang's murderer, Yuwen Huaji, was marching toward Luoyang with a large army. The court was in consternation. Already facing the threat of Li Mi, now an even more vicious threat was coming. An advisor, Gai Cong, suggested to the court that Emperor Tong offer Li Mi an official position in the Sui court provided he resist Yuwen Huaji. Since the Sui in Luoyang were not strong enough to overthrow Li Mi, not to mention Yuwen, the idea was for both of them to weaken each other and then the Sui court might be able to overcome the victor. Presumably, Li Mi would defeat Yuwen. But the court knew Li Mi's forces were made up of diverse groups, and some of them would be open to bribery. The court appointed Gai Cong as emissary to offer an official position to Li Mi.

Yuwen Huaji reorganized his forces at Huatai (Huaxian Henan). He set up a base there under his commander, Wang Gui, and stored his supplies and war materiel. He then marched north to Liyang (Xunxian Henan), a stronghold of Li Mi. Commanded by Xu Shiji, Liyang was too small to withstand an assault. Xu withdrew his forces west to Cangcheng (south-west of Xunxian Henan), where there was a great granary. Yuwen Huaji crossed the Yellow River, took Liyang and then sent a force to besiege Cangcheng. Xu Shiji reinforced Cangcheng's fortifications with a ditch and stockades. He communicated with Li Mi using fire signals. Li Mi organized a force of some 200,000 foot and horse and brought them to within striking distance of Yuwen's army from the west. However, Li Mi still had to worry about the forces to his west in Luoyang. While Li Mi kept his force in place, threatening Yuwen but not moving, Xu Shiji had his men excavate tunnels under his ditch and stockade, the soldiers bursting out in Yuwen's camp and lines, burning equipment and war machines. This relieved some of the pressure on Li Mi's main force, but he was pleased when Gai Cong arrived with the offer of official recognition. He responded with pledges of loyalty to Emperor

Tong and the Sui Dynasty, and requested that he be sent against Yuwen Huaji as atonement for his previous derelictions. As a sign of loyalty, Li Mi sent a captive commander of Yuwen Huaji to the emperor in Luoyang. As a symbol of unity, the Sui administration granted Li Mi the title Lord of Wei and made Xu Shiji Grand Commander.

Being part of the Sui administration relieved Li Mi of concern about his western flank. Now, in July, he could concentrate against Yuwen Huaji. Scouts told Li Mi that Yuwen's force was running low on supplies, so Li Mi sent envoys with an offer of peace. Yuwen saw this as the solution to his supply problem. Believing he could be resupplied without a problem, Yuwen kept issuing full rations. A little later, a deserter from Li Mi's camp told Yuwen that Li Mi was deceiving him. Yuwen was furious. As soon as he could, he mobilized his troops, deployed them across the Yongji Canal and marched to the foot of Tangshan Mountain (Qixian Henan). He had trapped Li Mi's army, and in the morning he forced a battle. Yuwen's attack included an arrow storm. An arrow struck Li Mi, who fell from his horse. Li Mi's men fled, except for Qin Shu Bao, who, with his followers, protected the fallen Li Mi. Qin's men rallied Li Mi's forces, who pushed back Yuwen's men to pull Li Mi out of danger. But Yuwen held the field.

Yuwen, concerned about supplies, sent foragers to Ji and Dong commanderies to gather food by any means. Li Mi was undeterred. Sending envoys to some of Yuwen's sub commanders, he informed them of his new relation with the Sui administration in Luoyang. Wang Gui, Yuwen Huaji's commander at Huatai, defected to Li Mi, along with his territory. The news shocked Yuwen, who started to march toward Huatai to retake the land. While on the march, Yuwen's cavalry commanders, with tens of thousands of troops, pulled out and went over to Li Mi. Only some 20,000 troops remained with Yuwen. He retreated to Wei Commandery (south-east of Hebei and north-west of Shangdong). Li Mi posted some of the defecting troops to keep Yuwen isolated.

In the Imperial Court at Luoyang

In Luoyang, Sui Chief Minister Yuan Wendu believed that Li Mi was trustworthy and loyal. Under Yuan's guidance, the court granted Li Mi his high honours. But Wang Shichong, the former favourite of Emperor Yang and now head of military affairs, did not like or trust Li Mi. Wang became even more upset when Li Mi defeated Yuwen Huaji. He believed that Li Mi was going to grab supreme power and was making Yuan Wendu into a fool. Wang was sure that once Li Mi did gain power, he would be killed. An associate of Wang let Yuan Wendu know that Wang distrusted Li Mi and Yuan. Rather than confront Wang, Yuan and his confidant Lu Chu decided to have him killed because they assumed that he was planning to grab power and kill them. Yuan and Lu set a plot in motion: the court would request that Wang Shichong present himself, and then guards would slay him. However, one of Yuan's conspirators, Duan Da, agreed with Wang. He sent his son-in-law to Wang, informing him about Yuan's plot.

Late at night on 15 July 618, Wang Shichong brought a select band of soldiers to the Hanjie Gate of the palace and attempted to force entry. Yuan Wendu, hearing of this, rushed to the emperor and deployed guards to defend the palace. The emperor immediately confirmed Yuan's orders. He had the palace gates locked and demanded resistance to Wang Shichong's attack. Guard commanders were not so inclined. Commander Baye Gang led all of his troopers out of the palace and surrendered to Wang. Other commanders ordered resistance to Wang's force, but quickly surrendered. Yuan Wendu commanded the soldiers who guarded the imperial person. Leading his crack troops, Yuan moved to the attack. He intended to march his force to the Xuanwu Gate, leave the palace and go around to hit Wang's force in their rear. But the commander of the gate garrison claimed he could not open the gate because his men had lost the keys. Yuan had to turn his unit around and head for the Taiyang Gate, on the other side of the palace. By that time, dawn was breaking.

While Yuan was hurrying through the Qianyang Hall, heading toward the Taiyang Gate, Wang's men broke through that gate and seized most of the palace except the imperial residence, the Zhiwei Palace. Wang's men killed the guards who resisted but let go those who fled. Coming to the Zhiwei Palace, Wang massed his troops to break through the Xingjiao Gate. A representative of the emperor appeared at the wall top. He demanded to know why Wang was attacking his emperor. Wang swiftly dismounted his horse and bowed deeply. He replied that, with profound apologies, he knew that Yuan Wendu and his fellows had conspired to kill him: 'I request that Yuan Wendu and Lu Chu die. Then shall I submit to the Imperial Law.'

Duan Da stepped up and ordered Commander Huang Tao Shu to arrest Yuan Wendu and deliver him to Wang Shichong. As he was escorted from the Palace, Yuan yelled, 'I am going to die. The Imperial Person will die soon!' The emperor cried as he waved Yuan on. As soon as Yuan was led out of the Xingjiao Gate, soldiers cut him down. Then Duan Da ordered the gates to open. Wang Shichong with his soldiers made a formal entry into the imperial palace. Wang had his men relieve and expel the guards who were there. The emperor, sitting in state in the Qianyang Hall, received Wang Shichong. Wang pledged loyalty to the emperor, who appointed him as prime minister.

As these events unfolded, Li Mi was marching with an impressive escort to Luoyang. He expected to receive the office of prime minster, promised by Yuan Wendu. But then news came of the morning's events and Li Mi turned his cavalcade around. He retraced his steps to Jinyang, a small town to the east of Luoyang. Li Mi grieved for Yuan Wendu and began to blockade Luoyang with the intent of overthrowing Wang Shichong.

References

Chinese sources: *Suishu*, 2, 4, 8, 64; *Jiu Tangshu*, 53, 64; *Xin Tangshu*, 1, 20, 84-85; *Zizhi Tongjian*, 175, 178, 180-83.

Bingham, 51, 54, 56-57, 59, 61-72.

Fitzgerald, 12-30.

Graff, 162-63.

Hung, 13-15.

Chapter 8

War for Domination I

Tang Advances East

While rumours had swirled through Daxing for months, finally unquestioned evidence came that Emperor Yang was dead. The Sui Emperor Yang You resigned the imperial office on 15 May and offered to recognize Li Yuan as emperor. Li Yuan assumed the imperial office on 21 May as founding emperor of the Tang Dynasty. Later Chinese historians refer to him as Emperor Gaozu. The new emperor organized his administration, appointing his chief advisors as ministers. His eldest son, Li Jiancheng, became Crown Prince, with second son Li Shimin as King of Qin and fourth son Li Yuanji as King of Qi. The Tang changed Daxing's name back to the older Chang'an. The former Sui Emperor became Lord of Xi.

After the death of Emperor Yang became known, the Tang faced a serious threat from the Qin Dynasty under the Xue family on the north and west fringes of the Wei River valley. In June 618, Xue Ju, Emperor of the Qin Dynasty, seized Jingzhou Commandery (Jingchuan Gansu). Li Yuan, Emperor Gaozu, appointed second son Li Shimin commander-in-chief of the expeditionary force to repel the Qin offensive. Li Shimin marched to Gaozhu (Changwu Shaanxi) and built a strong fortified camp with ditches and palisade. In July, Xue Ju's army advanced against Gaozhu, with outriders reaching Binzhou (Binxian and Xunxian Shaanxi) and Qizhou (near Fengxiang Shaanxi). Li Shimin intended to outwait Xue Ju, but he came down with malaria and relinquished command, with the instruction that his commanders, Liu Wenjing and Yin Kaishan, should not engage in battle. Shimin saw that Xue Ju was running low on supplies and would have to retreat in a little while, so the Tang forces should defend but let Xue defeat themselves.

But Liu and Yin thought that by gaining a victory, they could greatly enhance their reputations. After some time, they advanced out of their fortifications and deployed on a plain south-west of Gaozhu. They set up their battle lines ready to attack the Qin. This was just what Xue Ju wanted. He marshalled his forces for battle while sending a small but strong unit to hide in the rear of the Tang force. On 9 July, the Qin attacked and defeated the Tang at the Battle of Qianshuiyuan (south-east of Changwu Shaanxi). Half the Tang army was killed, along with many good officers. Li Shimin had to return to Chang'an. He removed Liu Wenjing and Yin Kaishan from command and threw them out of the army.

In August, Xue Ju sent his son, Xue Ren Gao, to follow up their victory by advancing on Ningzhou (Ningxian Gansu) and besieging the town. Hu Yan, commander of Ningzhou, held out. Xue Ren Gao withdrew because news came that the Tang defeat had unsettled Guanzhong. Xue Ju decided to concentrate his forces to invade Guanzhong to overthrow Tang power. But Xue Ju died suddenly and Xue Ren Gao became Qin Emperor. He called off the offensive, preferring to mobilize larger forces. Establishing his capital at Xizhu (north-east of Jingchuan Gansu), the new emperor prepared his attack. At the same time, Tang Emperor Gaozu again appointed second son Shimin to command an expeditionary force to eliminate the Qin. Both sides took some months to refurbish and prepare their forces.

By early autumn 618, Wang Shichong's forces in Luoyang faced short supplies. After discussions with the regency council and Emperor Tong, Wang intended to attack Li Mi and capture the granary at the juncture of the Luo River with the Yellow River. He thought that Li Mi's forces could not withstand a powerful attack. Battles with Yuwen Huaji had depleted Li Mi's army and his only reinforcements were doubtful units picked up from Yuwen's wreckage. Wang selected out of his massive garrison a force of some 20,000 men, spearheaded by 2,000 crack heavy horsemen. These troops had followed Wang for years and many came from the same Iranian Central Asian background as he. Wang sanctified a new shrine to the Lord of Zhuo, one of the founders of the ancient Zhuo Dynasty, who had originally founded Luoyang. Through the ceremony, Wang proclaimed that he who fought would win great distinction, but he who refused would die of the plague. (One of Wang's subordinate commanders observed, 'Wang likes spells and incantations just like a wizard or old witch.')

Wang marched out of Luoyang on 9 September 618. He led his force east, along the south side of the Luo River, passing Li Mi's blockade. Wang then crossed to the north side of the Luo River and continued on east. Here the Luo River flows parallel to the Yellow River for quite a distance before merging with it. As he marched at speed to the east, Wang had the Tongji Canal protecting his left and the Luo covered his right. Before sunset on 10 September, Wang reached his destination and camped some 20 miles from Luoyang, south-west of Yanshi. His position was secure, with the Tongji Canal looping around to cover his left, front and right, as it flowed into the Luo River. The canal stretched all the way back to Luoyang, providing a means of transport for supplies which could relieve distress in the city. To the north, level ground gave way to rough country, which also stretched back to the city. Wang and his force were deep behind Li Mi's lines.

Li Mi's force, mostly infantry, was encamped at Jinyong fort about 6 miles from Luoyang when Wang began his advance. Li Mi marched his field force, about 40,000 men, east to Yanshi, where he camped on the heights of Mangshan. He called his commanders together to analyze options. The question was whether they should fight with Wang's force or evade them until time ground down Wang's force? Wang's force was powerful, but Li Mi now had its supplies blocked. Li Mi's problem was that he led a coalition of bandits, warlords and landowners, and needed to follow their decisions. His commanders decided to let Wang make the first move but then attack him, thus collecting plunder. Li Mi stayed in his main camp on the upper reaches of Mangshan. His subordinate commander, Shan Xiongxin, camped in the plain just north of the walls of Yanshi. The two camps supported each other: If Wang attacked Li on Mangshan, Shan could hit his flank and rear; if Wang struck Shan, Li could hit him in flank and rear. If Wang retreated across the canal, both forces could hit him from two sides.

Li Mi organized his forces. In the camp on the Mangshan Hills, Li Mi kept his personal guard and his main body of heavy cavalry under Commander of the Inner Line Cheng Zhi Jie. Shan Xiong Xin, Commander of the Outer Line with the main force of light cavalry, held the camp north of Yanshi. Before dawn, in the rain, Wang Shichong threw three pontoon bridges across the Tongji Canal and sent several hundred heavy cavalry, backed up by light cavalry, across the bridges to attack Shan's camp. Li Mi ordered Pei Xing Jian, his second in command, to lead a force made up of Li Mi's personal guard and Cheng Zhi Jie's heavy cavalry to reinforce Shan Xiong Xin. When Wang's army launched their attack on Shan's camp, Pei and Cheng charged into Wang's force. An arrow hit Pei and he fell from his horse. Cheng rode to his aid. Cheng killed several of Wang's horsemen and his guards held off the rest. Cheng pulled Pei up and put him on his own horse, and the two of them started to return to Li Mi's camp. However, some of Wang's cavalry wheeled about and charged toward Cheng and his guards. A pursuer struck Cheng with a lance. Cheng grabbed the lance, broke off the handle and killed the pursuer. He, Pei and their guards rode back to safety. At dusk, both sides sounded the retreat, returning to their respective camps. Li Mi's men were exhausted, and many were wounded. Li Mi believed that Wang's forces were equally hurt, so did not post a watch that night.

During the night, Wang sent 200 heavy cavalry to penetrate the Mangshan Hills and hide in the ravines near some brooks. At the same time, in his camp, Wang ordered all his soldiers to water and feed their horses and sharpen their weapons. At dawn on 10 September, Wang Shichong held a grand ceremony to encourage his men. Wang marshalled his horse and foot into battle formation and marched against Li Mi's camp. Li Mi roused his soldiers and ordered them to move out of the camp and into battle formation. But before his troops achieved combat readiness, Wang's army charged. Before the fight, Wang had found a man who looked like Li Mi. He had the man tied up and placed on a horse. When his charge had disrupted Li Mi's units, Wang had the man brought out as his soldiers yelled, 'We have Li Mi!' and 'Live long!' At that signal, the hidden 200 heavy cavalry rode down the hills and fired Li Mi's camp. Li Mi's army disintegrated.

Li Mi escaped the carnage and fled to Luokou with some 10,000 men. Wang Shichong then attacked Yanshi, where a defector opened the town gates and let in Wang's army. Wang next took his troops to Luokou. Li Mi saw his power disintegrate, and he and his followers fled again. Li Mi's subordinate commander, Wang Bo Dang, retreated from his stronghold of Jinyong and took his army to Heyang (south of Mengxian Henan). He sent word to Li Mi that he had a safe refuge. Li Mi marched to Heyang and collected what forces he could there. In a commanders' conference, Li Mi proposed that they move north to the lands between the Yellow River and the Taihang Mountain (between Shanxi and Hebei), so he could link up with Xu Shiji in Liyang and recover all his lands. But the consensus was that defeat had broken their power and they should best join Li Yuan and the Tang. Li Mi and some 20,000 men marched to Chang'an and pledged loyalty to the Tang. Li Yuan welcomed Li Mi, making him Lord of Xing and Minister of Palace Supplies.

Tang Attacks to the North

In late October, Shimin marched his army to Gaozhu to his former base, where he settled his forces in the fortifications. Xue Ren Gao sent his commander, Zong Luo Hou to oppose Shimin. Zong's force of many light cavalry was unable to force its way in against Shimin's fortifications. For some sixty days, Zong kept Shimin's force confined to their camp. Xue Ren Gao then arrived with reinforcements, heavy cavalry and siege equipment. But with such a large mass of men, Xue had to be concerned about bringing up sufficient supplies, especially as winter was coming. As his supplies became critical, some of Xue's commanders decided they could not be successful. Liang Hulang defected to the Tang, bringing his soldiers with him. Besides his men, he brought news to Shimin that Xue's commanders were in disagreement. Now, said Shimin, was the time to attack.

At dawn on 7 November, Li Shimin sent Commander Pang Yu to deploy his infantry in battle formation near Qianshuiyuan. They dug field works and prepared to receive the Qin attack. Zong Luo Hou led his light cavalry in attacking Pang Yu's infantry, shooting arrow storms against the dug-in infantry. Li Shimin saw the Qin cavalry using up their arrows against Pang's infantry, and that the Qin forces were weakening themselves as they continued to try overwhelming them. The Tang infantry suffered but held. At the critical moment, astride his massive warhorse Baitiwu, armoured and waving his great sword, Li Shimin charged out, leading forty elite heavy cavalry, followed by a mass of heavy and light cavalry. Coming out of the dust behind Qianshuiyuan, the Tang force struck Zong Luo Hou's army in the flank. Li Shimin's wedge broke in and then through Zong's formations as Pang's infantry suddenly lurched forward and collided with Zong's front. Zong's army shattered, with several thousand killed.

Having won this Second Battle of Qianshuiyuan, Li Shimin immediately organized a force of some 2,000 heavy cavalrymen and started to pursue the defeated enemy. Shimin's uncle, Dou Gui, warned him about rashness leading to failure, but Shimin pushed passed him and spurred Baitiwu on, leading his 2,000 men. At that time, Xue Ren Gao was at his capital of Xizhu on the banks of the Jingshui River. When Shimin quickly reached the town, Xue deployed his men in front of the town walls. Shimin deployed on the opposite side of the Jingshui River. Suddenly, several formations of Xue's army defected and went over the river to the Tang side. Xue withdrew into the town and prepared for a siege. At dusk, Shimin's men approached the walls and blockaded the gates. That night, many men fled the town by climbing down the walls and surrendered to the Tang. Xue Ren Gao saw his power eroding. The next morning, he opened the gates to Li Shimin. Later, Li Shimin explained that the soldiers who fought for Xue at Qianshuiyuan were the best Xue had. By moving against Xizhu so quickly, Shimin reached the town before the fleeing soldiers could, and so had to fight only the weakest of Xue's force.

Li Shimin placed two brothers of the Qin Emperor in command of the surrendered troops and appointed them to government offices. Emperor Tang Gaozu sent orders to Li Shimin to execute all of Xue Ren Gao's followers because of the great damage they had done to the Tang. But Li Mi interceded with the emperor, supporting Li Shimin's clemency. On 22 November, Li Shimin made a formal entry into Chang'an and was received by his father, the emperor.

Death Comes to Li Mi

Xu Shi Ji, subordinate commander of Li Mi, still held the town of Liyang. Li Mi sent his follower, Wei Zheng, to convince Xu Shi Ji to surrender Liyang to the Tang. Xu Shi Ji did so, but gave the census records of households, people, horses and landholdings to Li Mi to give to the emperor. This showed that it was Li Mi who relinquished the town to Emperor Tang Gaozu. The emperor gladly received the town and gave special favour to Xu Shi Ji. He elevated Xu to membership in the Imperial House of Li, so from then on he was Li Ji. Li Mi felt that the Tang did not value his worth. His official position, overseeing banquets for the imperial family, seemed insulting. Li Mi sounded out some commanders, finding several who were also dissatisfied with the Tang, including Commander Wang Bo Dang.

Since lands east of the Xiaoshan Mountains remained under the control of Li Mi's commanders and the loyal Zhang Shan Xiang still held Yizhou (Xiangcheng Henan), Li Mi decided that he could reconstruct his holdings if he could raise some troops.

Pointing out to Emperor Gaozu that Wang Shichong at Luoyang was a threat, Li Mi offered to lead an army to destroy him. He added the inducement that since he already held the allegiance of some eastern commanders, he could bring the whole area under Tang domination. The imperial court discussed this offer. Many ministers did not trust Li Mi, saying, 'This is like releasing a harnessed tiger back into wild mountains. He will never return.' The emperor decided to let Li Mi go and fight with Wang. If he fought and won, the emperor said, so much the better. If he went on his own, his greed would do him in and the Tang would be rid of him. Li Mi set out with a small but well-trained force. Always subtle, Emperor Gaozu then sent an envoy carrying instruction that Li Mi was to return to Chang'an, but the expedition was to continue. As expected, this precipitated Li Mi's decision to strike out on his own.

Li Mi immediately killed Emperor Gaozu's envoy when he came to his camp. On 30 December, Li Mi reached the town of Taolin. He wrote to the governor of Taolin explaining that the Tang Emperor had recalled him and asking if he could leave his family in the town. The governor granted Li Mi permission. Li Mi then had his bravest men dress as his wife, concubines and domestic servants. Once in the town, they attacked the garrison and delivered Taolin to Li Mi. He took all the soldiers and food. His force then marched east toward the Nanshan Mountains (Shenxian Henan). Li Mi wrote to his former subordinate, Zhang Shanxiang, who held Yizhou (Xiangcheng Henan), telling him that he was coming.

Tang officer Sheng Yanshi informed his superior, Shi Wanbao, commander in Xiongzhou, that he thought killing Li Mi was easy. If Shi gave him command of 3,000–4,000 troops, said Sheng, he would bring the heads of Li Mi and his commanders, saying, 'I have a secret strategy.' Shi assigned the troops to Sheng. Mobilizing his troops, Sheng marched to Xiong'ershan (south of Yiyang Henan). Once there, an officer asked Sheng why they were in the south at the Xiong'ershan Mountains when all they heard said that Li Mi was marching east to Luozhou. Sheng responded that the rumours were Li Mi's subterfuge to hide the fact that he was going to Zhangshan at Yizhou.

Li Mi continued to march east through Shanzhou (Shanxian Henan), meeting no resistance. He then turned his march south toward the Xiong'ershan Mountains. Li Mi believed he had got through the danger zone and could now march quickly. Sheng Yanshi had occupied a rough pass on the road to Yizhou. He posted archers in the heights, with infantry armed with swords and spears hidden along the road. He ordered his officers to wait until Li Mi's men had marched half their numbers across a brook that flowed through the pass, and then attack. Sheng's force destroyed Li Mi's army, and he collected the heads of Li Mi and Wang Bo Dang. He sent the heads to Chang'an and received from the emperor elevation to Lord of Geguo. The emperor sent Li Mi's head to Li Ji in Liyang. Li Ji responded with a letter requesting permission to bury Li Mi. This was granted, and Li Ji held an imperial funeral for Li Mi.

Wang Shichong Becomes Emperor of Zheng

After he had defeated Li Mi, Wang Shichong controlled the administration and commanded the army in Luoyang. While Emperor Sui Tong reigned, Wang was the real power in the state. That Wang would soon take the state as his own was evident. Some gravitated closer to Wang to gain his favour; others, despairing of Wang's favour – saying that Wang was more a sorcerer than a ruler – defected to the Tang. On 9 January 619, Wang moved a force against Guzhou but did not press the siege other than a dilatory blockade. The real reason for the campaign was to allow Wang to organize support for his assumption of the throne. On 12 March, Wang sent Duan Da to request from Emperor Tong the Nine Symbols of Imperial Power: the imperial chariot, embroidered robes with sun and dragons, the bow and arrows, personal guards, musical accompaniment, red-painted gates, battles axes and five-toed dragons. The emperor refused to consent, but Duan Da announced that Wang was now elevated to King of Zheng and had received the Nine Symbols.

On 2 April, Duan Da presented Wang's request that Emperor Tong retire and recognize Wang as emperor. Tong refused but said that Wang should just take the title. On 5 April, Wang announced that Emperor Sui Tong had surrendered the throne and retired. Wang Shichong was now emperor of the Zheng Dynasty. Wang appointed his eldest son to be Crown Prince and made his younger son King of Han, and ennobled his whole family along with many supporters. The former emperor was held under house arrest. Wang soon discovered a widespread conspiracy among his officers, who plotted to restore the Sui Emperor. Those involved and their families were executed. Wang's brother, Wang Shiyun, convinced him that so long as the former emperor was alive, he would be a threat. Wang Shiyun sent his nephew, Wang Renze, with his servant to force the former emperor to drink poison. Yang Tong begged for his life, imploring Wang Renze to remind Emperor Wang of his promise of life to his former emperor. Wang Renze did send Yang Tong's request to the palace, but Wang Shiyun denied it emphatically. Yang Tong begged to see his mother, but that too was refused. Finally, praying to the Buddha that he never be reborn in an imperial house, Yang Tong drank the poison. But it was ineffective. Wang Renze ordered him strangled instead.

Dou Jiande Proclaims Himself Emperor of Xia

Yuwen Huaji, after Li Mi's death, tried to capture outlying areas that had been under Li Mi's influence. In spring 619, he attacked Yuan Baozang and attempted to seize his lands, but Yuan surrendered to the Tang instead. Emperor Gaozu sent his nephew, Li Shentong, against Yuwen, who could not withstand the Tang attack and retreated east to Liaocheng (in western Shandong). Yuwen still carried with him Empress Xiao, widow of Emperor Yang, and Prince Yang Zheng, Emperor Yang's grandson. In Liaocheng, Yuwen allied with Wang Bo, who was impressed with Yuwen's treasures. Li Shentong followed and put Liaocheng under siege. But the local strongman, Dou Jiande King of Xia, arrived, pressured Li Shentong to withdraw back to Tang territory and put Liaocheng under strict siege. When Dou prepared to storm the town, Wang Bo opened the gates to let him enter. Liaocheng fell into Dou's hands. He received Empress Xiao with a bow, representing himself as 'your subject'. Dou arrested and immediately executed anyone connected with Emperor Yang's murder, except Yuwen Huaji and his family. He took these people and the imperial family to his capital, Xiangguo (Xingtai Hebei). There, in a public ceremony, he had Yuwen Huaji and two of his sons beheaded. Yuwen Huaji's only words were, 'I have never done any harm to the King of Xia.'

Dou was held in high regard by his allies and enemies. Even the *Old Tang History*, written under Tang auspices, praised Dou Jiande for his justice and moderation:

> 'Every time that Dou Jiande was successful in battle or in capturing a city, the treasures he received were all divided for the soldiers, and he did not personally take anything. His daily life was frugal and simple. He did not feast on meat, instead eating vegetables and unrefined grain. His wife, Lady Cao, wore only cloth, not silk, and had less than ten servant girls.'

Dou respected and honoured Empress Xiao and Prince Yang Zheng, but he disbanded the crowd of Emperor Yang's concubines and what remained of Yuwen's army. Dou had regularized his administration, using former Sui officials, centralizing decision-making and enforcing a single set of regulatory guidelines. He received recognition of his title of King of Xia, which he gratefully accepted, from Emperor Tong in Luoyang. He was also allied with Wang Shichong, but when Wang took the throne for himself and then killed former Emperor Tong, Dou renounced any relation with Wang and assumed imperial style without taking the imperial title. He elevated Emperor Yang's young grandson, Yang Zheng, to be Lord of Xun and gave the posthumous name Min to Emperor Yang. Dou Jiande, left on a limb by Wang Shichong's usurpation, sought an alliance with the Eastern Turks. The Sui Princess Yicheng, wife of the Shibi Khan, had requested that he send Empress Xiao and Prince Yang to her. Dou did so, along with Yuwen Huaji's head.

The lands to the north of the Yellow River fell either to Tang or Zheng. Dou decided that he needed to round out his holdings in that direction. He launched an offensive and pushed the Tang back west. By autumn 619, Li Shentong, Tang commander in the north Yellow River, had to withdraw to Liyang. There he joined Li Ji, the former Li Mi commander, who gained Emperor Tang Gaozu's favour. In winter 619, Li Ji caught Dou Jiande in an ambush and repelled him. But Dou, rein-forced, counter-attacked and stormed Liyang, capturing Li Shentong, Li Gai, Li Ji's father, and Princess Tong'an, Emperor Gaozu's younger sister. Li Ji escaped, but returned in a few days because Dou held his father. Dou kept Li Ji in com-mand of the town guard, but still held Li Gai as a hostage. He kept Li Shentong and Princess Tong'an in custody, yet treated them honourably and allowed them comfort. Dou controlled most of the lands north of the Yellow River and east of the Taihang Mountains, except for an enclave run by Li Yi, formerly Luo Yi but granted the Tang family name by Emperor Gaozu. Guarding his fortifications in the rough country, Li Yi managed to hold his own despite many attacks.

Li Ji, looking for a way to end Dou Jiande's rule, suggested that Dou attack the lands of Ming Haigong, a peasant ruler who recognized Emperor Wang at Luoyang. These lands were the commanderies of Cao and Dai (modern Heze Shandong). Li Ji planned to have allies ambush Dou when he crossed the Yellow River, but Dou stayed behind to attend his wife Empress Cao's delivery. Li Ji's ally did not know this and attacked the convoy which Cao Dan, brother of the empress, commanded. The ambush failed even to kill Cao Dan, and Li Ji fled to the Tang. Dou caught and executed Li Ji's accomplices, but did not kill Li Ji's father, Li Gai, because he appreciated Li Ji's loyalty. For the moment, Dou Jiande's realm was at peace with rising prosperity.

In 620, Dou attempted to subdue Li Yi but failed. He blamed his commanders, some of whom he executed. In the autumn, Emperor Gaozu made peace with Dou Jiande, who returned Princess Tong'an to the Tang but kept Li Shentong in cus-tody. Dou considered making an alliance with the Eastern Turks. They could attack the Tang from the north while Dou would attack through the Taihang Mountains. But the Chuluo Khan died before any real decision was made.

Reference

Chinese sources: *Suishu*, 70, 85; *Jiu Tangshu*, 53-56; *Xin Tangshu*, 84; *Zizhi Tongjian*, 183, 186.
Fitzgerald, pp.50-59.
Graff, pp.162-171.
Hung, pp.61-69.

Chapter 9

War for Domination II

The Fight for Taiyuan

The Eastern Turks remained interested in extending their power into the Yellow River Valley. In April 619, their ally, Liu Wuzhou, marched south to take Bingzhou, near Taiyuan, Shanxi. Liu had taken Mayi with Turkish support when Sui power faltered. He had established his main base north of modern Yuci, Shanxi, and intended to seize the towns that surrounded Taiyuan, letting the local Tang capital fall into his hands. He commanded a strong force of light cavalry with a core of heavy cavalry. Fourth son Li Yuanji commanded the Tang force in Taiyuan. He had ordered Commander Zhong Da to attack Liu Wuzhou's base, but Zhong replied that he was sure to suffer defeat. The Tang force was only infantry because their cavalry was near Chang'an. Li Yuanji insisted the order be carried out. Liu's force made short work of the Tang infantry and captured Zheng Da, who promptly switched sides. On 18 April, Liu led an assault against the walls of Bingzhou, but the Tang forces held. Liu continued to probe the Tang defences around Taiyuan; on 19 May, he took the important town of Pingyao, which allowed him to cut Taiyuan's southern communications route.

Liu Wuzhou renewed his offensive in Shanxi in June 619, capturing Jiezhou (Jiexiu Shanxi). He recruited Commander Song Jingang and his army. Song had commanded a territory in Yizhou (Yixian Hebei) but ran afoul of Dou Jiande. Dou threatened him, and Song took his family and men off to Liu Wenzhou. Liu, who appreciated Song's well-known tactical ability, received him with honour and appointed him King of Song. In response, Song divorced his wife and married Liu's sister. He then marched an army of 30,000 men to Bingzhou and took over the siege.

In Chang'an, Emperor Gaozu found the news about events at Taiyuan disturbing. He ordered Imperial Commander Li Zhongwen to gather a force and repel Liu Wuzhou. Liu's base at this time was at Queshugu (south of Jiexiu Shanxi). Li's army was on the march when Liu's light cavalry came in sight. Li quickly deployed his army, while Liu's cavalry appeared to be somewhat confused. Li's force charged Liu's cavalry, which broke and fled the field. Li gave chase, driving his soldiers pell-mell toward the fleeing enemy. But Liu had hidden reinforcements, and combining the fleeing force with the fresh troops, his cavalry turned and attacked

Li's soldiers. Li's army, overstretched and disorganized, disintegrated. Liu's men captured Li Zhongwen. Li managed to escape and returned to Chang'an. The emperor received him with honour and reappointed him as commander. While he continued to support Li Zhongwen, Emperor Gaozu considered him not up to independent command. Prime Minister Pei Ji agreed to take overall control, with Li Zhongwen as second in command. Pei marched to Jinzhou (Linfen Shanxi) and prepared his campaign.

Pei Ji advanced his army against Jiexiu, reaching the town on 12 September. Song Jingang took over direct command of the town to face Pei. The Tang forces set up camp in Dusuoyuan (in the Mianshan Mountains, south-west of Jiexiu Shanxi). Water for this camp came from streams in the mountains. Song's scouts soon found this out, so he sent special troops to find the streams' headwaters and divert them. With his water supply cut, Pei organized a new camp with a better-protected water source. When, however, he marched his soldiers from the old camp to the new one, his army became disorganized. Out of the hills came Song's army, smashing Pei's force. Pei Ji, almost alone, made it back to Jinzhou. He requested that the emperor punish him, but Gaozu affirmed his appointment as Commander of Hedong (most of Shanxi).

While Song fought with Pei, Liu Wuzhou advanced against Taiyuan with a large contingent of Turkish light cavalry. Fourth son Commander Li Yuanji decided that he had best return to Chang'an. He set out on 16 September, taking his wife, concubines and children. As guards for his Dynastic Highness, he also took the best soldiers. He left Liu Dewei in command with poor soldiers and short supplies. When Li Yuanji and his column were well out of sight, Taiyuan capitulated to Liu. After taking Taiyuan, Liu ordered Song to advance against Jinzhou (Linfen Shanxi). Song swept through Jinzhou, then through Jiangzhou (Xinjiang Shanxi) to Longmen (Longmen Shanxi). This town sits on the eastern bank of the Yellow River and is a main crossing into Guanzhong. When Song had reached the Yellow River, another commander of Liu Wuzhou, Wang Xingben, took Pufan (Puzhou Shanxi). This is an important crossing point of the Yellow River and also leads into Guanzhong. By holding Longmen and Pufan, Liu Wuzhou threatened Chang'an and the Tang regime. By October, Liu and Song were mopping up resistance in Shanxi. The Tang Commander-in-Chief of Shanxi, Pei Ji, ordered all the people, supplies and livestock collected in fortified strongholds. He ordered the destruction of all the rest of the farms, villages and crops in the fields, but this started a series of peasant rebellions and Tang lost all Shanxi.

At the imperial court in Chang'an, Emperor Gaozu and his council decided to withdraw all forces from Shanxi and reinforce Guanzhong's defences. However, second son Li Shimin objected, saying, as famously recorded, 'Taiyuan is the foundation of the Imperial Regime and of the State.' Li Shimin announced that with 30,000 men he would defeat Liu Wuzhou. The emperor agreed with his second son and assigned him the troops he needed. On 20 October, Emperor Gaozu held a grand ceremony at Huayin in the Changchun Palace, celebrating the start of Li Shimin's campaign. In November, the Yellow River froze; Li Shimin led his troops across the ice near Longmen.

He took his troops to Bobi (south-west of Xinjiang Shanxi) and built a strongly fortified camp. He faced Song Jingang's army, which also encamped. Song did not attack because Shimin's camp was too strong, but Song believed he had pinned the Tang force and so contained it. On the other hand, Shimin saw where Song had stationed his main force and believed that Song's men were pinned until the Tang moved. Song's hope to blockade the Tang force was foiled when Shimin released an announcement that he had come to expel the rebels and their foreign allies. Suddenly, carts appeared at the Tang camp, bringing supplies which the Tang purchased. Li Shimin kept his force in camp, avoiding any major engagement. He personally reconnoitred Song's camp, killing soldiers who came out to capture him with long arrows shot from his great bow.

While Li Shimin and Song Jingang still faced each other in January 620, Tang Commander Qin Wutong attacked Pufan, which was held by Wang Xingben. Wang led his army out of Pufan to repel the Tang, but Qin's force pushed him back. Qin immediately blockaded Pufan. The garrison of Pufan had not received supplies for some time, and Wang knew that there was no possibility of reinforcements or supplies. He tried to organize a breakout from the town, but the soldiers were not interested. On 14 January, Wang Xingben surrendered to Qin Wutong. Emperor Gaozu made an entry into Pufan on 17 January, where he awaited Li Shimin. When Li Shimin came, the emperor and son conferred about strategy. After seeing to the execution of Wang Xingben, father and son departed on 29 January, Gaozu to Chang'an and Li Shimin back to Bobi.

After some two months of waiting, Tang officers came to Li Shimin and requested permission to attack Song's force. Shimin replied that Song had a large army at hand but was a long distance from his base. Song was a skilled commander with a brave army, he went on. Shimin added that Liu Wuzhou was occupying Taiyuan and Song protected Liu, but supplies were short. When Song ran out of supplies, he would have to withdraw. Then they could attack. Song Jingang ran out of food on 14 April. Organizing his troops, Song pulled out of his camp, marching north. When his scouts told Shimin that the enemy was withdrawing, he mobilized his crack cavalry, which consisted of many light bowmen with a solid core of heavy horsemen. Sitting on his great warhorse, Teginbiao, Li Shimin gave the signal to advance. The Tang force hit Song's rearguard under Xun Xiang at Luzhou (Houzho Shanxi). The Tang scattered Xun's force. The Tang then charged on. For a day and night, the Tang pursuit continued. In eight different skirmishes, Li Shimin's men repelled Song's rearguard attacks. When the Tang reached Gaobiling (south of Lingshi Shanxi), Shimin's commander, Liu Hongji, grabbed Shimin's bridle, saying that the men were tired and hungry and needed to stop the pursuit. The supply train was following and would come soon. Li Shimin responded that Song was at the end of his resources; his officers and men were dispirited: 'Such chances are hard to come by but easy to lose.' Should they stop, Shimin added, Song would catch his breath and develop a plan to cope with them. Shimin signalled the advance to continue.

Li Shimin caught up with Song in Queshugu, south-west of Jiexiu Shanxi. The armies met in a large disjointed battle. The Tang killed or captured tens of thousands of Song's men, but Song escaped with his best troops. That night, the Tang finally made camp. Li Shimin had not eaten for two days and had not taken off his armour for three. His personal supply had only one goat, which he shared with his entourage and guards. Li Shimin rested and resupplied his force, continuing his march to Jiexiu on 23 April. Song deployed his 20,000 troops beyond the town's south gate. Shimin ordered Li Ji to attack Song's battle front, while he took some heavy cavalry out of Song's sight, manoeuvring around the town wall. Li Ji's attack failed to break Song's front line until Shimin's heavy cavalry hit Song's force from behind. Song's men disintegrated, but Song escaped. Three thousand of Song's men were dead on the field.

Li Shimin pursued Song for 10 miles, But Song fled quickly and Li Shimin lost him. On the way, however, the Tang came to the fortress town of Zhangnanbao. When he demanded entrance, the local commander refused to let him in, saying that he was a loyal Tang officer holding out for the return of the Tang. Li Shimin took off his helmet to show them who he was. The garrison holding the walls cheered as the commander ordered the gates to open. They were now rescued from the hostile force they had constantly faced. They prepared food for Li Shimin and the whole army.

Once Song had left Jiexiu, the local commanders gathered their troops and surrendered to the Tang. Li Shimin took the soldiers and officers into the Tang army. After Liu Wuzhou had heard that Song Jingang fled in defeat, he went to join the Turks. Song collected the men left by Liu, but they refused to fight, so Song followed Liu and went to the Turks. But the Turks had little patience with failed warlords; soon both Liu and Song were dead. Li Shimin made a formal entry into Taiyuan and re-established the Tang administration, rewarding loyalty. By the end of May, Li Shimin had returned to Chang'an.

The Tang Attacks Wang Shichong

In the court at Chang'an, Emperor Gaozu and his advisors improved and extended the imperial administration. Their objective was to increase agricultural production to generate the wealth with which to build a large military force. The main task was to strengthen imperial control of the commanderies. Since Emperor Yang had abolished the provinces, the commanderies remained the basic administrative unit. The Tang civil officials sought control of the *fubing* (fighting man) holdings, integrating them into the Tang system of headquarters units. A commander titled *Zhechong Du Wei* (senior district authority) ran each headquarters. He controlled the 'fighting men' by organizing them into *dui* units. These were fifty men of like service. Six to eight *dui* joined into a *tong*; 1,000 men made a *Ying*. *Ying* was the largest permanent unit, but they combined to form *Jun* (armies). Ad hoc organizations formed army subdivisions. Most *fubing* soldiers were cavalry, both heavy and light.

The most important Tang military force were horsemen. The Tang could easily conscript foot soldiers, porters, labourers and garrisons, but expert riders and fierce mounts were hard to come by and expensive. As a form of commandery under the Tang, the administration organized 'bridle' or 'loose rein' commanderies. These were in the north, along the great loop of the Yellow River and in the north of what is now Shanxi. Here, where China abuts the steppe, tribes of horsemen received subsidies to raise horses for the Tang. Because of their access to horses, particularly strong mounts for heavy cavalry, the Tang had a significant advantage over other claimants for the universal throne. Mobilizing foot and horse, Emperor Gaozu saw that either the Tang administration must move forward or other candidates for the imperial throne would gain similar advantages.

The emperor announced on 1 July 620 that Tang forces would remove the rebel Wang Shichong and bring the Eastern capital, Luoyang, into Tang control. He appointed Li Shimin commander-in-chief of the expeditionary force. By 21 July, Shimin and his army had reached Xin'an (Xin'an Henan), approaching Luoyang from the west. Wang's forces avoided battle with the advancing Tang. Rather, they pushed rearguards at Shimin's forces in bitter skirmishes. In one minor engagement, Shimin was separated from his guards and, after a hard fight, returned to his troops covered in dust. The sentries challenged him when he tried to enter his camp. He had to take off his helmet and speak before they knew who he was. At this time, Gaozu sent envoys to Dou Jiande to negotiate a non-aggression treaty. Dou and his advisors considered a war between the Tang and Wang Shichong's Zheng Dynasty something to their advantage: the war would weaken both powers and leave the field open to Dou's benefit. Dou returned Princess Tong'an, Gaozu's younger sister, with an honour guard and accepted the offered treaty.

Scouts came into Luoyang with continuing news of the Tang advance. Wang had expected something like this since the Tang forces began to overwhelm their enemies near Taiyuan. Wang Shichong mobilized a field force of some 30,000 men, then established eight fortified sites, strongly garrisoned, surrounding Luoyang.

The idea was that when Tang forces came to besiege Luoyang, the garrisons could hinder their supplies and harass their rear.

Li Shimin's vanguard under commander Luo Shixin marched to Jijahe, just west of Luoyang. There he dug in, besieging the town but keeping his own forces well defended on all sides. Wang marched out of Luoyang with his main field force to confront Luo, digging entrenchments facing Luo's camp. On 28 July, Li Shimin led an elite force of heavy cavalry to reconnoitre Wang's camp when he heard that Wang himself led a reconnaissance force around Luo's camp. Leading his horsemen, Shimin drew his great bow and shot long arrows at Wang's force, hitting some of Wang's personal guards. Wang's force broke and fled, pursued by Shimin's riders, who captured the commander of Wang's rearguard. The next day, Li Shimin brought his whole field force to Luo's camp and Wang withdrew back into Luoyang.

Observing the lay of the land, Shimin detached four strong units with orders to establish fortified camps that would block major routes into Luoyang and keep in check Wang's eight garrisons. While these forces established themselves, Shimin took his field force to the Beimang Mountain, just north of Luoyang, and dug in there. On 4 August, a Tang detached force took Huilou, a town on the main route east of Luoyang, blocking that route. Wang Shichong sent his son, Wang Yingxuan, to retake the town, but he failed. To keep the Tang force in the town, the younger Wang had his troops dig in and block the town's egress to the west with a crescent-shaped earthwork nearly surrounding Huilou. As their forces skirmished in the distance, Li Shimin and Wang Shichong met, with strong forces accompanying them, near Qingcheng and negotiated from horseback. Wang offered some rectifications of the boundary between them, but Shimin demanded Luoyang. Both sides withdrew.

Letting the dust settle a little, Wang decided to scorch a few Tang feathers. On 21 August, Wang led a raiding force of light cavalry into Beimang Mountain. Unfortunately for Wang, Li Shimin was waiting for him. With some 500 heavy cavalry, Shimin was near the tomb of Emperor Huanwu of the Wei Dynasty, hidden, and looking at Wang's massive force beginning to spread out in the broken countryside. Suddenly, Wang discovered the Tang force and attacked, shooting arrows and throwing spears at them. One of Wang's personal retainers, a big man on a powerful horse, lowered his lance and charged at Li Shimin. Yuchi Jingde, who was accused of disloyalty by others but was supported by Shimin, made his horse leap forward, levelled his lance and struck Wang's man off his horse. Wang's horsemen backed off, but Yuchi led a charge of armoured cavalry straight into the enemy's milling mass and broke through. Li Shimin rallied his force, wheeled about and drove through the light cavalry again and again. The arrows and spears of Wang's force were ineffective against the Tang armour. Reinforcements soon arrived from the Tang camp, hitting Wang's force in the flank and scattering them. Wang withdrew, leaving some 1,000 dead and about 6,000 prisoners.

The expertise of Yuchi Jingde was well known before he joined the Tang. He was renowned for his abilities on horseback. He deflected lances and spears, often just grabbing them out of his opponent's hands. Fourth son Li Yuanji, still in disfavour for his less than successful defence of Taiyuan, sought a match with Yuchi to prove his martial ability, but Yuchi grabbed Li Yuanji's spear three times in succession.

The Tang forces were slowly strangling Wang's hold on power. Li Shimin was in no great hurry to come to grips with Wang, preferring just to let him bleed. The Tang commander, Luo Shixin, captured Xiashi fortress, a little over 4 miles north of Luoyang, on 15 October. Luo then tried to take Qianjin fortress, also just north of Luoyang. The defenders of Qianjin repulsed Luo and shouted insults at him from the top of their walls. At night, Luo had 100 soldiers carry thirty infants to the fortress gate. Amidst the infants' crying, one soldier said to the guards, 'Open the door, we have come from the Eastern Capital to join the Tang.' Of course, the door remained closed. Then another soldier said, 'This is Qianjin Fortress, we are at the wrong place.' Then the thirty soldiers with the crying infants left. The defenders saw them leave and, considering them refugees, decided to go out and plunder them. They opened the gate and went out, intent on the loot they would get. But Tang soldiers, remaining behind and hidden, jumped out, killed the defending soldiers, entered the gate and seized the fortress. A little later, Wang's commander in Guancheng (Zhengzhou Henan), Yang Qing, saw which way the wind blew and switched sides, bringing his fortress and garrison with him. Li Shimin sent Li Ji to receive the town. Wang's eldest son, Wang Xuanying, at Hulao at the time, marched his troops to recover Guancheng, but Li Ji pushed him back and he had to return to Hulao.

Dou Jiande Enters the Struggle: Li Shimin Besieges Luoyang

Wang Shichong saw his position eroding. He sent an envoy to Dou Jiande, soliciting his aid. Wang had taken advantage of Dou when he was campaigning on his frontiers by seizing Liyang from him. Dou responded by grabbing Yinzhou from Wang, so the two potentates were not on good terms. Since Dou Jiande had already sought an understanding with the Tang, he was not moved by Wang's appeal. However, his chief strategist, Liu Bin, formulated far-reaching plans. With the House of Li as the Tang Dynasty in Guanzhong, the House of Wang as the Zheng Dynasty in Luoyang and the House of Dou as the Xia Dynasty in Hebei, Liu Bin saw a straightforward balance of power. Now that Tang was pushing Zheng to destruction, clearly Xia would be next. 'When the lips are gone, the teeth become cold,' quoted Liu Bin. But since the current struggle weakened both Tang and

Zheng, Liu Bin suggested implementing 'the laughing third option'. Xia could take over Zheng and so become superior to Tang. Liu Bin continued:

> 'The country is in upheaval. Tang holds Guanzhong. Zheng [Wang] has the lands south of the Yellow River. Xia [Dou Jiande] has the land north of the Yellow River. The three powers are about equally strong. They are like three legs of a tripod. But Tang has attacked Zheng and since autumn has been doing well. Zheng is weakening. So Zheng will fall, but after Zheng falls, Xia will succumb to Tang. Let go of your hatred of Wang. Send your army and rescue him. If Zheng attacks Tang from inside and Xia attacks from the outside, we shall destroy Tang. With Tang gone, Zheng falls to Xia.'

Dou Jiande sent envoys in January 621 to Wang Shichong and Li Shimin. One envoy assured Wang that Dou was mobilizing his forces to come and rescue him; the other informed Li Shimin that he had to withdraw his army from investing Luoyang and return to Tongguan Pass. Wang sent his nephew with a major delegation, presenting Dou with gifts of gold and jade. Li Shimin imprisoned Dou's envoy and gave no response, but sent word about Dou's threats to the court in Chang'an. Emperor Gaozu ordered his forces in Shanxi to advance against Dou's northern towns to distract Dou. However, Dou had left strong garrisons in those towns. The combat between Li Shimin and Wang Shichong continued. On 28 January, Wang's light cavalry was again raiding Tang patrols in Beimang Mountain. Li Shimin, at the head of a detachment of his special heavy cavalry, ambushed Wang's force, crushing it. On 3 February, Tang forces captured a major supply convoy coming to Luoyang.

Now that it was late winter moving into early spring, Li Shimin judged the time proper to assault Luoyang's walls and take the city. Because the Eastern capital properly belonged to his father, Emperor Gaozu, Shimin sent a personal messenger, Yuwen Shiji, to the Tang court in Chang'an, requesting permission to take Luoyang. The emperor responded, 'Return and tell the King of Qin [Li Shimin] that the purpose of attacking Luoyang is to end the war. When Luoyang is taken, he is to seal all public property for imperial inspection. Then all jade and silk shall be distributed among the officers and men.' By February 621, Shimin transferred his base camp to Qingcheng Fortress, in the middle of Xiyuan, an imperial estate west of Luoyang. Before the Tang soldiers could complete the necessary trenches and barricades, Wang Shichong led out of Luoyang's west gate a field army of some 20,000 men, deploying them along the banks of the Gushui River, opposite Qingcheng. The Tang officers, very concerned that they faced defeat, sent word to Li Shimin. The supreme commander was at the tomb of Emperor Wei Xuanwu, on a promontory from which he could see his camp, Luoyang and Wang's army.

Shimin rode swiftly down the hills and came to Qingcheng while his men watched Wang's forces deploy into attack formation. Shimin called his senior officers together. He told them that it was Wang Shichong who was in a bad position, despite appearances. Wang was deploying his last best troops, Shimin went on. Wang was desperate, and if he lost now, he would never be able to send out another army. Shimin ordered the work on the camp's trenches and rampart continued with all due haste. He ordered senior commander Qutu Tong to organize a force of 5,000 heavy and light infantry to immediately attack Wang's army across the Gushui River. He told Qutu to signal with smoking arrows when he was engaged. Shimin mounted his great warhorse, Saluzi, ordered his *ying* of black armoured heavy cavalry to be ready and led them south, out of sight, to turn east, facing Wang's south flank and rear.

When Qutu's smoke arrows broke into the sky, Shimin led his 1,000 heavy cavalry in a wild charge against Wang's army. Despite the fact that the total Tang force was merely some 6,000 against Wang's 20,000, the Tang's superior abilities and high morale shook Wang's lines. Li Shimin's cavalry broke through Wang's ranks and emerged on the other side of Wang's lines, only to regroup and charge back through their opponents. Shimin and about thirty of his personal guards became separated from the rest of his force. Wang's few heavy cavalry spotted Shimin and made for him. An arrow hit Saluzi, Shimin's horse, who could no longer gallop. Qiu Xinggong, Shimin's companion, turned his horse and, with his composite bow, shot arrows at Wang's cavalry, hitting and killing several. Wang's cavalry turned back. Qiu leaped from his horse and shoved Shimin up on it. Shimin sped away to Tang lines. Armed with a *chang dao* (staff sabre), Qiu swung the weapon this way and that, shouting loudly and clearing a path through the enemy infantry, killing any who got too close. He brought his commander's horse to safety, then pulled the arrow from Saluzi's front.

Wang made a great effort to hold his army together, but it broke apart under the Tang hammer blows. The struggle, from their exit from the west gate to the final break-up, lasted from morning until noon, when Wang had to withdraw the army back into Luoyang. Many thousand, dead or captive, did not return. Wang immediately saw to the preparations for a fierce siege. The throwing machines on the wall were put into condition and armed with many 40lb stones. Their range was about 200ft. He saw to the placing of numerous massive eight-bow large arrow launchers with a range of some 500ft. The walls and city were ready for the Tang onslaught.

Li Shimin marshalled his forces, dug trenches, set up throwing machines and prepared assault equipment. For ten days, Tang forces probed, scouted and tested the defences, day and night. Throwing machines and arrow projectors struck at the walls, but the Tang command found no soft spots. The Tang command staff went to Li Shimin and told him that the forces were running out of supplies, units had become disorganized and the campaign was dragging on too long for the men. They suggested that the main bases be garrisoned and the field army return to their Tang homeland. Li Shimin heard them out and then gave his orders: 'We came with a great army. We need to eliminate Wang Shichong. All the eastern towns are in our hands. Luoyang is isolated. The city shall fall. Until Luoyang is taken, the army remains. Anyone who retreats or suggests retreat shall be executed.' Officials in Chang'an informed the emperor about Li Shimin's problems. Emperor Gaozu secretly wrote to Li Shimin, suggesting he withdraw. Li Shimin replied by telling the emperor that he would take the city.

Li Shimin understood that Wang Shichong was holding out waiting for Dou Jiande to come. Shimin wrote to Wang, telling him to surrender soon or his fate would be terrible. Wang sent no reply. In early March, the commander at Guancheng (Zhengzhou Henan) surrendered the town to Li Ji and the Tang. About the same time, a Tang night attack took Hulao, at the end of the Hulao Pass to the east of Luoyang. They captured Wang's relative, the King of Jing. The Tang lines tightened around Luoyang so nothing could get in. Supplies ran out and the population starved, even high officials. But Wang Shichong held on, waiting for Dou Jiande's army to push back the Tang.

Back in early winter 620, Dou was involved in a campaign against a local strongman in Shandong. He concluded the campaign in late winter 621, garrisoning fortresses and concentrating his forces. In March, Dou began his march to rescue Wang Shichong. He reached Huazhou (Huaxian Henan), which was held by Wang's forces. Joining with Dou's army, the combined force continued west, occupying Guanzhou (near Zhengzhou Henan) and Yangzhai (Yuzhou Henan) by 24 March. As Dou marched his army along the Yellow River, he directed his supply ships to keep pace. Wang's forces in the area joined Dou's army. Soon Dou had concentrated 100,000 men at Chenggao (Sishui, Xingyang Henan).

References

Chinese sources: *Suishu*, 70, 85; *Jiu Tangshu*, 53-56; *Xin Tangshu*, 84; *Zizhi Tongjian*, 183, 186.
Fitzgerald, pp.50-59.
Graff, pp.162-71.
Hung, pp.61-69.

Chapter 10

Tang Victorious

Li Shimin Weighs Tang's Next Move

When word of Dou's approach came to Tang headquarters, Li Shimin, his subordinate commanders and their staffs sat down to consider their options. The question was whether to attack or retreat. Either path led to possible disaster or a great victory. Individual staff members, along with commanders Xiao Yu, Qutu Tong and Feng Deyi, presented one option. Their soldiers were tired, they said. Wang Shichong was holding out behind high and well-defended walls, and Dou Jiande was coming with a victorious army to rescue him. They would be caught between front and rear, so they should withdraw to their home to refit and regroup; opportunity would come to attack again. Then Field Commander Gao Xiaoke responded that the best option would be a fast and massive effort to occupy the barrier at Hulao Pass to block Dou Jiande. He went on that once they destroyed Dou, Wang would fall because he had no food or hope. Staff officer Xue Shou pointed out that both Wang Shichong and Dou Jiande still commanded significant forces. If Dou managed to unite with Wang, bringing in supplies and horses to Luoyang, the two of them could easily defeat the Tang. The land would remain divided, and there would be a war without end.

Xue then presented his campaign plan. Firstly, he said, they need to divide their forces. They should pull the best troops and powerful cavalry out of their lines and organize them into a field force. The weaker troops and support groups should remain in the siege lines around Luoyang. There, they should strengthen the lines and fortify their camps. If Wang Shichong attacked, they needed to defend positions rather than fight. Secondly, Commander Li Shimin should take the field force to Chenggao and wait for Dou Jiande. When they came, Li Shimin would attack and defeat them. Thirdly, with the defeat of Dou, Wang would be out of moves: he would surrender, and within twenty days the war would conclude. Li Shimin listened to his commanders and staff. He dismissed the meeting with the remark that he would make the necessary decision.

After some time, messengers recalled the commanders and staff to the meeting place. Li Shimin entered and issued his orders. He explained that Wang Shichong had run out of supplies. Morale was low, and ruler, ministers and officers were in disagreement. They did not have to attack the city; it would fall soon enough. Dou

Jiande had managed successful campaigns. His army was brave and well-disciplined, but it was tired. They could block Dou at Hulao Pass. If he could not force a way to Luoyang, the city defences would collapse within a month. That way, they gained more men. If they didn't hold Hulao Pass, then Dou would reach Luoyang and join Wang. They could not defeat that joint force. Li Shimin'd mind was clear: this was his decision.

Campaign of Hulao Pass

Li Shimin began his new campaign on 24 March 621. He had drawn out of his forces around Luoyang the best infantry troops and light cavalry. These he added to his black heavy cavalry force. He appointed fourth son Li Juanji to be commander of the siege, with Qutu Tong as a military advisor. Leading a mixed advanced guard of 3,500 men, Li Shimin marched out of camp at noon. The army marched past Beimang Mountain and Heyang (Mengxian Henan) and on beyond Gongxian (north-east of Gongyi Henan). Wang Shichong, standing on Luoyang's wall, saw Li Shimin's force on the march but did not know where he was going. On 25 March, Li Shimin entered Hulao Pass (just west of Sishui, Xingyang Henan). There his troops dug in, preparing defences for the main force which slowly arrived.

At midday the next day, Li Shimin, in full black armour with flag carriers, led 500 of his black heavy cavalry out of the pass toward Dou Jiande's camp. In the rough country beyond the pass, he had his forces spread out on the ground on either side of the road, hiding in ambush. He and four guardsmen rode on toward Dou's camp, some 6 miles away. His close companion, Yuchi Jingde, rode next to him. Shimin remarked as they went forward that he with his bow and Yuchi with his lance could hold off a myriad of men, but his plan was to beat a quick retreat when the enemy realized they were there.

The five rode on toward Dou's camp. Sentries saw them approach. When the five were about a half a mile away, Li Shimin yelled, 'I am the King of Qin' (telling them that he was Li Shimin). His soldiers unfurled their banners, which identified them as Tang. A group of Dou's light cavalry urged their horses toward the five. Li Shimin drew his great bow and shot an arrow that struck the group's leader, unhorsing him. Dou saw all this and was impressed with such impertinence. Waving to his commanders, he ordered six units, some 6,000 men, to capture the insolent enemies. Li Shimin and his four companions watched Dou's soldiers form up and begin to advance toward them. Li Shimin told his companions to stand still. Then he turned and said that the three guardsmen should go, and he and Yuchi would hold the rear. The three turned and slowly rode down the road, while Li Shimin and Yuchi waited for the cavalry force to come closer. Shimin then again drew his great bow and shot an arrow that hit and unhorsed another of Dou's men. The cavalry stopped for a moment. Shimin and Yuchi drew back, and the cavalry then came forward. Shimin shot again, unhorsing another. The cavalry stopped again. Repeating this, Shimin pulled Dou's cavalry force back into the rough country on either side of the road.

Waiting in ambush, Li Ji and the heavy cavalry let Dou's cavalry drive deep into the rough ground before he gave the signal and the warriors flung themselves onto their opponents. The conflict was brutal but short. Some 600 of Dou's men lay dead on the road, and the rest fled. Having thus announced his arrival, Li Shimin sent a letter to Dou Jiande. It said:

'You occupy land belonging to the Tang. But, you care for Li Shentong, our relative, and have honourably sent Princess Tong'an back to Chang'an. There is no hatred between us. Yet, you ally with Wang Shichong, so repudiating your word. We will destroy Wang Shichong. You have brought your whole army to rescue him. You act for the benefit of others! They use your resources, so wasting them for yourself. Be clever! Today was a mere contest of vanguards. We block your path to Wang Shichong. We shall stop you. We hope you halt your offensive. I tell you, you will be sorry if you do not take my advice.'

In reply, Dou Jiande fortified his camps, put scouts out to keep an eye on the Tang, and settled down to stockpile supplies. Dou exercised his troops and prepared for his coming offensive against the Tang. He also fortified and garrisoned his lines facing the Hulao Pass.

The south bank of the Yellow River, from the mouth of the Luo River to the valley of the Sishui River, is a complex area of water-cut loess hills. The wind, rain, creeks and rivers have sculpted a land of flat plains interrupted by high rounded hills and deeply indented rough country. Between the Yellow River and the foot-hills of the Song Mountain, the Sishui River flows along an escarpment that rises in the west. To the east, another escarpment rises some 60ft, topping out to a level plain stretching further east. The rough country to the west contains complexes of routes and ways fit for small numbers of people. But the only way through the country for a large group of men and supplies was a river ravine that ran down to a small plain abutting the Sishui River. This ravine, from the escarpment's crest to the Sishui River, is the Hulao Pass (Tiger Trap Pass).

Dou encamped his army some 10 miles east of the pass, near where the Yongli Canal entered the Yellow River. His forces were comfortable and easily in reach of his supply fleet. He decided to wait out Li Shimin. Dou knew if he attempted to manoeuvre over the escarpment to the north or south, his infantry would become exposed to Shimin's cavalry while they were strung out. He decided not to risk it. After sitting in front of Hulao Pass for a good month, Dou Jiande's commanders questioned whether this was the correct strategy. Ling Jing, an advisor and officer, offered another course of action. Rather than attempting to break through Li Shimin's considerable forces, he suggested, Dou's army should decamp and march north, cross the Yellow River and occupy the towns on the north side. Then after regrouping, Dou should march west, bypassing the Taihang Mountain, and descend into the lands of Fen and Jin (Shanxi). Seizing local towns, they could then easily occupy Pujin on the Yellow River. This manoeuvre would accomplish three important results: Tang's strength was here, and the march would encounter only weak forces; they would gain lands and people, increasing their power; and they would threaten Guanzhong. The Tang would have to withdraw to protect their capital.

Representatives of Wang Shichong reacted to this suggestion quickly. They pointed out to Dou Jiande that Ling Jing's operation would take a year: Luoyang would be finished by then. Dou dismissed Ling Jing, rejecting his plan. But whispers from the inner court said that marching north, uniting with the Turks and threatening Guanzhong was good for Dou Jiande – let Wang Shichong be destroyed. Dou should look out for himself. However, Dou rejected this path.

Near the end of April, Li Shimin's supplies ran low. The Tang had to decide whether to solidify their position on the Sishui at the expense of their siege lines at Luoyang, or somehow defeat Dou. The Tang unleashed their light cavalry to harass Dou's supply lines, more to hold their opponent's attention than cause actual damage. The Tang were very short of fodder for the horses. Li Shimin understood he needed a decision soon. Either he had to retreat and give up the campaign, or somehow precipitate a battle. To see the actual condition of Dou's forces, Li Shimin dressed as a common light cavalry soldier and personally reconnoitred Dou's positions. What he saw was encouraging. He moved some of his best units to locations out of sight to Dou's scouts. On 1 May, he sent his 1,000 best horses out of his encampments to an island in the Yellow River, where they could graze. Surely Dou's scouts would see this. He hoped Dou would conclude that the Tang had run out of fodder and were now going to hold the pass on foot.

Combat At Hulao

Dou decided that his best course of action was to break through Hulao Pass and advance on Luoyang; his commanders were eager and his men were ready. The time had come. At dawn on 2 May, Dou Jiande had horns sound and drums beat. His army mobilized into battle units and deployed. When his forces reached the east bank of the Sishui River, they formed up along a line from where the Sishui empties into the Yellow River and then extending upstream along the Sishui for more than a mile to a defendable hill known as Magpie Mountain. Dou had a small number of heavy cavalry but a strong force of light cavalry. His main strength was heavy infantry. He concentrated his best infantry units opposite Hulao town, facing the town on three sides. When Dou gave the signal, the beating of drums sounded along the whole front as marching feet and cheering voices announced the advance of his large force. Taking position at the ready, they threatened to cross the Sishui River and overwhelm the Tang.

Li Shimin gathered his staff and commanders on a promontory that overlooked the whole valley of the Sishui River. Shimin pointed out different units and leaders of Dou's army and spoke about how impressive the whole looked. But he said they were from north of the Yellow River, and reminded his officers they had never fought really well-trained, hardened troops. He said that despite advancing against a strong enemy, they were talking and joking and were not well disciplined. Shimin believed Dou's forces underestimated their opponents. He gave orders to keep their garrison in the town, and sent messengers to the island in the Yellow River to have the steeds return. Shimin ordered his men to remain in their defensive positions and let Dou's forces wait. His soldiers would keep their formation for hours, but eventually they would become hungry and thirsty. Then Dou's army would withdraw, and when they did, the Tang would attack. Shimin said that when noon passed, they would win.

In the middle of the morning, Dou sent 300 armoured cavalrymen across the Sishui River. They came, flags flying, clad in rich trappings, on prancing horses. A spokesman, under a banner of truce, rode up to the camp rampart. He issued a challenge to the Tang heavy cavalry to come and do battle with real warriors. Shimin let Wang Junkuo take 200 armoured horsemen out and spar with Dou's cavalry. They did so for some time, and then each side decided to return to their camps. As Dou's troopers withdrew, one of their commanders rode a horse which used to belong to Emperor Yang of the Sui Dynasty. The horse's armour was shiny gold, blazing in the sun. The rider pranced his horse back and forth to show off. Li Shimin, observing all of this, said to Yuchi Jingde, 'That is an excellent horse.' Yuchi offered to go and get the beast, but Shimin refused and said that he was not going to lose a warrior for a horse. However, Yuchi did not listen. With two cavalrymen, he rode out and captured the horse and rider, bringing both back to Li Shimin.

By now, the morning was over. Dou Jiande's formations had been in position since early sunrise. When the sun reached its zenith, Dou's troops became restless through thirst and hunger. Seeing the well-manned Tang fortifications, they did not want to advance, preferring to go back to their camps. Li Shimin then judged the moment to move had come. His horses were back, his units were formed and his men were ready. Calling forth Yuwen Shiji, Shimin ordered him to take 300 heavy cavalry and ride in front of the enemy's west wing. Once past their flank, he was to turn south. If the wing stayed firm in position, he was to ride back and return. If the wing began to retreat, he was to engage them, keeping them well occupied.

Li Shimin watched Yuwen Shiji ride out past Dou's west wing, which began looking confused. Some men dispersed, while others tried to form up into units. Seeing this, Shimin said, 'Now, we attack!' He put on his black armour, mounted his warhorse, Shifachi, and rode to the fore of his force of black-armoured heavy cavalry. Li Shimin giving the signal, drums began to beat, flags started flying, and the Tang army launched forward out of Hulao Pass, crossed the Sishui River and struck Dou's lines. At that time, Dou Jiande, along with his ministers and commanders, was holding morning court. The Tang heavy cavalry had cut through Dou's infantry and suddenly appeared. The ministers and staff panicked, running this way and that, while the commanders tried to return to their units. The whole camp erupted in commotion. Dou, who was keeping his heavy cavalry force in reserve, ordered them to advance against the Tang. But their commander was looking for them in the middle of the confused mass of panic-stricken courtiers. When the Tang cavalry hit Dou's troops guarding the camp, the disorder became complete. Dou's men bunched up to defend against Shimin's heavy cavalry, only to become targets for the horse archers, or they dispersed to defend against the archers, only to be ridden down by the heavy cavalry. Shimin's cousin, 18-year-old Li Daoxuan, charged into the mass of Dou's infantry until he emerged out of their rear. He then turned around and cut his way back to the Tang lines. His horse killed under him, Shimin had him remounted, and the whole force of heavy cavalry followed him through Dou's lines: 'His armour was thick with arrows like the quills of a porcupine.' As the fighting and confusion continued, 'dust filling the sky', Li Shimin and three of his companions rode through the fighting forces up to an eminence behind the battle lines. There, they unfurled a great banner with the character 'Tang' on it. This sight was the final blow to Dou's soldiers: hot, tired, thirsty, surprised and out-fought, now with their enemy in the rear, they had had enough. Slowly at first, then in large masses, they fled the field, leaving 3,000 dead. Li Shimin ordered an immediate pursuit, and Dou's men surrendered as Tang forces approached them.

Dou's army soon broke up; units dispersed and the whole became a mass of fleeing individuals. The Tang captured 50,000 of Dou's men, but the same day, Li Shimin released them all, telling them to go home. Pursued, Dou Jiande was hit by an arrow in his leg and fell from his horse. A Tang officer was about to finish him off when he yelled who he was. The soldiers bound him and threw him on a spare horse they had picked up. They took him to Li Shimin, who had Dou's wounds bound and sat him down. Shimin asked Dou why, when the Tang's quarrel was with Wang Shichong, had he come to attack him? Dou responded, 'I came here to save you the trouble of going all the way to get me.'

Fall of Luoyang

The Tang placed Dou and his principal commanders in cages mounted on wagons and drove them to Luoyang. Li Shimin had them paraded around the foot of the city walls. Wang Shichong, standing on the walls, saw Dou Jiande. He heard from Dou's lips the sorry story of defeat. The two would-be emperors saw in each other's eyes their doom. They broke down and wept. Shimin then sent one of Dou's chief commanders into the city with terms for Wang. Wang and his family would receive honourable exile. Except for a select few, his men could either join the Tang or go where they pleased. Wang called together his ministers and commanders to discuss their situation. Wang wanted to choose an elite force and break out of Luoyang, heading south, but his commanders did not think they would be successful, considering the state of their horses and men. They accepted Li Shimin's terms. The next day, the great gates opened. Wang and his ministers, dressed in plain white, with Wang's coffin carried beside them, walked out of Luoyang to the gates of the Tang camp. They all knelt down and put their foreheads on the dirt. Li Shimin said to Wang, 'You kept saying how you would like to meet that "boy". Well, here is that "boy", what are you going to do about it?' Wang abjectly apologized. As Wang and his entourage left Luoyang, Tang officers and troops entered to secure the city and prevent looting.

On the following day, Li Shimin entered Luoyang. He sent clerical staff to collect documents from the Sui Dynasty, but someone had seen to their destruction. He also sent officials to seal the storehouses and collect all gold and silk, which he would distribute to commanders and soldiers. Shimin also ordered the arrest of a dozen or so of Wang's ministers and commanders, whom he accused of serious crimes. Li Ji tried to intercede for one who had been his friend, but Li Shimin refused. Shimin had all the accused ministers and commanders executed on the banks of the Luo River.

Dou's wife and political officials had escaped from his defeat, making their way to Hebei. There, some suggested that they enthrone Dou's adopted son as emperor and continue the struggle. But the resources for another effort were not available. On 10 June, Dou's main holdings surrendered to the Tang, soon followed by outlying territories.

On 9 July, Li Shimin made a grand ceremonial entrance into Chang'an. He rode at the head of his army, wearing golden armour. Twenty-five of his chief commanders followed, each wearing decorated armour. Then came the army: the

1,000 black-armoured heavy cavalry, followed by 9,000 heavy and light cavalry, then 30,000 infantry, each in their units, with sparkling armour and trappings. Drums sounded and different coloured flags waved. Li Shimin led the procession to the great ancestral temple where the Emperor Gaozu sat enthroned. Li Shimin presented Wang Shichong and Dou Jiande to the emperor. Then he presented the imperial Sui chariot. The emperor held a great banquet, at which he presented Li Shimin with the title Grand Commander of Ever Victorious Strategy. Servants brought Wang Shichong before the emperor. He recognized Li Shimin's promise of life and exile. The emperor set Wang, his sons, brothers and nephews free of their chains and assigned them to exile in Sichuan. Dou Jiande was taken to the market place and executed.

Wang Shichong and his eldest brother lived in a guest house near Chang'an while they waited for the move to Sichuan. On 12 July, Dugu Xiude, Administrator of Dingzhou (Dingzhou Hebei), led his brothers to the house. Dugu pretended that he had a message from the emperor for Wang Shichong. The brothers Wang came out of the house. Dugu Xiude swung his sword and killed both Wangs. Dugu later explained that he killed the Wangs in retaliation for the death of his father in 619, but the emperor dismissed Dugu from all positions and authority.

References

Chinese sources: *Jiu Tangshu*, 2, 54; *Xin Tangshu*, 85; *Zizhi Tongjian*, 189.
Fitzgerald, pp.70–89.
Graff, pp.172–77.
Hung, pp.94–101.

Chapter 11

Imperial Consolidation

Li Shimin Organizes for Victory

Li Shimin's victory at Hulao and conquest of Luoyang solidified Tang power but left many areas of the Chinese lands as autonomous or independent states. Separate states had ruled in the lands of the Yellow and Yangzi River valleys since the defeat of the Jin Dynasty in 317 until the Sui Dynasty united the Chinese lands in 589. Then, under the Sui Emperor Yang, the empire collapsed again by 618. Some modern commentators suggest that the idea of a united Chinese Empire was simply the result of a series of military campaigns over centuries, not necessarily a profound drive in Chinese ideology. But we should remember that Emperor Sui Wen said: 'At the end of Wei there was chaos and loss and the empire's territory was divided like a melon.' Emperor Wen meant the entire area of both the Yellow and Yangzi River courses were 'the empire'. Emperor Tang Gaozu followed in the footsteps of the founding emperors of former and later Han, Wei, Jin and Sui. The Tang Dynasty, from the beginning, intended to unite all the Chinese lands.

Even stronger than the Sui, the Tang forces under Li Shimin had both a tactical and strategic advantage that their competitors lacked. As a member of the northwest aristocracy, Li Shimin was brought up with horses, and his followers knew how to breed and train warhorses. The 1,000-strong black-armoured heavy cavalry unit, well drilled and aggressive, was the crucial tactical piece on Shimin's side of the battle board. No other power in China had the resources to manage such a unit.

Li Shimin's strategic advantage was even greater. He and his principal officers were well-versed in Chinese war literature. Chinese handbooks of war, including Sun Tzu's *Art of War*, present strategic advice about military operations. In many ways, Li Shimin's campaigns illustrate many features of Sun's methods of understanding the proper practice of the military art. In a basic sense, Chinese war theory recommends that military situations be recognized as a problem to be solved through complex thought. Every factor involved in the problems of war is to be analyzed in relation to other factors so the commander may generate a favourable balance of forces. Thus, terrain determines commitment; commitment affects numbers; numbers depend on supplies; supplies balance forces; force balance sways victory (*Art of War*, chapter 4, trans. Jonathan Clements). We must never doubt, however, that bold moves and hard fighting are what, in the end, won the battles. Li Shimin, in his old age, liked to point out that he killed over 1,000 men by his own hand.

Battle Against Liang

Sichuan had remained under the direction of Sui officials while the rest of the Sui dominion fell apart. These officials remained loyal to Emperor Yang until he was dead; they then recognized the Tang regime in Chang'an in 618. Down the Yangzi, beyond the gorges, a restored Liang Dynasty under Emperor Xiao Xian held the middle Yangzi and further south. The south had been independent for centuries, except for the brief period under the Sui dominion. The old House of Liang had ruled the south from 503-555. Emperor Xiao Xian of the restored Liang Dynasty commanded a strong infantry force. He saw the Tang occupation of Sichuan as a threat. In 619, Liang pushed up the Yangzi Gorges to invade Sichuan, but met with failure. The court at Chang'an decided to overthrow the Liang regime. The Tang high command collected some well-trained infantry and assigned them to an imperial cousin, Li Xiagong, a civilian administrator. The command also appointed an expert military officer to assist Li Xiagong. This was Li Jing, who was adopted into the imperial clan. He was a son of a Sui commandery governor and nephew of the great Sui commander, Han Qinhu, who had lead in the Sui campaign against Chen in 589. Li Jing was a clever youth, well acquainted with military literature, and had administrative experience.

In 619, the court appointed Li Xiagong as area commander in Xinzhou, in south-eastern Sichuan. He brought Li Jing as his second in command. Once settled in, the two Lis ordered the collection of a large army and the construction of a fleet of warships by local watermen. The officers trained their men for water combat during 620. They intended to drive down the Yangzi and destroy the Liang forces in 621. However, a series of revolts suddenly broke out in the Liang realm. Emperor Xiao Xian knew about the Tang preparations, but thought that they would wait until late spring when the Yangzi flood in the gorges abated. Xiao Xian certainly thought the enemy would not risk their forces in the autumn flood, so sent his army to the south to suppress the rebellions. But the Tang commanders decided to attack during late autumn 621. They would assault the Liang capital, Jiangling, before the Liang army could return from the south.

In late autumn 621, the Yangzi River was high but slowly lowering. Li Xiagong commanded some 2,000 war junks and Li Jing headed the infantry army. Directing his war junks through the gorges, Li Xiagong led his fleet down the Yangzi. When the fleet landed on the shore beyond the gorges, Li Jing marched the army through their narrows. Xiao Xian had failed to defend the gorges, thinking he had plenty of time before the Tang would move. Seizing a town just some 60 miles from Jiangling, Li Xiagong and Li Jing prepared their forces and put them in battle formation. When news of the Tang advance came to the Liang court at Jiangling, the high command panicked. Immediate orders went out to the southern army to return by forced marches. The Liang war fleet mobilized and worked their way up the Yangzi. The Tang waited for the Liang fleet at the mouth of the Qing River. As the Liang fleet deployed for an attack, the Tang fleet launched their assault, with the current carrying them along. Li Xiagong's fleet broke through the Liang line of ships, capturing 300 of them and killing 10,000 men. The Tang command believed that the Liang capital had no major defensive forces. Their whole force moved down the Yangzi to attack Jiangling. By the time the Tang army and fleet arrived, the Liang had mobilized another fleet, pulling it together from many different sources. Li Jing, moving his force as quickly as possible, attacked the Liang fleet before it was readied for battle. The fleet was burned, and the surviving crew withdrew into Jiangling. Li Jing put the town under siege, but remained concerned that the Liang southern army was on its way.

Li Jing ordered all the Liang ships – broken, bloody and burned as they were – launched on the river, to float down to where the Liang army, coming up from the south, was marching. When the floating pieces of wreckage appeared, the Liang commanders saw them as evidence of defeat. One of the Liang commanders who saw the wreckage, Gao Shilian, was the maternal uncle of Li Shimin's consort, the Princess Zhangsun. He was a former high official of the Sui Dynasty, a commander in Annam. When the Sui Dynasty collapsed, he led a body of troops north, reaching the Yangzi. There, the Liang Dynasty invited him to join their forces, and he had no choice but to agree. Now, he and the other Liang officers began to consider their options.

In Jiangling, Liang Emperor Xiao Xian saw Li Jing's siege lines. The relief forces should have arrived, and the emperor believed that they were not going to come. He decided to surrender to the Tang. Xiao Xian ordered the gates of Jiangling opened, and he and his court submitted to Li Xiagong on 10 November 621. Xiao Xian said: 'I alone should suffer death. My people have done you no injury. You should leave them in peace.' Li Xiagong and Li Jing took the town over. They accepted the local authorities so long as they submitted to the Tang. The easy terms were readily accepted by the rest of the Liang towns and the Liang armed forces. Li Jing took a small expeditionary force through the former Liang dominion and accepted the submission of the Liang south, Annam and the valley of the West River. By the end of 621, the south submitted to the Tang and Xiao Xian was executed in Chang'an.

Rebels Gain Power: Liu Heita and Xu Yuanlang

After Dou Jiande met defeat and death, some of his commanders and soldiers, having fled the field and escaped the hands of the Tang, collected together in Hebei,
north of the Yellow River. There, they founded an independent state, raising taxes
and dispensing justice. They sent Tang officials away. Concerned that the rebellion
might spread, Emperor Tang Gaozu summoned Dou's former high commanders
to come to Chang'an. Many of these officers lived in Tang lands unaffected by the
rebellion in Hebei. The former senior commanders Fan Yuan, Dong Kangmai and
Gao Yaxian met. Fan Yuan made the point that Wang Shichong had surrendered
Luoyang, then the Tang executed him and his commanders and ministers. Dou
Jiande had surrendered, and the Tang also executed him and the officers whom
they got into their hands. Fan Yuan felt if they went to Chang'an, the Tang would
execute them too. He added that they had lived through a hundred battles, and
they should have died long ago. Life itself meant little; but honour, they must
preserve. Dou had captured the Tang Emperor's cousin, and had treated him well
and sent him back. The Tang then executed him. Fan Yuan said they should avenge
him.

The three former officers gathered together in a secret spot and cast spells
in a bid to penetrate the curtain of the future. The portents were clear: their
efforts would succeed if they were led by a man named Liu. The three travelled
to Zhangnan (Linzhang Hebei) to confer with Liu Ya, a former commander of
Dou Jiande. They begged him to become the leader of their rebellion, but Liu Yan
refused, saying that he had had enough of upheaval and war. The three killed him
to keep him quiet. Another former commander of Dou Jiande, Liu Heita, lived in
Zhangnan. The trio found him in his vegetable garden. He quickly agreed to their
plan. Liu Heita immediately took a steer, slaughtered and cooked it. Fan Yuan,
Dong Kangmai, Gao Yaxian and Liu Heita mutually pledged faith and loyalty over
the meal as they ate and drank.

Liu Heita had been one of Dou Jiande's better commanders. He quickly organized some hundreds of men into a force, and on 16 July 621 he took over the
town of Zhangnan. As his successes accumulated, Liu Heita added to his dominion. On 12 August, he took Shuxian (Xiajin Shandong). As Liu increased his
power, Tang governor Quan Wei of Weihou (Daming Hebei) mobilized an army
to defend his area. Liu defeated and killed him and took over Quan's army, supplies and town. Many of Dou's former officers and men came to join Liu Heita.
His army grew to more than 2,000 trained soldiers. Having a high platform constructed in Zhangnan, Liu officiated at a grand ceremony to commemorate Dou
Jiande. All present pledged to avenge Dou and recognize Liu Heita as supreme
commander.

During the war of the Tang with Dou Jiande, the lands of Yanzhou (Shandong) were part of the dominions of Xu Yuanlang, who had been a rebel and branded at the time of the collapse of the Sui Dynasty. Xu had established a well-run state by the time Li Shimin defeated Dou Jiande. Xu recognized reality and submitted to the Tang. Emperor Tang Gaozu appointed Xu as chief commander of forces in the Yanzhou area and elevated him to Lord of Lu by imperial edict. But Xu was worried about how long this arrangement would last. Hearing of Liu Heita's successes, Xu Yuanlang initiated a secret alliance. On 26 August, Xu proclaimed his independence from the Tang and affiliation with Liu. Siting his capital at Rencheng, Xu accepted the position of chief commander of forces in his lands. Local leaders, landowners and officials in eastern Henan and western Shandong supported Xu's move toward independence. On 7 September, Xu Yuanlang proclaimed himself King of Lu.

The Imperial Court at Chang'an slowly received news about the collapse of Tang power in the north-east. The rise of a clique of Dou's former officers was bad, but the apparent defection of Xu Yuanlang was worse because it showed the weakness of Tang prestige. Emperor Tang Gaozu issued orders to mobilize a powerful army in Guanzhong and instructions to the towns in the east to increase their garrisons. By September 621, Li Shentong led a strong army out of Guanzhong toward Jizhou (Hengshui Hebei). He joined forces with Li Yi, commander–in-chief of the Tang military in Youzhou (south-west of Beijing). Li Yi, formerly Lou Yi, had seized Zhuo Commandery during the troubles in the time of Emperor Yang. When Li Yuan proclaimed the Tang Empire, Lou Yi pledged his loyalty to the Tang. Emperor Tang Gaozu granted Lou Yi the imperial name Li. Li Shentong and Li Yi collected an army of 50,000 men to fight Liu Heita.

The combined Tang army marched south to Raoyang (Raoyang Hebei). There they found Liu Heita and his forces. The Tang had a much larger army but only a core of trained infantry. Liu Heita's smaller army was better trained. They faced each other along the banks of the Rao River. Li Shentong extended his men along a 2-mile front, while Liu Heita concentrated his men in a single strong formation. A storm blew in the next morning. The wind, rain and sand favoured the Tang side. Li Shentong launched the Tang attack, charging Liu Heita's infantry. Liu's lines wavered, but the wind changed suddenly and Liu's infantry lunged forward, breaking the Tang line. Li Yi, on the Tang west wing, hit and defeated Gao Yaxian's force, but still had to withdraw because of Li Shentong's defeat. Li Yi pulled back to Gaocheng (Hebei). Liu Heita pursued Li Yi, who retreated to Youzhou. The Tang army lost two-thirds of its men. Liu Heita's victory magnified his strength.

The rebel force advanced and took Yingzhou (Hejian Hebei). They captured Li Xuantong, a 19-year-old Tang aristocrat officer. Liu Heita wanted him to join his forces, but Li Xuantong refused. Liu confined Li but gave him enough food and left him in the hands of friendly guards. Li Xuantong got on well with his guards, showing them different dances. Then he asked for a sword to demonstrate a particular sword dance, but in the dance, Li Xuantong used the sword to kill himself.

Continuing his advance, Liu Heita captured the Tang base at Jizhou (Hengshui Hebei). Sitting in the Tang eastern base, he sent letters to all of Dou Jiande's former officials and commanders, telling them to come and join him. Many of those who received the letters killed local Tang officers and joined Liu. Liu organized an army of 30,000 well-trained men. He marched north against Zongcheng (Weixian), where Li Ji stationed his field army. As Liu advanced, Li Ji saw that his army was not strong enough to face Liu. Li Ji withdrew to Mingzhou (Yongnian Hebei). Liu followed Li Ji and brought his army to battle. Defeating Li Ji, Liu's army killed 5,000 Tang soldiers. Li Ji only narrowly escaped. On 14 December, the local officials in Mingzhou seized the town and presented it to Liu Heita. Within the next ten days, Liu Heita captured five more major towns, rounding out Dou Jiande's former dominion. On 1 January 622, Liu Heita proclaimed himself King of Handong, with Fan Yuan as his prime minister and his capital at Mingzhou.

The Tang Counter-Attack

The rebels' success shocked the Imperial Court. Emperor Gaozu issued orders to mobilize his crack troops. He appointed second son Li Shimin, King of Qin, and fourth son Li Yuanji, King of Qi, as supreme commanders and sent them to crush the rebels. Li Shimin rode his warhorse Juanmaogua at the head of his 1,000 black armoured heavy cavalry when he took formal leave of Chang'an. The Tang force reached Huojia (Huojia Henan) on 8 January 622. Liu Heita's scouts told of the vast strength of the Tang forces and that Li Shimin led them. He withdrew his army from Xiangzhou (Anyang Honan), pulling back to his capital, Mingzhou, so that when he finally met the Tang in battle, he would have reinforcements and supplies at hand. Li Shimin occupied Xiangzhou and moved on to Feixiang (Feixiang Hebei). From there, he advanced along the Mingshui River, coming within striking distance of Liu Heita's capital.

The Tang commander in the north, Li Yi, in Youzhou (Beijing), had increased his army to 40,000 men. When Li Shimin approached, Li Ji marched south-west to join him. Liu's scouts reported that Li Ji was on the march. On 27 January, Liu marched out with a large army to intercept Li Ji's army. He appointed his prime minister, Fan Yuan, to take charge of their capital with a garrison of 10,000 troops. Liu camped that evening at Shahe (Shahe Hebei). The Tang commander in the area near Mingzhou, Cheng Mingzhen, confirmed his information that Liu Heita and a powerful army had left his capital. Cheng then organized a formation with sixty large drums and hid them near the river about half a mile from Mingzhou.

Li Shimin as emperor.

Informal view of Li Shimin.

A large Tang warship.

A Tang temple.

Reconstruction of Xuanwu Gate.

In the morning, Cheng had the drums start to beat, slowly getting louder and louder. Soon the drums sounded like thunder. Fan Yuan thought a massive army was coming. Panicking, he sent an urgent message to Liu Heita to immediately return because his capital was under grave threat. Liu found the news disturbing. He left 10,000 men to continue the march north with his second in command, his younger brother. Liu turned around with his best troops and hurried back to his capital. Li Ji found Liu's younger brother and his army on 30 January. The soldiers fought on the banks of the Xuhe River. Li Ji crushed Liu's force, killing about 8,000 men. Li Ji marched southward, taking over many areas formally recognizing Liu Heita's rule.

Liu Heita's commander of Mingshui Commandery, Li Yuan Huo, surrendered the district capital to the Tang. Li Shimin sent Wang Jun Kuo with 1,500 cavalrymen to Mingshui as a garrison. In mid-winter, Liu Heita, after running back and forth between his army in the north and his capital under spurious threat, moved to reoccupy Mingshui Commandery. He called for and got reinforcements, and proceeded to lay Mingshui town under siege. Wang Jun Kuo and his cavalrymen were the only troops in the town, but a moat 50ft wide protected the town walls. Liu's engineers began to build two tunnels under the moat, and at the same time they constructed a circumvallation protecting his siege lines.

Li Shimin hurried to Mingshui to relieve Wang Jun Kuo and his men. Three times he tried to break through Liu's line, but was thwarted. Shimin called a council. He was very concerned that his friend and comrade in arms, Wang Jun Kuo, and his cavalrymen would be overwhelmed. He asked for ideas. All agreed that when Liu's tunnels reached under the walls, Mingshui would have to surrender. A young commander, Luo Shixin, offered to replace Wang Jun Kuo. The Tang forces communicated with their garrison in Mingshui with signals from a nearby hilltop. Li Shimin ordered Wang to break out at a given moment. At that time, Wang Jun Kuo and his personal guards sortied out of Mingshui while Luo Shixin and 300 elite troopers fought their way into the town.

For the following eight days, heavy snow prevented any major Tang operations, while Liu's engineers continued to excavate their tunnels. On 25 February, Liu's men seized Mingshui. Liu offered an honourable surrender to Luo Shixin, but Luo refused and was quickly cut down. Li Shimin paid a hefty ransom for his cavalrymen and the body of Luo, and gave Luo a grand funeral. In March, Li Ji and his army, held up by the snow storms, joined Li Shimin on the south bank of the Mingshui River. There, the Tang built fortified camps, one for Li Shimin's force and the other for Li Ji's.

The two forces observed each other across the Mingshui River. Tang supplies came down the Yellow River valley from Luoyang. Liu's supplies came from Yizhou (Xixian Hebei) and nearby settlements, moving south by water and land.

The Tang commander of Yongning, Cheng Mingzhen, kept sending raiding parties to disrupt Liu's supplies. For many days, the two forces kept watch on each other. Li Shimin expected Liu Heita would offer battle when his supplies began to run low. Shimin sent a crew of engineers up the Mingshui River to build a dyke, holding back a significant amount of water, ordering the engineers to be prepared to break the levee on a given signal.

At the same time, Liu Heita organized a strong force of heavy infantry, arming and training them. He also sent scouts to reconnoitre the Tang camps. Liu understood that the strength of the Tang was the military talent and heavy armoured cavalry of Li Shimin. Eliminating Shimin would allow local powers to hold out against the expanding Tang Empire. But Li Shimin was a brilliant and bold fighting man. On his great warhorse in his black armour, with his companion guards, Li Shimin was a magnificent fighter. Despite the danger of poison, a stab in the dark or an arrow out of nowhere, Shimin's men were loyal and his servants were incorruptible. Instead, Liu decided to see if using Shimin's strengths against him might lead to his destruction. Seeing how attached Li Shimin was to his underlings, Liu set up a trap in which, by attacking a subordinate, Liu would bring Shimin and his cavalry to battle before they saw what they were attacking. Then, by surrounding his heavy cavalry force with a heavy infantry force, Liu hoped he would see Shimin fall.

On 23 March, Liu Heita's forces were ready. Out of the dawn, Liu led his light cavalry forces, masking a strong unit of heavy armoured infantry. The light force heartily attacked Li Ji's camp, beating drums and sounding horns, with many flags waving. Li Shimin immediately mounted Juanmaogua and called his armoured cavalry together, leading the attack against the rear of Liu's attacking force. Liu then sprang his trap: the light cavalry faded away and the heavy infantry deployed, surrounding Shimin's compact unit of heavy cavalry. Wheeling about, Shimin led an attack, using all the tricks that cavalry had to break infantry, but the horsemen faced solid ranks of shields and spears held by regular armoured infantry. Shimin's black armoured cavalrymen were stymied. Slowly, the circle of infantry contracted. Seeing his beloved master in trouble, Yuchi Jingde organized Tang heavy infantry from both camps and led an attack against one point on Liu Heita's circle. Shimin's force, taking casualties, concentrated on the same point from inside the circle and broke out. Liu's plan had nearly worked: he had taught the great Tang commander a lesson in the art of war.

Three days later, as the sun reached its zenith, Liu Heita led out 20,000 men across the Mingshui River to the south bank. Then he deployed his army threatening Li Shimin's camp. Shimin led his black armoured heavy cavalry out of his camp, covering the deployment of his infantry. Shimin brushed Liu's cavalry aside, but then faced Liu's heavy infantry phalanx. The Tang heavy cavalry had already met these men three days before, and Shimin was wary of engaging them. He sent his archers and swordsmen forward, but they simply held their own without denting Liu's phalanx. A signal was sent to the men at the dyke, who began opening the river's flow. By evening, the rising water disrupted Liu's heavy infantry phalanx. Then the black cavalry charged and broke Liu's army. Liu Heta and his personal guard of about 200 horsemen turned and fled the field.

The Tang Consolidate their Hold on the East

The collapse of Liu Heita's power left local potentates facing the power of the Tang Dynasty. Li Shimin immediately threatened to attack Xu Yuan Lang, King of Lu. But before he could organize his offensive, word came from Chang'an that Emperor Gaozu had recalled Li Shimin for consultation. Shimin handed command over to fourth son Li Yuanji, and marched with his personal forces toward Chang'an. The emperor came out of the city to meet Shimin and waited for him at Changleban, east of the capital. This was a great honour for second son Shimin. On 9 April, Commander Li Shimin, at the head of his black armoured heavy cavalry, with drums beating and horns sounding, entered Chang'an. The emperor received him and Shimin handed over his report of his operations. Shimin, his men and the court celebrated the great victories until the beginning of summer.

In late June, Li Shimin led his troops to Liyang (Xunxian Henan), organized a large force and marched to Jiyin (orth-west of Caoxian Shandong). In July, Shimin launched his offensive against the Kingdom of Lu, taking ten cities and surprising the towns in the lands of the Huai and Sishui Rivers. Having secured most of the Kingdom of Lu, Shimin ordered subordinate commanders to mop up the rest.

Du Fuwei held power in a realm along the Huai and Yangzi Rivers. In 621, during the war of the Tang and Wang Shichong, Li Shimin requested Du Fuwei accept Tang rule. Du Fuwei sent envoys with his submission to Chang'an, and Emperor Gaozu appointed him supreme commander of the south-east and governor of the lands between the Huai and Yangzi Rivers. The emperor adopted Du into the imperial house, so he became Li Fuwei, King of Wu. In November 621, Li Fuwei sent Commander Wang Xiongdan to attack Li Zitong, who called himself Emperor of Wu. In battle after battle, Wang Xiongdan defeated Li Zitong, overran his lands and finally captured him. Li Fuwei sent Li Zitong to Chang'an, where Emperor Gaozu released him to exile.

Another local potentate, Wang Hua, occupied towns in south-eastern Anhui, calling himself king. Li Fuwei sent Commander Wang Xiongdan to eliminate King Wang Hua. When Wang Xiongdan advanced against Wang Hua, Hua fortified and garrisoned the narrow pass leading to his capital, effectively blocking Wang Xiongdan's advance. Hua's soldiers were veterans from many campaigns, trained and hard. Knowing this, Wang Xiongdan pulled his best men out of his battle lines and sent them into concealment in a ravine. The rest of his men, older and weaker, he sent to the pass to fight with Wang Hua's men. These men attacked as best they could, were repulsed and then withdrew to their camp. Wang Hua ordered his army to pursue, hoping to end the battle then and there. His men attacked the camp and fought until dark. Then Wang Hua withdrew his soldiers back to the pass. His surprise was complete when he found Wang Xiongdan's best men occupying the pass. Wang Hua, trapped between two forces, had to surrender. Li Fuwei then held the lands from the Huai River to the Yangzi River and the East China Sea. In early 622, with Li Shimin's victories in the east, Li Fuwei saw the need to go to Chang'an and present himself to the Tang court. Arriving in July, Emperor Gaozu received Li Fuwei. The emperor appointed Li Fuwei Protector of the Crown Prince and Imperial Governor of the South-east. His high rank was even superior to that of fourth son Li Yuan Ji. However, the court clearly indicated that Li Fuwei was to remain in Chang'an.

References

Chinese sources: *Jiu Tangshu*, 54; *Xin Tangshu*, 85; *Zizhi Tongjian*, 188–89.
Fitzgerald, pp.70–89.
Graff, *Medieval*, pp.171–74.

Chapter 12

Rivalry in the House of Li

Conflict Between Brothers

Since the founding of the Zhou Dynasty, concord among members of ruling families was of the highest importance. The House of Li was no different. United, they were successful, but should division arise, the House of Li could easily find itself in the same position into which they had thrust so many rivals. The three brothers, sons of the Empress Dou – Jiancheng, Shimin and Yuanji – had the usual sibling rivalry, coming from ambitious and driven parents. But imperial complications intensified the rivalry. First son Jiancheng, being eldest, was Crown Prince, successor to the throne. He was a sensitive, generous and honest man, but his taste was that of a Chinese gentleman who appreciated fine wine and beautiful women. Second son Shimin was like his Xianbei nomad ancestors. He preferred spending his time with horses in the countryside. When there, he was indistinguishable from his nomad companions, yet when he was at the imperial court, he was the high and mighty Chinese gentleman. Third son Xuanba had fallen off a horse at age 14 and died. Fourth son Yuanji was troubled. He was cruel like an unhappy nomad and manipulative like a dishonest Chinese official.

Unlike sibling rivalry in a rich family, however, most observers saw that this rivalry was mortal. If Jiancheng became emperor, Shimin, commander and victor, would dominate him. If Jiancheng caused him trouble, Shimin would exile him, or worse. Shimin, in any case, would send Yuanji to some comfortable distant place. From Shimin's perspective, both Jiancheng and Yuanji had good reason to find a way to remove him. The question might revolve around who struck first.

Emperor Gaozu was in his mid-50s in 622. His wife, Lady Dou, had died almost two decades ago, and he enjoyed the company of young beauties. Jiancheng also enjoyed young women's company, and some of his concubines were relatives of Emperor Gaozu's concubines. The ladies spread stories about the dour Shimin, who preferred horses and war to the delights of the inner court. The many virtues of Jiancheng and Yuanji were often repeated, but Shimin received only criticism. The emperor began to distrust his second son, saying: 'This boy has stayed away from me for a long time. He would rather command armies and fight on the frontiers. He pays too much attention to the literati. He is no longer the son I knew in the old days.'

Stories from the inner court were always popular in the towns and countryside. Rumours about Li Shimin facing imperial displeasure spread, percolating even to the Turkish camp. There, Liu Heita, his younger brother Liu Shishan and Commander Wang Xianhu decided to return to re-establish their dominion, now that Li Shimin appeared in disfavour. The Turks agreed to assist them now that they had little fear of the other Tang leaders. By mid-June, Liu Heita and the Turkish cavalry took Dingzhou (Dingzhou Hebei); in September, they captured Yingzhou (Hejian Hebei). On 17 October, Tang commander Li Daoxian met Liu in battle near Xiabo (Xiabo Hebei). Liu's forces defeated and killed Li Daoxian. When news of the Tang defeat came to Mingzhou, Liu's former capital, the Tang commander pulled out and withdrew his forces. Within a short time, Liu Heita recovered all the lands he had held. On 27 October, Liu marched into Mingzhou and re-established his dominion.

News of the collapse in the east upset Emperor Gaozu. He discussed the issue with his advisors. They decided not to call on Li Shimin, and looked to Li Jiancheng. The emperor, his advisors and Li Jiancheng's advisors all understood that Jiancheng was Crown Prince only because he was first born. If the Crown Prince was to have credibility, he needed to demonstrate military ability, otherwise second son Shimin would throw him into the shadows. By taking an appointment as commander-in-chief in the fight with Liu Heita, Jiancheng's prestige would increase. The court saw Liu as actually quite weak, with only some 10,000 trained soldiers and a flock of Turkish cavalry. Further, his supply situation was poor. Li Jiancheng should manage well.

On 7 November 622, Emperor Gaozu issued the order which appointed Crown Prince Li Jiancheng as commander-in-chief of the expeditionary force to the east and of all Tang forces to the east of the Xiaoshan Mountains (east of Shaanxi, west of Henan). In December, Liu Heita besieged Weizhou (Daming Hebei). Li Jiancheng and his younger brother, Li Yuanji, led a powerful infantry army to relieve Weizhou, arriving at Chongle (Nonle Henan). Liu Heita collected a massive if untrained army, withdrew from Weizhou and faced the Tang forces. Both armies encamped near each other and deployed, but neither would attack.

During the stand-off, Wei Zheng suggested to Li Jiancheng that when Li Shimin defeated Liu Heita the previous March, he had executed almost all of Liu's commanders and governors. He searched and found even those who fled. They were killed. He imprisoned all of these men's families. Thus no one responded to the offer of amnesty. Therefore, they should now release all these prisoners, give them a little something and send them back to their homes. Liu's force would then disintegrate. Li Jiancheng agreed and issued the orders.

Liu Heita saw that many soldiers were deserting his lines. Worrying that the Tang might launch an assault and expose him to attack in his rear from Weizhou, Liu withdrew from his position and began to march east to Guantao (south-east of Hebei) on the east bank of the Yongji Canal. Marching quickly, Liu's force would have to bridge the canal to get their army and supplies across. Li Jiancheng pursued. On 25 December, the Tang force caught up with the rebel army. Liu Heita directed his second in command to deploy in front of the canal to hold Li Jiancheng at bay while he led the bridge construction. The Tang pressed against Liu's force but did not overly exert themselves. Finishing the bridge, Liu ordered the army to withdraw. In the retreat, Liu's army disintegrated. The Tang charged across the bridge, but after about 1,000 Tang soldiers were across, the bridge collapsed. Liu Heita escaped with a few hundred men. Li Jiancheng sent his commander of light cavalry to pursue.

Liu, with only about 100 followers, arrived at Raoyang (Raoyang Hebei) on 3 January. The governor, Zhuge Dewei, an appointment of Liu's, invited them into the town, but Liu refused. Zhuge, with tears in his eyes, begged Liu to enter and to trust him. Liu relented, and entered with his followers. Food came, and Liu and his fellows relaxed, only to be caught and bound by Zhuge's men. Zhuge Dewei surrendered the town, Liu and his fellows to Li Jiancheng, who confirmed Zhuge in his governorship. Li Jiancheng had Liu Heita and his brother, Liu Shishan, executed in Mingzhou market. Just before his head was removed, Liu said, 'I would still be living a peaceful life, growing vegetables, if Gao Yaxian had not come. He led me to destruction.'

The Two Brothers' Alliance

When Li Yuanji had initially offered to have Li Shimin killed for Li Jiancheng's benefit, Jiancheng refused his offer. But as Li Shimin's power and prestige increased and Jiancheng received little credit for his victory over Liu Heita, the Crown Prince began to reconsider his position. Slowly, without informing Emperor Gaozu, Jiancheng started building up a strong military force of veteran soldiers. He called them his palace guards but organized them into teams which rotated through his palace, so instead of one formation of guards, he was able to double, then triple the number of men under his command. His palace had a major entrance called the Changlin Gate, so his army was called the Changlin Guards. Soon, however, he went too far. Jiancheng requested that his guard commander, Keda Zhi, secretly ask Li Yi, Tang commander in the east based at Youzhou (Beijing), to send the Crown Prince 300 well-trained, veteran armoured cavalry. Ever loyal, Li Yi saw to it that news of this reached Emperor Gaozu's ears. The investigation revealed Jiancheng's hidden army. The emperor was not happy. Guard commander Keda

Zhi received a minor post in distant Sichuan, where he was instructed to stay. The emperor chastised the Crown Prince.

Emperor Gaozu took his usual summer retreat to the Renzhi Palace a little less than 100 miles from the capital. Li Jiancheng was even more determined to garner armed forces to protect himself and increase his personal power. The commander in Qingzhou (Qingyang Gansu), Yang Wengan, was a former guard of Jiancheng and a friend. Secretly, Jiancheng requested Yang to mobilize some veteran formations to be ready to march. After the emperor had settled himself in Renzhi, Jiancheng sent some select military officers to deliver unique suits of armour to Yang Wengan. The officers gave the armour and Jiancheng's verbal order to take the standing troops and attack the Renzhi Palace.

The officers, trained and loyal soldiers of the Tang, stopped off at Binzhou (Binxian Shaanxi) and informed trusted authorities about their mission. An urgent message soon reached the emperor that the Crown Prince had ordered Yang Wengan to launch a rebellion while Jiancheng seized Chang'an. At the same time, other officials sent similar messages. The emperor immediately sent an order to Jiancheng to come straight to the Renzhi Palace. Jiancheng wavered between open rebellion and absolute submission; he chose submission and went to the Renzhi Palace to face his father. When he was about 10 miles from the palace, he dismissed his entourage and with just a few guards went to see the emperor. At the palace, Jiancheng knelt down and struck his head so hard on the floor that he passed out (or was it that he just fainted?). Emperor Gaozu ordered him into confinement and to receive only poor food.

The emperor sent Yuwen Ying to Qingzhou to summon Yang Wengan to the Renzhi Palace. Rather than enforce the emperor's orders, Yuwen told Yang everything that had happened. Yang saw his fate: either meekly bow his head and lose it or rebel and maybe survive. Yang Wengan rebelled. Using his town of Qingzhou as a base, he expanded his holdings in Gansu to include Ningzhou (Ningxian Gansu). On 26 June, Emperor Gaozu summoned Li Shimin and ordered him to crush the rebellion. At the request of Li Yuanji and many officials, the emperor ordered Li Jiancheng to return to Chang'an and reinstated his office. Leading a small but select force of his horsemen with covering infantry, Shimin reached Qingzhou. The rebellion simply collapsed. On 5 July, a subordinate commander killed Yang Wengan and sent his head to Chang'an. Local officials arrested Yuwen Ying, and he was also executed.

Controversy About Moving the Capital

Back in August 622, Eastern Turkish marauders raided the north-western frontiers of the Tang dominions. Their forces seized Dazhen Pass (south-east of

Zhangjiachuan Gansu). In Chang'an, Emperor Gaozu understood these events as uncontrolled actions by young Turkish warriors. Having come from the frontier area and being descended from nomad warriors, the emperor did not see a great threat. His forces were tied up in the east under Li Shimin. Rather than raise another army, the emperor appointed Zheng Yuanchou, Minister of Rites and Ceremonies, as envoy extraordinary to the court of Jiali Khan (Ashina Duobi), ruler of the Eastern Turks. Zheng offered beautiful presents in the form of gold, silver and silk if the Jiali Khan would protect Tang frontiers from raiding. Jiali Khan agreed to the terms, eventually sealed in a moving ceremony with Li Shimin present.

The next year there were several raids, and the year after even more. Some imperial advisors suggested that the administration remove the capital from Chang'an to a place deeper into China. By moving valuables, gold, silver, silk and beautiful women from Guanzhong, these advisors suggested the Turks would lose interest and leave China alone. Li Jiancheng and Li Yuanji supported the idea of moving the capital. Emperor Gaozu agreed to consider the idea. He sent Yuwen Shiji to Fancheng (Xiangfan Hebei) to evaluate the suitability of the site as an imperial capital. When Li Shimin got wind of this move, he stated his clear opposition. He felt such a move was simply a confession of weakness and the Turks would merely come further. The advisors inquired what Shimin would recommend. Shimin told his father that he would conquer the lands to the north of the desert in less than ten years.

Turkish Raids

During August 624, Jiali Khan (Ashina Duebi) and his nephew Tuli Khan (Ashina Shibobi) launched massive raids into Gansu. Emperor Gaozu saw this as a good time to begin testing Li Shimin's boast. He sent Shimin and his brother Li Yuanji with a strong select force to confront the Turks. As they marched into Gansu, rains began soaking the Tang. The roads were flooded, bridges were washed away and the land was drenched. The floods halted all the supply trains, and food was short. The Tang encamped at Binzhou village (Binxian Shaanxi) when the Turkish raiders suddenly appeared. Both sides were equally surprised they were so near to each other. Jiali Khan and Tuli Khan each led 5,000 horsemen. They deployed into battle formation, facing Binzhou. Tang scouts on the camp ramparts reported the numbers and formation of the Turks.

Li Shimin roused his forces, but Li Yuanji ordered his men to hold back. He told Shimin that they faced defeat and should prepare to escape from the camp. Li Shimin pointed out that the rains soaked the Turks too and the Tang had protected their bows from the wet. Shimin then mounted up 100 of his armoured cavalry. He put on his armour and rode out of the camp with flags flying and drums beating.

His men trotted toward the Turk force. Li Shimin formed them up facing the Turks, with only a narrow space separating them. He took off his helmet and called out to Jiali Khan:

> 'You pledged friendship with the Tang! You promised not to invade our lands! Here you are! I am King of Qin [Li Shimin's title]! Do you want to fight with me yourself? You and your force can attack us here but we will fight! Do you dare?'

Jiali Khan did not expect to find Li Shimin facing him. He did not answer, but only sat smiling on his horse. Li Shimin rode along the brook that separated the armies until he faced Tuli Khan. Shimin yelled at Tuli Khan: 'We, you and me, participated in a ceremony in which we burned incense and took oaths. You swore to me that you would share the good and the bad with me and we would help each other!' The Khan did not respond. Raising his hand as a signal, Li Shimin started to lead his force across the brook that separated the Tang and the Turks. Suddenly, a messenger rushed out from the Turkish lines and approached Li Shimin. Deeply bowing, he said that the mighty King of Qin need not come any further; the Turks were withdrawing right away. The rain had damaged the Turks' equipment, the going was rough, loot was hard to find and now they ran into the hard–fighting Li Shimin. The khans had decided to cut their losses, withdrawing to their camp.

Then it rained even more. In camp later that day, Li Shimin talked with his main commanders. He said that the Turks were good archers and brave soldiers, but rain and damp spoiled their bow strings until they could dry. He said the Tang, camped in the village, had kept their weapons dry inside walls and could cook with fire. They should use this opportunity to defeat the Turks. That night, in the continuing rain, the Tang army approached the Turkish camp. The Turkish lookouts, hiding from the rain, only saw the Tang force when they were very close. They quickly told the shocked khans. Li Shimin sent an envoy to Tuli Khan. The agent pointed out to the khan just how compromised was his position. Tuli Khan accepted Li Shimin's advice. At an emergency meeting of commanders chaired by Jiali Khan, Tuli Khan told them that it was best to make peace with Li Shimin because he was such an extraordinary fighter and commander. Jiali Khan and the commanders agreed. They sent Tuli Khan to work out the details, and he and Li Shimin became friends.

The Brothers Weaken Li Shimin's Influence

After Li Shimin had led his army back to Chang'an, his brothers agreed that either they had to get rid of Shimin or they would soon find themselves administering small districts in distant lands. Their friends and courts supported them, because should the crown prince and the King of Qi fall from favour, their roles and influence would diminish or disappear. At a major reception in the crown prince's palace, the brothers managed to poison Li Shimin's wine. Always careful, Shimin had only a little of the wine and felt the caustic poison. With assistance, he quickly went back to his palace. There, he spat out blood and took the prescribed antidote. Shimin made it known that he was not pleased. Emperor Gaozu even chastised Li Jiancheng for giving Li Shimin too much wine, before going to Shimin's palace to commiserate with him.

The emperor and Li Shimin talked about the rift between the very able King of Qin and his two not so able brothers, Li Jiancheng, the Crown Prince, and Li Yuanji, the King of Qi. They agreed that the solution was to remove Li Shimin from Chang'an. The emperor would recognize Li Shimin as viceroy in Luoyang and allow him the administration of the east from the Xiaoshan Mountains. When Li Jiancheng and Li Yuanji found out what Li Shimin and the emperor decided, they were horrified. With Li Shimin in command of the east from Luoyang, he would also control the south, leaving only Guanzhong and Sichuan for them. Then, in time, he would sweep them out of the way. They decided to make him stay in the capital and try to kill him.

The brothers huddled with their advisors and trusted high officials in the capital, drawing up a secret memorandum for the emperor. The memorandum pointed out that many of the prominent administrators supported Shimin. If he moved to Luoyang, they would follow, one way or another. This would cripple the administration and make the emperor weak. Using the influence of the brothers' lackeys in the government and favoured concubines who did not like the austere Li Shimin, the brothers induced the emperor to withdraw his order for Shimin's appointment at Luoyang. Li Shimin understood that he was an 'over-mighty subject', and he sought safety by biding his time. He would deal carefully with the brothers while maintaining his power base. That way, when things changed, he would simply assume supreme power.

The strength of Li Shimin's position did not escape the brothers. To weaken him enough to destroy him, they decided to encourage disloyalty among his officers. The Crown Prince sent a cart of silver and gold to Yuchi Jingde's house. This was followed by a letter which told Yuchi, 'I know you are a man of integrity. I wish to be your friend.' Yuchi responded to the Crown Prince:

'I was born poor. My experiences are quite different from yours. When the Sui lost power, I joined a rebel gang. I committed crimes against the Tang forces. It was the King of Qin who saved me and gave me a new life. I am a commander in service to His Excellency. I repay his kindness with loyalty. I cannot accept your gift. I can have no secret dealings. Of course, Your Highness will agree that anyone who betrayed his master for gain is despicable.'

When Li Jiancheng received Yuchi's reply, he decided that he needed to eliminate him.

Yuchi informed Li Shimin about Li Jiancheng's actions. Shimin told Yuchi that the next time someone offered him a gift, he should take it. Then he could tell Shimin what the brothers were planning. Otherwise, Shimin said, they would get Yuchi. But Li Jiancheng was done with Yuchi Jingde. Over the next month, several people tried to kill Yuchi, but they failed. Li Yuanji laughed at Jiancheng's efforts. But in full court and in front of the emperor, Li Yuanji accused Yuchi Jingde of treason back when the Tang were fighting for survival. Emperor Gaozu ordered the case investigated and Yuchi was jailed. The authorities found the charges correct, and Yuchi was sentenced to death. Li Shimin had to reach out to friends to save Yuchi. Li Yuanji further issued a formal accusation against Cheng Zhijie, commander of Li Shimin's cavalry. Emperor Gaozu appointed Cheng to serve as an officer in remote Gansu. Cheng Zhijie refused to go to his new posting, telling Li Shimin, 'If arms and legs are cut off, how will your Excellency survive? I stay at my post for you, even if I am executed.'

The brothers tried to bribe Duan Zhixuan, commander of Li Shimin's second army, but Duan refused the gift. The brothers then accused two of Shimin's chief advisors of malfeasance in office. They were ordered to work elsewhere and not communicate with Shimin. Li Shimin's officials and commanders told him that if he were removed from his position or killed, all of them and their families would become vulnerable to exile or worse. Two of his main officials – Fang Xuanling, Head of Examinations, and Zhangsun Wuju, Chief of the Legal Department – pointed out to Shimin that he was a superior person. He should be emperor, not the weak Jiancheng or, even worse, the foul Yuanji.

Suddenly, news came about raiders besieging Wucheng (Dingbian Shaanxi). At the imperial court, Crown Prince Li Jiancheng recommended that Li Yuanji take command of the imperial army. Emperor Gaozu issued the appointment and Yuanji took command of Li Shimin's army. Rumours exploded: the brothers were going to strip Li Shimin of power, then kill him. Shimin's officials were full of doubt, fearing for their jobs and their lives. The army commanders had no high opinion of Li Yuanji's abilities, while the rank and file were also unsettled. The administrators began making contingency plans to face an uncertain future. The struggle between the brothers had reached the critical stage.

Decision at Xuanwu Gate

With Li Yuanji's assumption of military command over Li Shimin's forces, the struggle between the brothers became mortal. Li Shimin summoned the commanders of the imperial armies and his official staff to the offices of the Kingdom of Qin. In the great hall of the office, Li Shimin presided over a meeting of these high officers and officials. His main advisor spoke, addressing Shimin. He said that Li Yuanji was ambitious and unprincipled with evil tendencies. He aimed at the imperial office. He was working with Li Jiancheng to kill Li Shimin, but once that happened Yuanji would kill Jiancheng and become emperor himself. The advisor added: 'But nobody will follow him and the Empire will descend into chaos. You, King of Qin, should be Emperor!' All the officers and officials made clear their agreement.

Li Shimin stood. He ordered a tortoise shell burnt to inquire if their actions were acceptable. Zhang Gongjin, a member of Shimin's personal staff, took the tortoise shell and threw it on the floor, saying: 'The purpose of divination is to gain heaven's help in making a decision. We do not need help. Are we just going to give up?' Li Shimin agreed. Shimin sent Zhangsun Wuji to summon Fang Xuanling and Du Ruhui to the Office of the King of Qin. But Fang told Zhangsun that neither of them was going to disobey the emperor's order to stay away from Li Shimin. The imperial order was clear: if they disobeyed, they would face execution. Zhangsun returned to Li Shimin and reported what he was told. Shimin became very angry. He called Yuchi Jingde, unbuckled his sword and gave it to Yuchi, telling him to behead Fang and Du if they didn't come to his office. Yuchi and Zhangsun went to Fang and Du and told them that Shimin was committed to cleaning up the political problem. All four disguised themselves as Daoist priests and made their way through the city that night.

During the daylight of 3 June, the planet Venus appeared. The White Tiger Star, as the Chinese astrologers called Venus, was very significant. The Head Astrologer told Emperor Gaozu that 'the White Tiger Star appears in the sky over Qin. This means that the King of Qin will become Emperor.' On that day, Li Shimin came to talk to his father, the emperor. Gaozu told his son of the sign in the sky. Shimin told his father about his concerns regarding his brothers. He went on that both Jiancheng and Yuanji were entertaining and being entertained by the emperor's concubines: 'I have done nothing to harm them. They want to kill me. They are upset that my victories over Wang Shichong and Dou Jiande have gained me fame.' Emperor Gaozu said that tomorrow he would summon the brothers to come to the palace and investigate the matter.

The next morning, Li Shimin rode out from his palace, leading a select force of his officers and companions. He ordered them to hide in buildings near the Xuanwu Gate of the Imperial Palace. In the night, however, an imperial concubine had sent a message to Li Jiancheng about the astrological sign and Li Shimin's accusations. Jiancheng sent a messenger to Yuanji, telling him to quickly come to his palace. The brothers discussed their options. Yuanji suggested they set their troops to stand at the ready, inform the imperial court that they were ill and could not go to court, then see how the situation developed. Jiancheng said that his guards were ready and that they should go to the court and see exactly what was going on. They mounted their horses, readied their guards and rode to the Xuanwu Gate.

When the brothers approached the Xuanwu Gate, they saw that things were not right. They turned their horses about and began to ride back to the Crown Prince's palace. Li Shimin rode out and yelled at them, 'Why are you not coming to court?'

Li Yuanji pulled out his bow and attempted to shoot at Shimin three times, but misfired and his arrows flew in all directions. Shimin drew out his bow, aimed at Jiancheng and shot, unhorsing him with a fatal wound. Yuchi, leading some seventy horsemen, charged out and shot an arrow barrage toward Yuanji, who fell from his horse. At that moment, Shimin's horse bolted, crashing Shimin into tree branches, and he fell off his steed. His breath knocked out, Shimin could not get up. Yuanji rose to his feet and ran toward Shimin. Grabbing Shimin's bow, he tried to strangle Shimin with the bow string. Yuchi rode up, and Yuanji began to run away on foot. Yuchi drew his bow, shot and killed Yuanji. Getting off his horse, Yuchi then cut off the heads of the two brothers.

While the imperial princes battled each other, some 2,000 guards of the Crown Prince and the King of Qi marched forward to attack the Xuanwu Gate. The imperial guards closed the gate and defended the wall. The attackers' commander, Feng Li, turned the force about and marched to the palace of the King of Qin. Just as they were about to launch a powerful attack, Yuchi rode up and displayed the severed heads of Jiancheng and Yuanji. The officers turned away and left; their men dispersed.

Shimin, quite recovered, sent Yuchi, still in his bloody armour with his sword at his side and spear in his hand, into the imperial palace. He walked straight into the great reception hall into the presence of the emperor. Gaozu was shocked. 'Who is in rebellion?' he cried. Yuchi replied: 'The Crown Prince and the King of Qi rebelled. The King of Qin has suppressed the rebellion and killed the Crown Prince and the King of Qi.' Emperor Gaozu turned to his advisors, and they spoke in low tones. It was obvious that Li Shimin now held power. Any effort to displace him would be bloody and short. The emperor ordered all fighting stopped, and sent his confidant, Pei Ji, to the palace of the Crown Prince. He ordered disbanded the forces of the Crown Prince and the King of Qi. Then the emperor summoned Li Shimin.

The King of Qin marched into the great reception hall in imperial regalia. Emperor Gaozu received him. Reaching out his hand and placing it on Shimin's head, the emperor said: 'I almost believed Jiancheng and Yuanji.' By imperial decree, the emperor ruled that all government affairs were in the care of Li Shimin. All the sons of Jiancheng and Yuanji were beheaded. All their subordinates and supporters received pardons. On 7 June, Emperor Gaozu elevated Li Shimin to

Crown Prince. Further, by imperial decree, the Crown Prince would now handle all military and state affairs. Taking over the Crown Prince's palace, Li Shimin took on most of the former Crown Prince's advisors and officers. Yuchi Jingde received all the treasures from Yuanji's palace.

Emperor Gaozu announced on 8 August that he was going to retire, and appointed Li Shimin to become emperor. Shimin declined the offer, but Emperor Gaozu insisted. The next day, Li Shimin ascended the imperial throne in Xiande Hall of the Crown Prince's Palace, becoming the second Tang emperor. When he moved into the imperial palace, the new emperor released a large number of the palace women, returning them to their homes and allowing them to marry. He named his beloved wife, Lady Zhangsun, empress on 21 August, and on 8 October, Li Shimin made his 8-year-old son Crown Prince.

The Achievements of the Tang Dynasty

With Li Shimin's elevation to the imperial office, the sequence of events which began with the rise of the Sui Dynasty came to a conclusion. Since the end of the Han Dynasty in 220, different regimes had divided up China 'like a melon', as Emperor Sui Wen said. The efforts of the Sui emperors failed because their administration changed too much, too fast, and ignored local conditions and needs. Li Shimin and his Tang family lived through the Sui failure. Li Shimin, bold and perceptive, took over the imperial administration and consolidated the Tang state while paying close attention to local conditions. While far from serene, the rest of Li Shimin's reign maintained stability and extended the imperial administration's power and reach. This foundation of power and prosperity served the Tang Empire well.

References

Chinese sources, *Jiu Tongjian*, 2, 38; *Zizhi Tongjian*, 188, 191-92.
Fitzgerald, pp.107-24.
Graff, p.184.
Hung, pp.110-31.

Conclusion

The great wars of conquest that swept across the Chinese lands in the early seventh century were not the only such conflicts at the time. The clans of horse lords slowly spread through Eurasia in the service of different states, tribal confederations and their own states. The Turks, experts in horse breeding and iron metal working, conquered Central Asia, overthrowing the Hephthalite Empire and establishing a nomadic state in Inner Asia. The Gupta Empire in India lost control, only to be succeeded by a series of warring states. The Sassanid Empire fought a long and bitter war with the Byzantines, who were already involved in terrible civil strife. Italy, Gaul and Britain were the site of a myriad of chaotic small wars. The explosive growth of Arab tribes and towns had begun to create unrest in the Arabian Peninsula. From small specialized groups of soldiers, the horse lords grew into dominating clans, their influence spreading with their horse-raising manors and fortified houses.

China's journey from chaos to order led Li Shimin, who became Emperor Taizong, to work toward settling his realm into peaceful patterns of life. The emperor's armies defeated the Eastern Turks in 629, after which he assumed the title of Tian Kehan, Divine Khan of the Eastern Turks, who recognized him as their khagan. Taizong, at the same time, established Buddhist monasteries at the sites of his major battles with the charge to pray for the souls of the fallen from both sides. His realm prospered; his people did well. Emperor Taizong died in 649. His son, Gaozong, succeeded Taizong and ruled until 683. One of Taizong's concubines became Gaozong's empress, and after his death became regent for child emperors, but then assumed the throne as emperor of the Zhou Dynasty. She became seriously ill and her regime collapsed in confusing court intrigue in 705. Her son by Gaozong became Emperor Zhongzong of the Tang Dynasty (who ruled from 705-710). While the court intrigues never stopped, the empire remained peaceful in the Chinese lands and waged successful wars on the frontiers.

As the decades passed, the *fubing* settlements and the imperial heavy cavalry connected to them disappeared, replaced by professional infantry soldiers and nomadic cavalry. The imperial government abolished all the remaining *fubing* settlements by 750. The imperial administration saw these developments as cost-effective while still providing security. The men who held the swords and shields did not agree. By 756, a great rebellion began ripping through the empire under An Lushan. The men on horseback despised the men in robes. The rebellions finally ended, but the problem remained: how could a civilian farming state accommodate the military power that cavalry provided without coming under the horse lords' domination? The recurrent theme played itself out many times; the most significant saw the Song succumb to the northern tribes and then the Mongols, and the Ming succumb to the Qing. In all of these struggles, we find that the efforts to preserve the structure of agrarian Ruist-run institutions by avoiding technological developments shaped Chinese war-making methods.

However, the Chinese way of war was, and is, simply the way of war. Wars are fought to achieve victory, and victory is the destruction of the enemy's ability to resist. Without victory, the war drags on and on. However, enemy is a political term. Military objectives and political objectives often differ. It may be, and often is, politically advantageous for a war to drag on. Thucydides wrote, 'The strong do what they will; the weak suffer what they must', and so it is, but this is a political decision and not a military one. For much of Chinese military history, war's objective has been the destruction of the enemy by all available means. At times, however, the question of just who is the enemy becomes confused. This is particularly true when China has many power foci. Then the problems revolve around that third level of friendship: my enemy's enemy, who he is and how is he to be found?

Accounts of Chinese history play out on the same ground for 3,000 years, from the Western Zhou Dynasty in 1046 BC through to the People's Republic in AD 1949. The same is true for Mediterranean-European history, but because we are far more familiar with the western sites then we are not likely to confuse the First Punic War with the Allied invasion of Sicily in 1943. The seemingly endless repetition of wars across the Chinese lands all tend to merge together in Western accounts. But, of course, to someone without an intimate understanding of European history, the recurrent campaigns across the French-German borders – from the Treaty of Verdun in 843 to the Battle of Berlin in 1945 – also becomes very confusing.

So while to the Chinese, just who was who and why is clear, western accounts miss the necessary detail to understand why this side is my enemy and that side is my ally. Without a detailed foundation, the nuances of political-military policies are a mystery. This examination of a specific series of campaigns points up the complexities faced by Chinese commanders while leading their armed forces toward their military objectives. This study leads to two basic conclusions: first, while local powers may be more than happy to control smaller areas, as soon as one power is able to overawe its neighbours, the thrust of policy is to achieve the unity of the Chinese lands; and second, Chinese administrations preferred the preservation of social order through hierarchal authority managed by experts. Technological innovations were all well and good, but they should not disrupt proper social relations.

Appendix 1

Chronology of Chinese Dynasties

T he main periods of Chinese history are identified as dynasties, the time in which a certain family held power. Given the intrigues and quarrels that incessantly swept through the imperial palaces, exactly who was the father of any given emperor might be a question, and imperial mothers came from many different backgrounds, but the dynasty, the institutional structure, remained as something real in political perception. Each dynasty had its own style and character, so for historical purposes they remain important symbols of a given time period. Some current commentators suggest that a different periodization other than dynasties might improve understandings of Chinese history, but so far none has appeared.

The following lists the Chinese dynasties and their dates.

Legendary founders of Chinese culture: before 2070 BC

The Three Dynasties: 2070–250 BC
  Xia Dynasty: House of Xia, 2070–1600 BC
  Shang Dynasty: House of Yin-Shang, 1600–1050 BC
  Zhou Dynasty: House of Zhou, 1050–250 BC
    Western Zhou, 1050–770 BC
    Eastern Zhou, 770–250 BC

Spring and Autumn period: 770–476 BC

Warring States period: 476–221 BC

Imperial Dynasties

Qin Dynasty: House of Ying, 221–206 BC

Han Dynasty: House of Liu, 206 BC–AD 220
  Western (or Former) Han Dynasty, 206 BC–AD 9
  Xin Dynasty: House of Wang, AD 9–23
  Eastern (or Later) Han Dynasty, AD 25–220

Six Dynasties: 220–420
  Three Kingdoms: 220–265
    Wei: House of Cao, 220–265
    Shu or Shu Han: House of Liu, 221–263
    Wu or Sun Wu: House of Sun, 222–280

Western Jin Dynasty: House of Sima, 265-317
Eastern Jin Dynasty: House of Sima, 316-420
Sixteen Kingdoms (in north 304-439)
Northern Dynasties: 386-581
  Northern Wei: Tuoba clan, 386-534
  Western Wei: Tuoba clan, 535-557
  Eastern Wei: Tuoba clan, 534-550
  Northern Zhou: House of Yuwen, 557-581
  Northern Qi: House of Gao, 550-577
Southern Dynasties: 420-589
  Liu Song: House of Liu, 420-479
  Southern Qi: House of Xiao, 479-502
  Liang: House of Xiao, 502-557
  Chen: House of Chen, 557-589

Sui Dynasty: House of Yang, 581-618

Tang Dynasty: House of Li, 618-907

Five Dynasties, 907-960
  Later Liang: House of Zhu, 907-923
  Later Tang: House of Li, 923-934
  Later Jin: House of Shi, 934-947
  Later Han: House of Liu, 947-951
  Later Zhou: House of Chai, 951-960

Northern Song Dynasty: House of Zhao, 960-1127

Southern Song Dynasty: House of Zhao, 1127-1279

Liao Dynasty: House of Yelu, 907-1125

Jin Dynasty: House of Wanghia, 1115-1234

Western Xia: House of Li, 1038-1227

Yuan Dynasty: House of Borjigin, 1271-1368

Ming Dynasty: House of Zhu, 1368-1644

Qing Dynasty: House of Asin Gioro, 1644-1911

Republic of China, 1911-1949

People's Republic of China, Mao Zedong, 1949-1976

Peoples Republic of China, 1976-

Appendix 2

Military Geography of China

This appendix is for readers who are unfamiliar with China's geography. The modern nation, the People's Republic of China, is a very large state. Medieval China was smaller but still large, about the size of Europe west of Russia. Each province has its own character and a history as complex as any European nation. There is a great variety of geological and topographic structures, with some unique to China. There are long winding rivers, fertile plains, high mountains, dense jungles, tall forests, harsh deserts, at times almost on top of each other.

The most important geographic features are the two main rivers, the Huang He (the Yellow River) and the Yangzi (the Long River).

The Yellow River is some 3,300 miles long, of which the lower 1,100, known as the middle and lower reaches, is the area of early Chinese history. The middle reaches start flowing north, then turn and flow east, then south, in the Ordos Loop. This is a rugged area with mountains and gorges. After hundreds of miles flowing south, the Yellow River turns 90° east, slowly emerging out of the rugged landscape into the great central plains. Here begins the lower reaches. From Zhengzhou Henan to the sea, some 480 miles, the Yellow River drops vast amounts of silt collected above in the loess fields of the upper and middle reaches. The result is that thousands of years of hydraulic engineering has constricted the river between levees, with the result that the river flows in a bed significantly above the level of the ground around it. Of course, if the levees break, there is a disastrous flood. During the time our narrative covers, the Yellow River flowed into the Gulf of Bohai, to the north of the Shandong peninsula, but in different times, the river has shifted its mouth some 500 miles to the south of the Shandong peninsula.

The Yangzi River, Chang Jiang or Long River, is some 4,000 miles long. Over much of its length the river actually has other names, but for the purposes of this book, I use the name Yangzi for the whole river. The Yangzi enters our narrative where the river enters Sichuan province, a fertile valley surrounded by mountains, some 1,700 miles from the ocean. Leaving Sichuan through a series of great gorges, the river enters a vast plain. As the river flows along hundreds of miles through the plains, tributaries come from the north and south, allowing river access almost to the Yellow River valley to the north and deep into the mountains to the south. Large lakes connect with the river, allowing the formation of complex transportation networks. Finally, the river enters the East China Sea.

The Three Strategic Regions and Four Key Areas of China

There are three strategic regions of China: the Central Plains along the middle and lower reaches of the Yellow River; the Yangzi valley from the great gorges to the ocean; and the great steppe extending from the Ordos within the loop of the Yellow River through Inner Mongolia to Manchuria. While each region produced a diversity of products, the Yellow River valley concentrated on wheat, the Yangzi valley on rice and the steppe produced horses. A power that controlled any one region was vulnerable to attack from either of the others. But a power that controlled two regions generally overawed the third. The steppe and the Yellow River were invulnerable to attack from the Yangzi. The Yangzi might hold its own against the north, but was not able to expand. The reason for this is that the northern horse solders could not attack the water-protected south and the southern infantry could not prevail against northern cavalry.

Who was going to win and lose these struggles depended on who controlled four key areas:

Guanzhong, the 'Land within the Passes', is the north-west Wei River valley, surrounded by mountains. This is the site from which the Zhou Dynasty, Qin Dynasty and Former Han Dynasty set out to conquer the Chinese lands. A natural fortress, military experts said that 20,000 men could hold the land against a million attacking soldiers. A power could use the land as a launching pad to attack in a number of directions or retreat into the land as a refuge from defeat. While Guanzhong was defendable, it was not very fertile.

Shandong peninsula, the ancient land of Qi, was a mountainous area with the ocean on three sides. The side connected to the central plain was protected by mountains and rivers. This stronghold was a counterweight to the 'Land within the Passes'. Any power, to consolidate its hold on the central plain, had to control Shandong. A defeated power could retreat and find safety in the peninsula.

The Sichuan valley, the ancient land of Shu, is on the upper part of the Yangzi. Sichuan is a fertile plain surrounded by formidable mountains. The only egress is down the Yangzi through the great gorges or from Guanzhong in the north, along the difficult Gallery Road. This natural fortress can easily exist as an independent state, but as a route from Guanzhong to a backdoor entrance to the Yangzi valley, it is too valuable to be left on its own.

The Fujian coast, the ancient land of Min-Yue, is south of the Yangzi. This is a mountainous coastal land, isolated and defensible, surrounded by the Wu Yi Mountains. Not until the Han Dynasty was it controlled by the Chinese. The land served as a refuge for a defeated power or as a base to attack the lower Yangzi.

Chinese Provinces

After the Qin conquest, Chinese administrators divided the empire into a number of provinces, many of which still exist, either in part or whole. For the purposes of my narrative, I identify places by current provinces and find it useful to know what the province names mean. The following is a list of the main provinces cited in my narrative, along with their meaning:

Shaanxi, 'the narrow (road) west': this is the land of Guanzhong, the 'Land within the Passes', to the west of the Yellow River's north–south run. The main area is the Wei River valley. (Official PRC English spelling has the double 'a'. This is to distinguish this province from its neighbour, Shanxi, with which it is easily confused.)

Shanxi, 'the mountain with land to the west': this is the land west of the Tai Hang Shan (mountain). The west of this land is on the north–south run of the Yellow River, with Shaanxi on the other side. The Fen River with its fertile valley is the heart of the province.

Henan, 'south (of the) river': this is a rich agricultural land south of the Yellow River. Luoyang and Kaifeng are major cities of the province.

Hebei, 'north (of the) river': this is a rich agricultural land north of the Yellow River. The later city of Beijing is in the north of this province.

Shandong, 'mountain (is to the) east': this is the land to the east of the Tai Hang Shan (mountain), the peninsula that extends out into the East China Sea. A varied land, there is some good farmland but also much rugged territory.

Sichuan, 'four rivers': this land is at the place where the Yangzi River enters traditional China. It is a rich agricultural valley surrounded by formidable mountains. The Yangzi exits through the great gorges.

Hubei, 'lake north (land)': straddling the Yangzi, this rich agricultural land is in part north of Lake Dongting. Lake Dongting is a wide section of a tributary of the Yangzi, very rich in fish and water creatures, with extensive marshlands. It is the heart of the ancient Kingdom of Chu.

Hunan, 'lake south (land)': south of the Yangzi, this is rich agricultural land. While most of the province is south of Lake Dongting, the south shore of the lake and its marshes are included.

Jiangxi, 'large river (to the) west': this is a lush valley of the Gan River, surrounded by rough hills. Under the Tang, it was called Jiangnanxi (Yangzi south-road to the west).

Jiangsu, '(province of the two cities of) Jiangning and Suzhou': now Nanjing and Suzhou, it was the ancient Kingdom of Wu. This was and is an urbanized province, with manufacturing, specialty goods and transportation systems.

Zhejiang, 'Zhe River': this coastal province is just south of the Yangzi River's mouth. Very rough, there are small valleys and high peaks. It is the ancient Kingdom of Yue.

Fujian, '(province of two cities of) Fuzhou and Jianzhou': now Fuzhou and Jian'ou, this is a rough, mountainous and poor coastal province, but very defensible. The ancient Kingdom of Minyue was a combination of a former ruling house of Yue settled among a non-Chinese people, the Min.

Imperial Frontiers: An Empire's Place in the World

The heartlands and outlands of the Great Realm were never in doubt, but just how far that might extend was always a question. In the north-east, the Liao River marked the usual extent of the realm. Often enough, military expeditions went beyond the Liao, to attack toward Korea or north into the rich lands of what became Manchuria. To the north, facing toward what is now Inner and Outer Mongolia, sat the region of the Long Walls. Made to mark the extent of imperial control, the Long Walls shifted back and forth as climate and politics changed. The early modern Ming Great Wall, a raised roadway and artillery line, marked only one of a number of possible frontiers. To the north-west, the lands of Gansu followed the routes to the far west lands of Central Asia. At times, the imperial power extended into Central Asia through the Gansu corridor, but most of the time Gansu was a frontier transit point. To the west rose great mountains inhabited by tribes and small states, sometimes brought into Chinese administration, sometimes not. To the south, jungles and hills held a myriad of cultures, often hostile to the realm as Han settlers slowly infiltrated the lands. All these lands on the north, west and south were possible targets of expansionist schemes or sources of frontier disruption. Practised administrators managed each frontier as seemed best in their time.

To the east, the great ocean ran the length of the realm for thousands of miles. If the deserts of Mongolia, the mountains of Tibet or the jungles of the south were viewed as lands of little use, the wide expanse of water appeared worse than the deserts. Here, the masters of the Primary Realm turned their backs. People in the towns along the coast dealt with seafarers from Japan, the Philippines, the East Indies, India and Africa. The rulers in their distant capital cities ignored the coasts. Trade, a source of revenue, was to be channelled into only certain towns, but that policy was often ignored. A pattern of benign neglect hovered over the long coasts. To the masters of the Primary Realm, the heart of the empire – the rivers and canals, the fields and towns – were important. The oceans were simply pathless wastelands.

Military Strategy in the Primary Realm

In the Age of Warring States (475-221 BC), the battling sides eventually broke down to two: the Qin and Chu. The Chu opposed the Qins' efforts to achieve supremacy. Essentially, the Chu attempted to build alliances that would block the Qins' struggles to expand west to east (the Qin used 'horizontal strategy'). Chu alliances therefore attempted to build blocks of states that ran south to north (the Chu used 'vertical strategy'). While Zhou's conquest of Shang was 'horizontal', there are few details. But, ever after, from the rise of Qin and the struggles of Han, wars of conquest always demonstrate both horizontal and vertical strategies. The keys are the rivers. The Qin fought down the length of the Yellow River; the Chu tried to block this. Once the Long River was integrated into the Chinese state structure, the river lines represented the main strategic axis around which campaigns revolved, from the fall of Han through to the fall of the Kuomintang.

The Great Cities of the Sui and Tang Dynasties

Chinese cities are different from those of the Near East and Mediterranean worlds. Rather than sprawling commercial sites like ancient Athens or Carthage, Chinese cities spread out in an orderly manner from a number of dominating ceremonial centres. There are few examples of cities in China with the irregular walls of Alexandria and Antioch, with gates here and there. Rather, Chinese cities sit four-square, with massive straight walls and gates at regular intervals. In modern China, at the centre of many modern commercial megalopoleis, there remains in good part the ancient city with its walls and ceremonial centres. In the oldest archaeological layers of recognizable Chinese type cultures, elements of the pre-industrial Chinese city are present. Excavations at sites along the Yellow River dated to the early second millennium BC reveal a culture now called Erlitou, with straight walled palace precincts, ceramic forms ancestral to later bronze vessels and a stratified social structure. If this culture doesn't represent the legendary Xia Dynasty, it would be hard to understand what it represents.

The Shang cultural assembly succeeded Erlitou remains with more complex but similar ceremonial centre precincts. The Zhou Dynasty overthrew the Shang regimes around 1050 BC. The royal regent, the Lord of Zhou, established a new city, Changzhou, near where the loess deposits along the Yellow River met the Central Plain. Here, where the Luo River flows parallel for some space along the Yellow River course, the Lord of Zhou founded his new holy city to restore cosmological balance by receiving the displaced Shang aristocracy and their followers along with the Sacred Nine Dings, symbol of supreme power. Ultimately, scholars codified the detailed planning and design in the *Artisan's Record* based on ideas in the *Rites of Zhou*. The basis of design was the concept of the Sacred Space. This was a square, representing the earth, subdivided into nine equal squares. Each square had a number, and so adding '1' through '9', gave the sacred total, '15'. The most important square, '5', was at the centre and subject to the outer eight squares, which were influenced by the twelve exterior sides. Even numbered sides were *yin*, odd were *yang*, and so maintained the balanced flow of *Qi*. The city and its parts were a physical representation of the cosmos.

The interior square ('5') was surrounded by a wall and was the 'inner city'.

The remaining squares formed the 'outer city' and were enclosed by a wall. Each side of the outer city wall had three equally spaced gates which led to three main streets criss-crossing the area, all leading to the inner city. Between each main street were two lesser streets, making a grid plan of some eighty-one equal blocks. Each block was considered a 'village' and functioned as a separate ward. The design presented in the *Rites of Zhou* remained the underlying pattern for urban structures throughout pre-industrial China.

The building materials of Chinese cities were very different from Mediterranean, Near Eastern or Indian cities. To the west of the Central Asian deserts and mountains, stone was often preferred for major construction. Iranians, Greeks, Romans and Indians vied with each other with raising buildings of great size and engineering expertise. The grandest of these structures were beyond human scale. In China, the human scale was never forgotten and stone was rarely a major structural component. The basic ingredients of Chinese architecture were earth, wood and clay.

Chinese architecture was all about post and lintel construction. Nothing else mattered. But the elaboration of post and lintel was amazing. The architects built on tamped earth foundations. These formed platforms raised above ground level to keep the wood high and dry. Faced and paved with stone, these provided stable bases on which to rest wooden post-columns set at regular intervals in modular systems of support. Between the posts, curtain wall units closed in the buildings. It was the connection of the post-columns to their lintels that made Chinese architecture unique. Rather than the splayed top of the Doric and the spread capital of Ionic and Corinthian columns, or the pointed arch and arabesque of medieval buildings, the Chinese developed the *dougong* method of interlocking structural wooden brackets to uphold heavy trusses supporting high roofs. First used in the Spring and Autumn times (771-476 BC), the *dougong* structure became very complex as time went on. The *dou*, a wooden block the size of the column upon which it sat, supported a *gong*, a bow-shaped member that supported the beam above it or another *gong*. The *gong* provided cantilevered support to the member above it, and the builders could repeat the structure many times, thus generating the unique eaves that are so visible on Chinese buildings.

The beams supported heavy roof trusses, whose rafters supported a clay tile roof. The builder designed his roof tiles so as to quickly drain water off and away from the building, while at the same time providing ventilation to the higher parts of the interior to prevent moisture build-up. These members were connected by joinery techniques and stayed in place through gravity, the weight of the structure giving stability to the building. There were very few nails and little glue holding these buildings together; rather they 'fell' into place and stayed there because their interlocking parts pressed the member together by force of gravity. The building was solid but flexible, and so proof against strong wind and earthquake. The wood was treated with a heavy lacquer coating which protected the member from moisture and insects. Chinese buildings, whether small or large, suffered from two major dangers: fire and moisture. Cities were often fired in war, leaving a wasteland which was never replaced. Rather than clear away rubble and detritus, Chinese engineers often found it easier just to build a new city in a nearby place.

The largest structures in all cities and towns were their fortifications. The Chinese constructed these fortifications out of beaten earth: masses of labourers excavated tons of dirt and clay, moved by wheelbarrows to where the wall was to stand. After the labourers dumped the dirt, other teams, using heavy pounders, beat the detritus solid. Wood frames held the dirt in place as the wall rose. Finally, the wall was about as wide as it was tall. A stone facing held the earth in place. The workers made provision for gates. Over the gates they built tall wooden towers which provided protection for defenders.

Emperor Wen Builds Daxing (Great Prosperity)

Soon after seizing power, Emperor Wen began organizing an imperial administration based on consistent standards and merit. Such an imperial organization needed a setting. The emperor decided to build a whole new capital city to display the achievements of the new empire. The old sites of the Qin and Former Han capitals were in the 'Land within the Passes'. The Han city, Chang'an, was a fought-over ruin. Rather than try to rebuild that site, Emperor Wen found an empty site and began building a new city in 582. He named the city Daxing (Great Prosperity). The city was a rectangle 6 miles by 5 miles, surrounded by 20ft-high walls. Each wall side held the three great gates according to the ancient designs. The city streets cut the area into 108 wards and two marketplaces. Walls, 10ft high, enclosed each ward, which held anything from numerous private residences to one major residence. The lesser streets were 80ft wide; larger streets were 325ft wide, and the great north-south way was 500ft wide. Along the north side of the rectangle, Emperor Wen built three palace complexes, one in the centre with two flanking structures. Near here were the administrative offices, the centre of Sui Wen's empire. When Li Yuan assumed the imperial title in 618, he gave the old name, Chang'an, to Emperor Wen's city. Later, the Tang Emperor Taizong rebuilt the palaces, constructing a new grand building complex, the Daming Palace.

Emperor Yang Builds the Eastern Metropolis

The Northern Zhu Emperor Xuan, brilliant but unbalanced, decided his expanding empire needed a capital on the Yellow River to oversee Shanxi and Hebei. He started to build a city near the site of old Luoyang in 578, but his father-in-law Yang Jian convinced him to cancel the project in 580. Once Xuan had died,

Yang Jian, becoming Emperor Wen, built his new capital at Daxing in 582-583. His son, Emperor Yang, saw the need of a second capital, just as had Emperor Xuan. In early 605, he decreed the construction of a new grand city where the central plains meet the loess fields near the Yellow River. His head engineer was Yuwen Kai, a Xiongnu, but not of the former imperial clan. Yuwen Kai had been a main architect of Daxing and personally oversaw the design and construction of the Ancestral Temple and Summer Palace. On 18 February 606, Emperor Yang accepted the city, now named the Eastern Metropolis, as completed.

Seven hundred thousand soldiers and conscript labourers built the fortification walls of the Eastern Metropolis surrounding the whole city, with two further rings surrounding the imperial residences and administration offices. Another 100,000 constructed foundations of the great halls and enclosed courtyards. There were also some 100,000 carpenters, masons, metal fabricators and tile setters. When suppliers, transport workers, and other specialty trades were included, some two million people worked on the construction project, often in relays for a month at a time.

Yuwen Kai's basic design was to reflect the structure of heaven as seen in the circumpolar constellations. North of the Milky Way (toward the polar pivot), the Chinese see the Three Houses (Sanyuan), within which are the Purple Dominion and the Fruitful Dominion. The Luo River, which ran through the city, was the Milky Way; the administrative offices enclosure was the Fruitful Dominion and the imperial residence the Purple Dominion. Streets and gates followed in projecting these ideas as the foundation of the city plan. Emperor Yang's hope was to generate the power with the designs of the Book of Changes to bring the empire into harmony with the heavens. Significantly, the placing of the court complexes was not symmetrical like Daxing, but off-centre to the north-west. While some see the asymmetrical design of Yang's Eastern Metropolis as an unfinished version of Daxing, we should remember that Later Han Luoyang had a similar layout. On a practical note, Luoyang's imperial quarters were sited on the highest point of ground with the urban area, and so easily drained water, whereas the imperial quarters of Daxing, centred as they were, ended up at the lowest point in the urban area and had drainage problems. That was why Emperor Taizong built the Daming Palace, which was constructed much higher than the old Sui Palace complex.

The two capitals reflected very different building styles. Daxing was severe, simple, with its lines straight and bold. The Eastern Metropolis was extravagant, curved and built in the 'southern' style:

'Luoyang unequalled in splendour used the curvilinear and angular southern style of Liang and Chen. High walls, bridges floating across Luo River, high towers soaring over golden gates and ivory battle towers.' (Suishi, 24)

The great hall of the Eastern Metropolis imperial palace, the Qianyang, was some 400ft long and 75ft wide, with a rooftop 140ft high. (The near contemporary Hagia Sophia in Constantinople is 270ft long by 240ft wide, with a rooftop 180ft high.) The Qianyang sat on a triple raised terrace, had huge wide columns, patterned beams and jade decorations.

Daxing had some million inhabitants. The Eastern Metropolis had more than 600,00 people in 103 wards.

References

Arthur Cotterell, *The Imperial Capitals of China* (New York, 2007).

Liang Ssu-ch'eng, *Chinese Architecture* (Cambridge MA, 1985).

Paul Wheatley, *The Pivot of the Four Quarters, a Preliminary Enquiry into the Origins and Character of the Ancient Chinese City* (Chicago, 1971).

Fu Xinian et al, *Chinese Architecture* (New Haven CT, 2002).

Victor Cunrui Xiong, *Capital Cities and Urban Form in Pre-modern China, Luoyang 1038 BCE to 938 CE* (Abingdon, 2017).

Victor Cunrui Xiong, *Emperor Yang of the Sui Dynasty* (Suny, 2006).

Appendix 4

Chinese Art of History

In the vast collection of dynastic Chinese literature, there is a body of records called *Zhengshi lei* (*Accurate History*). Today, these are known as the *Twenty-Four Dynastic Histories*. With commentaries and notes, this collection holds thirty-six works. These works of history, from the beginnings of Chinese society through to the Qing Dynasty, are massive and of high quality. The Chinese body of historical texts is the largest collection of pre-industrial historical writing in the world. Interestingly, the whole is written in, more or less, the same language, the unique Chinese ideograms that are hard to learn but exceptionally expressive. Here is a repository of some of the greatest written works ever made. The ancient Shang (*c.* 1600-1046 BC) recorded divination answers, sometimes in considerable detail. The succeeding Western Zhou (1046-771 BC) recorded lengthy documents on bronze vessels, indicating a significant written tradition. The Spring and Autumn period (771-476 BC) saw the emerging Ruist teachers who expounded about human affairs and government. These people collected, collated and presented numerous documents that they said were from the Western Zhou leadership. That these documents are the actual words of Zhou leaders as they appear, or are enhanced versions of such documents, or are simply made-up compositions, has long been an interesting controversy. Still, they represent the beginning of a tradition to find answers to current problems by looking at the past. Of course, to do that adequately meant that the present should be accurately recorded so the future may understand what went on.

The *Shiji*

The first systematic work of general history was the collection written by Sima Qian in the reign of Emperor Wu of the Han Dynasty. Based on the initial collection of his father, Sima Tan, this work is now titled *Shiji* (*Scribe's Records*). Presented in about 94 BC, the *Shiji* became the architype for later Chinese histories. Sima Qian divided his work into main chronological units. For those periods when the evidence was legendary or sparse, Sima composed vivid narrative chronicles. For the Qin and Han dynasties, Sima used four different formats. The first, 'Basic Annals', a chronological compilation of important documents, recounted major events and political decisions. The second, 'tables', are chronological representations of major events following the documents in the 'Basic Annals'. The third are biographies of different classes of people, including detailed biographies of emperors, their consorts and important children. Following these, there are biographies of main officials, army officers and important political figures of action or thought. There are also biographies of artists and entertainers. Finally, Sima Qian composed 'Treatises', monographs explaining particular issues or events in detail. This four-fold structure is repeated in the subsequent *Dynastic Histories* from Ban Gu's *History of the Former Han Dynasty* to the *Ming Dynasty*, written under the Qing.

The *Shiji* holds some 526,000 Chinese characters. It is longer than the Hebrew *Holy Scriptures*. The succeeding *Dynastic Histories* are of a similar size. They are more of an encyclopedia of the age than a narrative. Each history holds a variety of narratives as events are viewed from the perspectives of the lives in the biographies. Of course, some biographies are better than others and some histories are better than others. But the sum total of the dynastic histories represent a major achievement of human endeavour.

Tang Histories

Following the fall of the Han Dynasty (AD 220), the succeeding regimes, fighting among themselves, did not devote much time to scholarship, although some authors wrote a few important histories. An interesting author of the Western Jin Dynasty, Chen Shou, wrote a series of biographies from the Three Kingdoms Period (AD 220-280), which he lived through. Fan Ye composed a monumental history of the Later Han Dynasty under the Liu Song Dynasty in 445. A number of histories of the ephemeral Northern and Southern Dynasties were written by their successors. It was the new imperial power that dominated all of the Yellow River and Yangzi lands, the Tang Dynasty, that extended the *Dynastic Histories* by producing eight dynastic histories from 636-659. These included Liang, Chen, Northern Qi, Northern Zhou, Jin, Northern Dynasties, Southern Dynasties and the History of the Sui Dynasty. Compiled by the academics of Chang'an, these histories set a high standard for their successors. The rulers of the Tang Dynasty maintained a strong sense of history and kept fine records.

With the final collapse of the Tang in 907, a struggling series of regimes succeeded one another in northern China, while a series of independent states rose along the Yangzi and in the south. This is the age of Five Dynasties and Ten Kingdoms (907-960). The founding emperor of one of these regimes, Shi Jingtang of the Later Jin Dynasty, decided to demonstrate his legitimacy by ordering the writing of the *History of the Tang Dynasty*. His imperial chancellor, Zhao Ying, started the project, and the next emperor's imperial chancellor, Liu Xu, completed the task. Liu Xu presented the completed project to Emperor Chu of the Later Jin in 945. The Liao Dynasty overthrew the Later Jin in 947.

The work on this *History* was rather slipshod, with older chronicles, monographs and biographies just stitched together. The erudite scholars of the Northern Song Dynasty (960-1127) harshly criticized the Later Jin's *Tang History*. The editors, important scholars Ouyang Xiu and Song Qi, produced their massive *Tang History*, starting their work in 1044. The editors expected their *Tang History* would replace Later Jin's *Tang History*. With Bi Sheng's development of moveable ceramic type in about 1040, Song books were printed. The old *Tang History* was not widely distributed and became very scarce, but because the old *Tang History* contained material whose sources were lost, the book was revived during the Ming Dynasty as the *Old Tang History* and the Song product called the *New Tang History*. Both are included in the *Twenty-Four Dynastic Histories*.

The *Zizhi Tongjian*

The development of printing led to a rapid growth of historical studies because sources became more available. Emperor Yingzong of the Northern Song commissioned the eminent historian Sima Guang to produce a comprehensive history of China. With a staff of outstanding scholars, Sima Guang wrote a narrative account of Chinese military and political history from 403 BC to 959 AD, including information from the 'official' histories and many other sources. This work took nineteen years to produce, and contained 294 volumes and about three million Chinese characters. Sima Guang presented the final work to Emperor Shenzong in 1084 AD. The work is titled *Zizhi Tongjian* (*The Mirror for the Perceptive*). The work has survived complete in numerous editions: eight volumes of the original manuscript are in the National Library of China, Beijing.

The Mirror started a new line of historical writing in China, the use of straight narrative to describe events. The two sorts of historical writing continued to exist, side by side, down to the end of Imperial China. Chinese publishers began producing shortened narrative histories, emphasizing important people and events for students taking exams. A number of these were translated into English at the end of the nineteenth and beginning of the twentieth centuries. Of particular note is the Rev. John Macgowan's *The Imperial History of China Being a History of the Empire as Compiled by the Chinese Historians* (Shanghai, 1906) (available from Internet Archive).

Reliability

The value of an ancient work of history is in its reliability: how well the work recounts a series of events, including personalities, actions and geographic details. If the work includes documents that represent various official statements, that is added value. Questions of bias, partisanship or wanting to have certain people appear in a good light are interesting, but are to be expected. Before the development of printing, all histories were very expensive to produce, particularly the *Chinese Accurate Histories*, most of which needed a staff of archivists and numerous copiers. While human bias is to be expected, all these works were made, not to satisfy a few people at a given time, but to provide an understanding of a certain period for all time, as they do. Denis Twitchett, in his *The Writing of Official History under the T'ang* (Cambridge UK, 1992), demonstrates that teams of scholars carefully collected the records from which other scholars carefully wrote the texts. Of course, none of this is perfect, but as a totality, the *Twenty-Four Dynastic Histories* are as accurate a series of works as exist from pre-industrial times.

Chinese Military Handbooks

Chinese military commanders were literate. Like their Mediterranean contemporaries, they had to read lists: names, supplies and geographical locations. Before and during the Spring and Autumn period, military leaders were hereditary nobles. They learned their business as apprentices in family armies. As war's intensity increased during the Age of Warring States, experts replaced noble officers. They were more intent on victory and found success the only road to status. Text books were part of Chinese pedagogical methods. '*How to do it*' books of all types appeared in Confucius' time, and military books were no exception. As in any field of expertise, experts talk, argue and steal ideas from each other.

Such texts were not made for individual study. A large and cumbersome packet of bamboo strips held together by thread was not something for an officer to sit in an easy chair and ponder. Professional scribe book-makers constructed these texts for some material remuneration. Commanders rented or bought the texts for their units. Lectors read the texts to a group of officers and staff. After every statement, the commanders would discuss the section, giving examples and questioning their subordinates about their comprehension of the statement. Year after year, generation after generation, the same texts were read and discussed. Given the expense of producing the text and the importance attributed to its contents, it is clear that the text was stabilized soon after its composition. Indeed, while many critics questioned the textual reliability of Master Sun's work because the oldest extant copies were from the time of Bi Sheng's invention of printing (990-1051), the recovery of a text from the time of the Former Han Dynasty demonstrated remarkable textual continuity.

Most officers spent their time drilling their units and teaching personal combat tactics with different weapons. Staffs oversaw logistics. Nevertheless, some commanders needed familiarity with basic war strategy, as did the civil officials who dealt with the military. Taken together, *The Art of War* and other handbooks speak of methods of warfare that engage enemies on all fronts: direct combat, cutting supplies, confusion concerning main effort, misinformation of all kinds and efforts to undermine enemy morale. Beyond all this, the texts are clear that the objective of war is the destruction of the enemy's war-making capacities. The thirteen chapters of Sun Tzu's work are thoughtful, direct observations of best-practice military actions. These include planning, the decision of going to war, strategies of attack, dispositions, the need for momentum, identifying weakness and strengths, principles of deployment, different variables, how to set forces on the march, the proper utilization of terrain, different situations that confuse operations, the use of fire and espionage.

The basic strategies depicted in the handbooks were turned into an abstract board game, *Weiqi*. This is the game now best known in the west by its Japanese name, Go. Played on a board usually of 19x19 intersection lines, one player puts a black stone on an intersection and the other player puts a white stone on an unoccupied intersection. This continues. As the board fills, one player is able to remove his opponent's stones from intersections. While essentially a simple game, the possibilities of attack and defence are infinite. Created before the Age of Warring States, all educated Chinese were expected to play the game, including politicians and commanders.

These military texts and this game, along with the history of which they are a part, should be a corrective to certain Western concepts that war is not part of Chinese culture. Consider Roger Ames' statement in his *Sun-Tzu the Art of War* (Ballantine, 1993), an excellent translation and study of the texts of the traditional *Art of War* with the recovered *Yin-Ch'üeh-Shan* texts (p.629, eBook): 'This abiding interest in military affairs [concerns of the *Art of War*] is a particularly curious situation for a culture in which warfare is neither celebrated or glorified, and in which military heroism is a rather undeveloped idea.'

Warfare is just as much a part of Chinese history as it is of Mediterranean, Near Eastern, European and every other people who write histories. Chinese military monuments exist from all ages of Chinese history. One of the greatest military monuments of all time is the Forbidden City (*Zijin Cheng*) itself. A vast and meticulously constructed concentric fortress, each structure in the complex can deliver cross-fire to defend the Dragon Throne. The main gate (*Wumen*) is a triumphal arch emphasizing military power. All city gates in traditional China were monumental military structures. The tombs of emperors and their processional ways featured soldiers and memorialized conquests. The Chinese novels, *Three Kingdoms* and *The Water Margin*, depict war leaders in a sophisticated heroic manner. So, as we saw before, military aspects of Chinese culture are discounted not because of what happened in China, but because it suits the predispositions of many European and American commentators.

Much the same attitude pervades the translations and analysis of Chinese military texts. Spoken Chinese is a direct and clear language. Military affairs need direct and clear directions and description. Yet many translations of classical Chinese military handbooks use philosophical and indefinite English words to render the Chinese text. As an example: Sun Tzu's *Art of War*, translated by Lionel

Giles, Barton Williams and Sian Kim, translates Chapter One, sections three and four, 'The art of war is governed by five constant factors, to be taken into account in one's deliberations, when seeking to determine the conditions in the field. These are: (1) The Moral Law; (2) Heaven; (3) Earth; (4) The Commander; (5) Method and Discipline.' Contrast that wording with Jonathan Clements' Sun Tzu, *Art of War*, same chapter and sections: 'War is governed by five crucial factors, which you must consider and implement: Politics, Weather, Terrain, Leadership, Training.' To use Master Sun's work as a philosophical guide is interesting, but ignores the work's basic purpose: to win wars.

Military Handbooks in the West

At the western end of Eurasia, Mediterranean societies also produced military handbooks, but with a different emphasis. Military leaders were members of the privileged and educated elite who ruled collectively in varied forms of republics, oligarchies or dictatorships. Under the Romans, both the Republic and Empire (200 BC–AD 250, the Second Macedonian War to Valerian's Persian War), the military depended on tactical proficiency for success: find the enemy, attack and drive him into the ground. The main operational strategic problems were managing supplies, site engineering works and collecting the revenue from selling the defeated as slaves. The elite gathered information from campaign histories, such as those of the Athenians, Macedonians, Carthaginians and Romans themselves. These histories remain the basic sources of Classical military history and, indeed, lead into the modern study of military strategy. There is mention of theoretical works on the military, but none of these are extant.

The oldest handbooks that remain appeared during the High Empire (96–180 AD). These are by three near contemporary authors, Aelianus (also named Aelian), Frontinus and Polyaenus. Aelianus' work is an extensive drill manual, Frontinus gives a list of tricks to fool the enemy and Polyaenus has 900 stratagems, of which 833 remain. Not until Roman tactical superiority waned do we begin to see more comprehensive treatments of military affairs. In the fifth century, Vegetius' *De Re Militari* appears, followed in the sixth century by Emperor Maurice's *Strategicon*. Both these texts devote considerable detail to tactical considerations, but simply see war as unavoidable. At the same time, military commentators still produced detailed campaign histories (Procopius, Agathias and Theophylact). The main difference between the Roman and Chinese military literature is the decided Roman preference for avoiding 'useless' abstract thought, but rather discussing issues directly without a general frame of reference which might hinder action.

We should be surprised, however, that certain ploys and recommendations appear in both Chinese and Roman military handbooks. We know the vast steppe tribal confederations were not based on ancestry. Someone with useful skills was always welcome, and there were plenty of people who needed to leave their homeland and find a new life. Underneath the movements of large armies, conquering tribes and powerful empires, there is a population of skilled, clever people moving about, looking for the best deal and a secure home. They left no writings but, if we look hard enough, we can see their footprints in techniques and ideas that move across Eurasia.

The Importance and Unimportance of Handbooks

Master Sun produced a significant aid for Chinese commanders. Yet we must remember that however clever, original and successful military understandings may be, without tactical success they are useless. Master Sun himself made this point, and it has come to us in the form of an amusing anecdote.

> King Ho Lu of Wu read the *Art of War*. Impressed, he decided to see if Sun could actually handle military affairs. Said King Ho Lu, 'Will you allow me to test your ideas?'
> Master Sun agreed.
> The king went on, 'Can you train women?'
> Master Sun said that he could.
> The king ordered the 180 young women in the palace women's quarters to come out and stand on the marshalling yard. Master Sun divided them into two companies, gave each woman a spear to hold and appointed two favourite concubines as officers for the two companies.
> Master Sun addressed the two companies, 'I assume you all know the difference between front and back, right and left hand?'
> The two companies replied, 'Yes.'
> 'When I say,' Master Sun continued, 'eyes front, you must look straight ahead. When I say, turn left, you must face toward your left hand. When I say turn right, you must face toward your right hand. When I say turnabout, you must turn right and face toward your back. Am I clear?'
> The two companies both said, 'Yes.'
> Master Sun then set in place the symbols of war, indicating that this was an official drill, and ordered the war drummers to begin beating. He ordered, 'Right turn!' The women burst out laughing.
> Master Sun silenced the drums and withdrew the symbols of war. He commented, 'If commanding words are not clear and direct, if orders are not understood, then the commander is at fault.'

Master Sun replaced the symbols of war, ordered the drums beaten. He gave the order, 'Left turn.' The women again burst out laughing. Master Sun commented, 'If the commander's orders are clear and direct and soldiers still disobey, that is the fault of their officers.' Master Sun ordered the two favourite concubine officers beheaded.

Now King Ho Lu of Wu was watching Master Sun's exercise. Seeing that his two favourite concubines were about to die, he sent a message to Master Sun, telling him that the king was satisfied with the Master's ability to handle troops and told him to stop the executions.

Master Sun responded, 'I have received the Royal Commission to be commander of the Royal Army. As a commander, I must judge military matters according to military necessity. To maintain discipline, I must overrule your royal command.' The two concubines were beheaded. Master Sun appointed two others as officers.

Then Master Sun ordered the drums to begin again. The women performed all evolutions ordered, accurately, quickly and silently. Master Sun sent a message to King Ho Lu, 'Your soldiers are now correctly drilled and disciplined. They are ready for your inspection. They will follow your orders, fighting through fire and water.'

King Ho Lu replied, 'The commander may cease the drill and return to camp. As for us, we have no wish to inspect troops.'

Master Sun replied, 'The King is fond of words but he is not interested in real achievement.'

The story concludes with King Ho Lu recognizing Master Sun's military ability. The king employed him as a very successful commander.

The point of this tale is that the basis of all military success lies in the quality and training of the troops; that in order to achieve this, political leaders need to understand the seriousness of developing such a force; and that this force is uniquely valuable and leaders need to use them very carefully.

Appendix 6

The Great Eurasian Routes

T he Great Eurasian Steppes stretch from the Hungarian Plains along the Danube to the Amur in Manchuria. To the urban dwellers along the shores of the grasslands, the steppe was a desert out of which storms of fierce and strange marauders suddenly appeared to plunder, kill and rape. To those who lived in the steppe and knew its nature, the grasslands were a road to almost everywhere in Eurasia. A horseman who started out of the Hungarian Plain near the Danube in early spring could be in central Mongolia at Lake Khovsgol before winter. People have moved across the steppe for many thousands of years. We know only what a few remains in excavated sites inform us, but these are enough to tell us that ideas, artefacts and people moved across the grasslands. With the coming of the horse, people moved faster. While there were many dangers, both natural and human, a small group of people could pass from one end of the steppe to the other. The valuable goods they carried were not material but knowledge: metal-working, medical techniques, religious enthusiasms and shaman tricks. An aura of holiness, either real or assumed, was always good protection. Along with the knowledge, they could also carry select products of great value.

View From the West

Most goods passed from hand to hand, from one group to another across the steppe. Pathways led to settlements and way stations. Herodotus gives the first evidence in the West of an awareness of routes east. His knowledge of geography was confused; he understood the world to be flat. But he repeated information that he did not understand. In his fourth book, chapters 17-36, 47-58 and 102-117, Herodotus described people who live beyond the Black Sea. One route went north to the arctic, another went east into the steppe. Herodotus' text is unclear about just where were the different peoples mentioned. The descriptions of some of the peoples seem attempts to say in Greek their names from unfamiliar tongues. Nevertheless, with all the account's imperfections, here are routes across the steppes.

Another surviving description of routes to the east was written around 60 AD, *The Periplus of the Erythraean Sea*. The *Periplus* (schedule of ports and cities in order of travel) list a country, *Thin*. The account runs:

> [T]he sea comes to a termination somewhere in Thin. In the interior of
> that country, quite to the north, there is a very great city called Thinae,
> from which raw silk, silk thread, and silk stuffs are brought overland
> through Bactria to Barygaza and also down the Ganges River to Limyrice.
> It is not easy to get to Thin and few and far between are those who come
> from there. The place lies under the Little Bear. It is said that it adjoins
> the remoter frontiers of the sea and the Caspian Sea, beyond which you
> find the Maeotian morass which has communication with the great sea.

Besides an interesting tale of a strange short people, the *Periplus* demonstrates a
solid basis of knowledge about routes to China, but without much detail.

About a century after the *Periplus*, Claudius Ptolemy's *Geography* discussed the
Far East. Taking information from Marinus of Tyre's work, Ptolemy traced a route
to China from the Euphrates River, through Mesopotamia, Parthia and north to
Bactria. Then the route turns north and west through mountains until it reaches
the stone tower which blocks the pass east. This is probably the town of Tashkurgan,
centre of a kingdom called Puli by the Chinese. Beyond Tashkurgan opens the land
of Serice, surrounded by mountains and rivers. The lands of the Tarim Basin seem
to be the lands of Serice. Then, further east, is Sinae. The lands of the Sinae are at
the end of the ocean and surrounded by *Terra Incognita*. Ptolemy also describes a
route to Sinae by sea, from India to the east, passing many towns on the way.

Silk was an important import from China to the Roman Empire. Especially
during the Julio–Claudian Dynasty, many aristocrats complained of the drain of
currency being sent east for the 'frivolous' luxury of silk cloths. In fact, Greeks on
the island of Cos had been producing a variety of silk for a long time. Bolts of silk did
come from China: Chinese silk was significantly finer than the Greek product, and
drove it off the market. Raw Chinese silk in bolts was bland and pale. Workshops in
Sidon, Tyre and Alexandria unravelled and spun the silk threads into cloth, adding
dye and design. Silk was expensive, but much of the cost stayed in the empire.

In fact, the most important import from China was steel. The Roman metal-
lurgists-alchemists did not have the tools to consistently create steel from iron.
Certain rare iron ores naturally processed into steel, but the metal workers did not
understand why. The Han Dynasty metallurgists had more efficient furnaces and
a better understanding of the compounds needed to produce better quality iron.
Moreover, they had more exacting measuring devices to reliably produce steel.
Large enclosed furnaces with double-acting piston bellows using bamboo nozzles
gave strong, steady streams of air. Coal cakes burned evenly and generated high
heat. The Chinese mass-produced cast iron and turned it into steel by applying
blasts of oxidizing cool air to the molten metal. This was the Hundred Refining
Method. Even more, the Chinese turned wrought iron into steel. They wrapped

blades in fruit skins, rich in carbon, small amounts of slag, charred rice husks and certain minerals. They sealed these packages in clay crucibles and heated them for a full day. The result allowed them to mass manufacture steel tools of all types. Chinese steel, either finished products or ingots, travelled across Eurasia. Pliny the Elder (34.41) pointed out, 'of all the different types of iron the Seres produced the most excellent variety and they send it to us along with their delicate fabrics and animal furs.'

View From the East

From the Spring and Autumn period (771-475 BC), the Chinese viewed their lands as the 'Middle Realms', situated between mountains, deserts, jungles and seas, inhabited by fierce uncultured peoples. The Warring States (475-221 BC) built long walls to keep such people away from their productive lands and towns. During the Qin Dynasty (221-206 BC), all the long walls were rebuilt and joined together. When the First Emperor Qin united all the Chinese realms into a single state, all the nomadic tribes in the north formed a single confederation, the Xiongnu. The Founding Emperor of Han (202-195 BC) forbad the trade of iron and weapons with the Xiongnu. The Han efforts to deflect the Xiongnu led to a severe defeat and the imperial administration decided to pay tribute rather than lose battles. Emperor Wu (141-87 BC), unhappy with the Xiongnu depredations and the heavy tribute, decided to go to war with them. The emperor and his military staff knew the Han horses were no match for the Xiongnu cavalry. They had bought good horses from the Yuezhi, but the Xiongnu had defeated and push them west. They had seen spectacular horses from the far west, the Heavenly Horses, big, powerful and bold. They decided to send an envoy spy to investigate the world in the far west.

The emperor appointed Zhang Qian, an official and diplomat, as envoy extraordinary and sent him west. Starting in 138 BC, Zhang led an expedition of about 100 people, including a Xiongnu guide, Ganfu, toward the west, but was halted and detained by the Xiongnu. Zhang lived with the Xiongnu for some ten years, studying their ways. He escaped with Ganfu, his Xiongnu wife and son, and continued to the west. Travelling past Lop Nor along the edge of the Tarim Basin, they came to Dayuan and the land of the Yuechi. When Zhang arrived, the Yuechi were in the process of taking over Bactria. They were not interested in becoming involved with the Xiongnu again. Zhang spent a year in Central Asia, investigating the many cultures and states, including the Seleucid Empire, Parthia, western India and the states of Central Asia. He began his return to China along the south edge of the Tarim Basin, but was again detained by the Xiongnu for another two years. Finally, in 125 BC, he and Ganfu returned to the imperial court.

Zhang submitted extensive reports, well written and factual, about the peoples and places he saw. This are contained in a number of sections of the *Shiji* and are an important source for Central Asia history. Zhang tried to lead an expedition to reach the west by way of Sichuan, but this proved impossible. His last expedition in 119-115 BC was to the Wusun people in Central Asia, which opened direct trade between China and the Parthians. The imperial administration was interested in bringing the powerful Central Asian horses to China. When this trade was interrupted by local disturbances, Emperor Wu decided to exert whatever military force necessary to bring back the horses. In 102 BC, he sent a force of 60,000 soldiers, along with a full complement of supply troops and 100,000 cattle, to bring Chinese order to the lands. By the reign of Emperor Xuan (74-49 BC), the Chinese began to directly administer the route to Central Asia through the Protectorate of the Western Regions. This was generally the lands of the Tarim Basin beyond the Jade Gate. The Former Han government initiated the administration of the Protectorate in 60 BC, and it lasted until AD 23, when the upheavals of the Wang Mang regime brought chaos. The restored Later Han Dynasty re-established the protectorate in AD 74 and maintained it until 106. Even when the official protectorate was not in place, Chinese merchandise and merchants continued to do business.

During the Liu Song Dynasty (AD 420-479), imperial scholars wrote the *Hou Hanshu*, the official history of the Later Han Dynasty. As part of this work, Fan Ye (398-445) compiled a treatise, 'Chronicle of the Western Regions', which included many reports of places and events in Central Asia. The accounts included towns and peoples from near China to the Mediterranean Sea. The work covers events up to AD 166.

View From the Centre

People in the ancient Mediterranean world looked east toward the silk lands. People in the ancient Yellow River great plain looked west to the lands of Heavenly Horses. The people living in Central Asia were aware of both these cultural foci to their west and east. We need to remember that the land routes were not the only nexus for merchandise transfer, but there were also sea routes leading from the Red Sea, Persian Gulf, the shores of the Indian Ocean in both Africa and Asia, to and through the islands of the East Indies and on to China and beyond. Central Asian emporia held merchandise from the Greco-Romans, Abyssinians, east Africans and what is now Malaysia, Indonesia, the Yellow River valley, Yangzi River valley, Siberia and Russia.

The rulers of the Iranian states, both in Iran and greater Iran, were not interested in expanding their power to non-traditional lands (the Achaemenid Empire being understood as traditional). Nor were the different states of India interested in expanding beyond the Sub-continent. The smaller states in Central Asia were never able to unite, and so could not expand anywhere. But in the cultural mix of the area, there were groups of people who strove for expansion and planting new settlements far from Central Asia. These were religious groups of people who believed they should expand their activities. There were Jews who slowly percolated across Asia to China. Then there were Christians, particularly Nestorians, who spread their good news from Eastern Rome to China. But the most important from a material viewpoint were the Buddhists.

Mahayana Buddhism was particularly prone to expansion through the spread of monastic settlements and individual missionary efforts. In the West, Zoroastrians in Persia and Christians in Eastern Rome repelled Buddhist missionary activity, but the East was open to their influence. The earliest contact with China appeared in the Later Han Dynasty (AD 25-220) during the reign of Emperor Ming (AD 58-75). The few contacts became a flood during the reign of the Kushan great king Kaniska, who expanded his dominion into the Tarim Basin, including Kashgar, Khotan and Yarkand. The missionaries, Parthians, Kushans, Sogdians and Kucheans, endeavoured to bring the Buddhists' truth to China. They translated their works into Chinese, both Hinayana and Mahayana texts. Almost forty such texts are known. The earliest such texts are attributed to An Shigao, a Parthian prince who lived in China about AD 148-170, who translated Hinayana texts. Lokaksema, a Kushan, translated the first Mahayana texts into Chinese in 167-186. These missionaries were followed by a number of Parthian, Kushan and Kuchean translators, whose work extend from the Later Han through to the Tang Dynasty. Bodhidharma (440-528) was an important figure in this process. He founded the Chan (Zen) school of Buddhism and is credited as the originator of physical training of the Shaolin monastery, Shaolin Kung fu.

While Central Asian Buddhists brought Buddhism to China, Chinese Buddhists began travelling to Central Asia and India to collect more texts and visit holy places. The first pilgrim was Zhu Zixing, who travelled to Central Asia in 260. Faxian made the trip to India to seek Buddhism instruction first-hand in 395-414. He wrote an account of his travels, *A Record of Buddhist Kingdoms, Being an Account by the Chinese Monk, Faxian of his Travels in India and Ceylon in Search of Buddhist Books of Discipline*. Faxian walked from China through Central Asia to India and passed through the Punjab to Pataliputra. He collected many Buddhist texts in India and Sri Lanka, and sailed back to China, but was blown off course in a storm, probably to Java. Sailing back to China was difficult, but Faxian finally got home and spent the rest of his life translating the writings which he had collected.

During the fifth and sixth centuries, many merchants found Buddhist teachings and practices helpful in their businesses. Buddhist monasteries provided merchant lodging and storage, and the travellers supported the monasteries.

The Great Eurasian Routes

The main foci of urban civilization in Eurasia – European, Mediterranean, Indian and Chinese – developed unique literary and cultural traditions. As modern understanding of world history progressed, the narrative structure of the sequence of events and various analyses of them became clearer. But the interactions of these foci remained unclear. Ancient literature from both the Mediterranean and China tell of peoples and tribes moving east and west. Historians in the nineteenth century worked on correlation of peoples mentioned in one place with those mentioned in others. Never perfect, there was always a great deal of speculation. In the twentieth and twenty-first centuries, archaeological and historical investigations have made these interactions clearer. There is still a lot of fog clouding these interactions. Nevertheless, there is sufficient evidence that people as individuals, small groups and whole nations passed back and forth along the great Eurasian routes, bringing products, ideas and methods of doing things to all the shores of the steppes.

References

Christopher Beckwith, *Empires of the Silk Road* (Princeton NJ, 2009).

Andre Bueno, 'Roman Views of the Chinese in Antiquity', *Sino-Platonic Papers*, No. 261, May 2016.

Craig Benjamin, *The Yuezhi Migration and Sogdia*, in Paola Raffetta (ed.), *Eran ud Aneran*, *Festschrift for Boris Marshak* (Transoxiana Webfestschrift Series I, 2006).

Fa-Hsien, *A Record of Buddhist Kingdoms*, translated by James Legge (Oxford, 1886).

John Hill, *Through the Jade Gate-China to Rome, A Study of the Silk Routes 1st to 2nd Centuries CE* (John Hill, 2015).

Raoul McLaughlin, *The Roman Empire and the Indian Ocean* (Barnsley, 2014).

Raoul McLaughlin, *The Roman Empire and the Silk Routes* (Barnsley, 2016).

Mariko Namba Walter, 'Sogdians and Buddhism', *Sino-Platonic Papers*, No. 174, November 2006.

Taishan Yu, 'A History of the Relationship between the Western and Eastern Han, Wei, Jin, Northern and Southern Dynasties and the Western Regions', *Sino-Platonic Papers*, No. 131 (March 2004).

Taishan Yu, 'A Study of the History of the Relationship between the Western and Eastern Han, Wei, Jin, Northern and Southern Dynasties and the Western Regions', *Sino-Platonic Papers*, No. 173 (October 2006).

Taishan Yu, 'The Origins of the Kushans', *Sino-Platonic Papers*, No. 212 (July 2011).

Henry Yule, *Cathay and the Way Thither* (London, 1866)

Henry Yule, *The Book of Ser Marco Polo the Venetian, Concerning the Kingdoms and Marvels of the East,* translated and annotated by Henry Yule, 3rd edition, revised by Henri Cordier (London, 1903).

Appendix 7

The Horse and the Steppe

The wars of the Sui and Tang reconstructed the Chinese Empire after some four centuries of independent and self-conscious local states with their own cultural institutions. The question is posed: what tool did the dynasts of Sui and Tang hold that allowed them to subdue the many states of China and crush opposition to their dominion? The answer is long and involved. It revolves around the emergence of the aggressive cavalry horse and the armoured warrior rider. The following appendix describes this development.

Steppe Peoples and Horses

Stretching from northern China across Eurasia to the Danube, the never-ending grasslands tied the Eurasian world island together. The steppe is a hard and unforgiving land. But for well-prepared groups of people with transport animals, the open plains are a highway to almost everywhere. The key to successful exploitation of the steppe was the horse, but here there is a series of important questions. There are many animals drawn into human contact, but very few which develop not only close economic relations but strong, life-long emotional ties. There are dogs, cats, elephants and horses. Domesticated horses came from the Eurasian steppe. The best guess is that about 4000–3500 BC a band of hunters merged with herds of wild horses and developed symbiotic relationships. Genetic studies indicate that these horses belong to a subspecies that no longer exists in the wild.

This animal appears to be the extinct subspecies of horse now called the Tarpan. The name comes from a Turkic term, either *Kazakh* or *Kyrgyz*, meaning 'wild horse'. The name distinguished this type of horse from feral horses, which were domesticated horses living without human control. Genetic studies also indicate that mares may come from many different horses, but stallions came from very few, perhaps only one progenitor. This suggests that initially one tribe developed the human-horse relation, and all subsequent horses are descendants from one or a very few original stallions breeding with varieties of mares. An important point here is the complex human-horse interaction, which involved careful breeding and care besides necessary training and instruction for both horse and person. The lives of those who live with horses revolve around horses and result in a 'horse oriented' lifestyle.

Horse raising and riding tribes developed a distinctive way of life. The force multiplier that horses gave these tribes allowed them to shape their human environment to ensure their continued dominance. They needed good land that otherwise might support independent farming families. They needed secure base camps, often fortified, to store feed and provide homes for riders. They needed time to learn and perfect riding and weapons skills. All these were available for the Horse Lords, because with their horses they could demand such things, and those without the beasts and the skills to use them could not successfully resist. There were horse people, and then there were the rest. Sheep, cattle and people were important, in as far as they served the Horse Lords. Dominating aristocrats, looking down on the rest of humanity from horseback, the horse tribes spread their rule wherever they could manage their mounts.

The Coming of the Horse Lords

The First Wave: Chariots

Evidence of horse domestication appears in Kazakhstan with the remains of horse legs and heads in tombs, dating to 4800 BC. By 3500 BC, in the same general area, there are clear indications of bridling and milking. The Afanasievo Culture (2900-2500 BC) used horses to draw wagons. They used copper and were herders and hunters. These people seem related to the succeeding cultures which had variants that inhabited lands from the Urals to the Altai Mountains. One of these, the Sintashta Culture, living on the lands of the Ural Mountains' eastern foothills in 2100 BC, suddenly built fortified sites. They also manufactured bronze worked accoutrements for chariots. Descending south, west and east, these chariot warriors began to make indelible impacts on all the societies with which they collided. A bowman riding a two-wheeled cart with a driver and accompanied by dozens of others is part of a conquering army.

The first dominions of the expanding Horse Lords were the river valley agricultural proto-urban peoples of the BMAC, the Bactrian–Magiana Archaeological Complex. Here was a Bronze Age civilization (c. 2300–1700 BC) similar to societies in the ancient Mesopotamian, Nile, and Indus River valleys. Located along the Amu Darya and extending into the neighbouring mountains and valleys, these people grew wheat and barley in irrigated fields, worked in copper and bronze and built large structures. The complex was similar and probably related to settlements in western Afghanistan, eastern Iran and the Indus Valley. A model of a two-wheeled cart pulled by some sort of bovine dates to 3000 BC.

The lands around the Amu Darya are excellent spaces to breed and train horses. The 'wild horse' mares bred with the slender, tall, fast horses of the oases and mountains. They developed into the Akhal-Teke breed, some 15 hands high; the

Buryat, some 14 hands high; and the Altai, some 13 hands high. The later Medes took some of these horses and generated the Nisean breeds, tall, swift, yet hardy.

The first wave of Horse Lords erupted out of the steppes some years after 2000 BC. These cart-riding killers set up numerous principalities in which they became 'shepherds of men' rather than owners of animal herds. Chariots formed the armed core of many tribes on the periphery of the steppe, and they descended on the agricultural societies that bordered the steppes. We first hear of them about 1500 BC, when the Hurrian principalities attacked many kingdoms in Asia Minor and the lands south of the Caucasus. Called the Maryannu ('young warrior') in the Near East, they brought the chariot, horse training for the chariot, armour and an aristocracy of leader-follower association style of social structure that they imposed over their subjects. They spoke Old Indic languages and established a number of long-lasting lineages. Similar groups entered the Indus Valley and Yellow River Valley, founding aristocratic chariot dominions. The chariot warriors spread from Wales to Shandong. Always, the crux of power for these good shepherds was the ongoing breeding and raising of horses.

With their horses, the chariot warriors spread widely, transferring their aristocratic ways and love of horses from one end of Eurasia to the other. But they faded. Disciplined units of armoured foot, with long spears, large shields and sharp swords, overcame the chariots' advantages. We can see this process in the literature that describes this time. Homer's *Iliad* describes chariot-riding armoured warriors who travel to the battle in their great chariots and then get off them to fight. The *Spring and Autumn Annals*, with the Zuo Commentary, describes the slow disintegration of an aristocratic society of chariot warriors in the face of rising armoured infantry armies. While the chariot warriors faded, their chariots remained as symbols of might and power.

The Coming of the Horse Lords

The Second Wave: Steppe Riders

Out on the steppes, tribes fought and merged into many configurations. Skilled workers in horn and wood, using slowly gained knowledge of chemical interactions, developed the composite bow. Small compared to a spear or longbow, the composite bow used by a horseman, joined together with many other horsemen, produced an irresistible army. Once leadership structures solidified and numbers grew, the armies of mounted archers swept across the steppes and into the settled lands that offered great opportunity for wealth and power. These mounted archers were members of various groups that emerged out of single Old Iranian tribal traditions. In China, they were called *Sse* or *Ssek*, the Persians and Indians called them *Saka* or *Shaka*, while the Greeks knew them as *Sakai*. We call them the Scythians, identifying them as different parts of the Scytho-Sarmatian family. These peoples kept herds of horses, cattle and sheep. They lived in tent-covered wagons and fought on horseback with bows and arrows. They lived in tribal groups, led by royal warriors accompanied by their comitati. These riding archers first appeared in the Near East in the early seventh century in northern Asia Minor. By 650 BC, Scythians under King Madyes reached the borders of Egypt. Scythian tribes joined with the Medes in northern Iran and fought in wars against Assyria, helping to capture Nineveh in 612 BC. By about 590 BC, Scythians tribes withdrew back to the steppes north of the Black Sea.

When the Scythian warriors first appeared in the Near East, they did not have defensive armour. They picked up the use of armour and metalworking from Near Eastern societies, using local products as models. Their preferred style of armour utilized leather corselets covered with overlapping scales of bronze or iron. At first, they protected their horses with large felt 'aprons' that covered their breast. Later, they overlay rider and horse with cloths covered in scales. The overlapping scales did not hinder movement, but gave two to three layers of protection.

All Scythians, men and women, shot arrows using the short composite bow. This was carried in a *gorytos*, a bow-and-arrow case. For the most part, Scythian cavalry fought light, in hide jackets and cloth headgear, shooting arrows in disciplined barrages. At their army's core was a force of armoured cavalry with long spears, swords and shields. The Russian expert on Scythian culture, E.V. Cernenko, describes their tactics. After the light horse charged the enemy, launching arrow storms disrupting the enemy formation, the armoured forces 'manoeuvre in battle, breaking through enemy ranks, regrouping in the thick of the action and charging to strike at the right place at the right time. When the enemy had been broken, the light armed mass of the Scythian horse closed in to finish the job.' The main tactical move was the charge of the armoured cavalry into the centre of the enemy force.

The Scythians and their Sarmatian cousins remained on the steppes north of the Black Sea until the coming of the Huns. Some think that these peoples merged with Slavic tribes to their north and became part of the Slavic peoples.

References

David Anthony, *The Horse, the Wheel, and Language, How Bronze-Age Riders from the Eurasian Steppe Shaped the Modern World* (Princeton, 2007).

Gina Barnes, *Archaeology of East Asia, the Rise of Civilization in China, Korea, and Japan* (Havertown PA, 2015).

E.V. Cernenko, *The Scythians* (Oxford, 1983), translated from Russian. E.V. Cernenko was Head of the Scythian Department of the Archaeological Institute of the Ukrainian SSR Academy of Science.

Barry Cunliffe, *By Steppe, Desert, and Ocean: The Birth of Eurasia* (Oxford, 2015).
H. Dani and V.M. Masson (eds), *History of Civilizations of Central Asia*, Vol. 1,
'The Dawn of Civilization: earliest times to 700 BC' (UNESCO, Paris, 1992).

Horse Breeding Becomes a Science

Macedonian Horse

Horsemanship in Classical Greece was important. Small valleys and limited pasture allowed few horse farms. But aristocratic Greeks loved horses, raced them bareback or riding chariots, and each major state had cavalry. The Greeks bred horses with their usual attention to system and method. Specialty stud farms in Asia Minor, Thrace, Thessaly, Sicily and Macedonia sent stock to the main ports in mainland Greece. In Athens, aristocrats formed the *hippeus*, a 1,000-man cavalry reserve from which the Athenians formed their cavalry forces. Each member of the reserve was obliged to keep two horses and a trained groom. Excavations have found about 1,000 official lead tablets in Athens, one per horse, which listed the owner's name on the outside. Inside, there was a description of the horse's colour, the design of the horse's brand and a monetary evaluation of the horse in hundreds of drachma. Athenian officials inspected each horse to see if it was properly fed, well-trained, obedient and fast. These tablets reveal that there were some twenty-five distinct brands representing different stud farms from all over the Greek world. Horse training and breeding were well-established Greek practices.

Greece south of Thermopylae has no areas that could serve as large pastures. Boeotia comes close but has to maintain the balance between farms and pasture. To the north, Thessaly supported a sizeable horse population but had little central control. Beyond Thessaly spread the Macedonian plains, which reached up into the southern Balkan Mountains.

Hesiod said: 'Macedon, rejoicing in horses, who dwells round about Pieria and Olympus' (Fragment iii *Catalogues of Women*, in Constantine Porphyrogenitus, *de Them.* 2, p.48B). The Macedonian lands have excellent pasturage and climate for raising large herds of horses. Moreover, there are extensive lowlands which produce grain needed for large, big-boned horses. The Macedonian Royal Dynasty, the House of Argead, was little removed from the rulers portrayed in Homer. While violence and upheaval were consistent factors in Macedonian society, the royal office of *Hippotrophoi*, Horse Breeder and Trainer to the King, was as old as the royal house itself. King Philip II seized power in 359 BC and proceeded to rebuild the kingdom into a centralized military state. Strategy was the king's pleasure and tactics his joy. He developed a unique phalanx structure based on lightly armoured, well-trained infantry who held a strong shield and an 18ft-long spear (*sarissa*).

King Philip also developed a unique and powerful cavalry force to use as an offensive force. Traditionally, Macedonian kings kept a guard of their most trusted nobles or their sons as the King's Companions (*hetairoi*). Philip organized this honour guard into an effective fighting organization. The King's Companions were now hard-fighting, hard-drinking warriors similar to their king. The king increased their numbers. At full strength, the Royal Companion cavalry was composed of eight *Ilai* of 200 riders, along with the king's *Agema* of 400. The men wore armoured cuirass, greaves and helmet. They did not carry a shield, but wielded a xyston, a 'cavalry *sarissa*', some 10ft long. This spear was made of cornel wood, providing strength and elasticity. The spear would break before unseating the rider in a collision. Since the spear had points on both ends, the cavalryman could turn the broken end and still be armed. Each rider also carried a sword. The main function of the Companion Cavalry was to deliver tactical shock attacks.

King Philip paid a great deal of attention to getting proper mounts for his cavalry. He encouraged a wide circle of recognized horse dealers to come to court. Importing many different breeds of foreign origin, Philip oversaw an extensive breeding programne to produce by cross-breeding the best horses for his style of war. Philip concentrated his breeding efforts at royal stud farms near Pieria and kept his herds on the grazing lands south of Pydna. Fine chargers from the royal stables held the King's Brand, a Hermes' staff (*kerykeion*) marked horizontally on rump or shoulder. Just as Philip experimented with breeding, so he encouraged the Companions to do the same. Each of them was a large landholder with horse ranches. The effectiveness of Philip's cavalry had a lot to do with strong, well-trained horses. Even more important was the single will of the unit, along with the discipline and eagerness to engage in violent action that gave Philip's cavalry a massive force multiplier. We can see King Philip's ideal cavalry horse on his tetradrachms, showing a large horse with a fine head and well-muscled anatomy. But, of course, the violent brutal man riding the horse made the weapon work.

Philip forced Greece into the League of Corinth and intended to lead a united Greek Macedonian force to push back the Persian Empire, perhaps to Mesopotamia. Philip was celebrating the marriage of one of his daughters when he was killed by a bodyguard. Macedonia, as usual in a succession crisis, tottered. One of Philip's sons, Alexander, seized the throne.

Alexander's Cavalry

Alexander was as deeply concerned about good horseflesh as his father. As a teenager, Alexander won a marvellous warhorse, Bucephalus. One of the horse traders accustomed to dealing with the royal court, Philonicus of Thessaly, offered a large young horse with a massive head. The horse was black with a white star on his brow. His eyes were blue and he came from a specialty breeding farm. What really caught King Philip's attention was the price. Philonicus wanted 13 talents (a talent was worth something like nine years' wages for a skilled workman), a simply amazing sum. The royal grooms could not handle the beast; it was too big and too powerful. Philip turned Philonicus down flat. But the young Alexander bet his father that he could control the horse. If he succeeded, Philip agreed to pay the price, but if he failed, Alexander would pay and be stuck with a useless horse. The famous story ends with Alexander turning the horse into the sun so the horse would not see his shadow, taking off his long cloak, talking softly to the beast and riding him bareback. Alexander named his horse Bucephalus after the ox head brand on the horse's rump.

This tale is not just an amusing anecdote. Alexander, Philip and the Macedonian horse lords were exploring equine behaviour in an effort to develop a cavalry force multiplier by producing more aggressive yet controllable horses. Uniting fierce aggressive horses to well-trained bold riders, covered by accompanying light infantry, produced an irresistible attack formation that could cut through heavy infantry. Over the centuries, as different tribes fought and experimented with different methods of fighting and tactical manoeuvre, some no doubt envisioned the same basic idea, but what made the Macedonian efforts more significant were the systematic methods used and recorded.

Training horses to be aggressive yet maintain rider control is very complex. Horses are herd animals that have ferocious predators. Their best defence is to avoid conflict. They have acute hearing and excellent eye sight, with 340° vision. They want to shy away and flee from threats, carrying their riders with them. For horse archers, such 'fight and flight' actions are just fine. Moving in masses of horses, a mounted archer force swarms toward their enemy, shoots an arrow storm and disperses, only to reform in another direction. This takes great skill and practice for the rider to know how to influence his horse's movements, but these follow the horse's instincts. The Macedonian programme for training aggressive horses had to break the animal from his natural inclinations. The only way for this training to develop the aggression yet tractability was to build on the personal trust of rider and horse. The emotional connection between warrior and mount was paramount. Even more than mounted archers or armoured steppe riders, the aggressive horse and warrior rider must live together, the rider raising the horse from colt, himself raised on horseback before he could walk.

Training inculcated obedience for both horse and rider through constant drill, in arena schooling, cross–country excursions and, most important, hunting. Organized hunts provided direction and practice in unit manoeuvres, long–distance movements and unit cohesion. The Macedonians preferred stallions rather than geldings or mares. Stallions had a better chance to intimidate the enemy's horses. If an enemy's horse submits to your horse, no matter how good a fighter, the enemy is lost. Further, all the horses in a formation must be well-trained. One horse that balks in a charge can upset the whole manoeuvre.

Rider and horse had to practice a number of basic moves which led to tactical success. Greek art and cavalry practice expect horse and rider to have 'collected stance'. Here, the horse shifts his centre of balance to his hind quarters. This lightens his forequarters so that he carries himself in an upright manner. The result is that the rider can shorten gaits, turn smoothly and shift gaits as he wants. Moreover, the flexion of the haunches gives more mobility yet lessens stress on joints. The rider sits straight up and stays centred on the horse for fighting, and the horse's movement adds strength to the rider's blows. The collected stance allows a skilled rider with proper saddle to have as much staying power as with the later stirrups. In order to fight effectively, the tactical formation needed to learn to execute the following moves as a unit.

First, the *Passage*: a compressed powerful trot with high supple leg action.

Second, the *Piaffe*: an elevated trot in place which maintains impulsion and rhythm. The horse may then rapidly burst forward yet stays in balance. (Just as a runner continues to jog in place at red traffic lights, so the horse needs to stay engaged under his rider's control all the time.)

Third, *Passage and Piaffe*: used together, these moves allow horse and rider to remain in balance for fighting while letting them respond to commands forward or to the side. The whole unit must maintain impulsion and rhythm during all of its movements.

The rider and horse need to learn a number of tactical moves, to be done as a unit or individually.

First, the *body check*: using the horse's body to push against the enemy's horse. Horses want to avoid such contact. The rider needs to train his mount to give and take this type of contact.

Second, the *shoulder barge*: a stronger body check, in which the horse hits the enemy's horse with his shoulder, with his body weight behind the hit, shoving the enemy's horse aside. The rider also needs to train his mount to withstand such hits.

Third, the *Levade*: a collected and controlled rearing up in which the horse rocks back on his haunches and raises his forelegs at a 45° angle. The rider remains balanced and uses his weapons. There are numerous Hellenistic statues which show this position.

Fourth, the *Courbette*: the horse rears straight up, flailing his forefeet, and then launches himself forward in a series of jumps. This move can overwhelm an enemy.

The new king united the Macedonian armed forces, and at the head of his aggressive armoured cavalry he beat the Greeks back into submission. Joining to his Macedonian army a large Greek force, Alexander began his campaign against

Persia. Sweeping through Asia Minor and the Levant, beating Persian armies one after another, Alexander fought his way through Mesopotamia into Iran and further into Central Asia. Here, the Macedonian armoured cavalry met the latest Scythian-style armoured cavalry, Greeks colliding with the ancient Inner Asian complex of urban-nomadic cultures.

Alexander in Bactria (329-327 BC)

Alexander initially simply swept through the Bactrian-Sogdianan lands as if he was just another potentate like the Persian Great King. Coming in spring 329 BC, he marched at the head of his Companion Cavalry, mounted javelin men, archers, Agrianians and two taxis of Foot Companions. The local powers in Bactria-Sogdiana could raise some 30,000 cavalrymen of all types, but they acknowledged this new great king and intended to continue to live as they pleased. Alexander reached the Jaxartes River without incident, even receiving a resupply of horses from Maracanda (Samarkand). Then, out of nowhere, local forces slaughtered a Macedonian foraging party. Alexander struck back hard, as was his wont. All sorts of local forces suddenly appeared and killed all the Macedonian garrisons along the Jaxartes. Sogdiana rose in rebellion.

The reason behind the sudden change in attitude puzzled the Macedonians. Modern commentators suggest that the founding of the fortified city of Alexandria Eschate (the farthest) convinced the locals that Alexander intended to eliminate the high degree of local autonomy enjoyed under the Persians. Alexander didn't care what the cause; he would not stand for such defiance. He attacked and took seven towns in two days, killing or enslaving the inhabitants. He intended to rule, not merely reign. Along with crushing what he considered opposition among his own people, Alexander reached out to overwhelm all local opposition. Beginning in spring 329 BC, Alexander secured his hold on the Jaxartes River, preventing reinforcements coming to his enemies across the steppe. He then marched east to Bactria to gain the Oxus River. He applied harsh scorched earth tactics, taking fortresses and destroying them, no matter how impregnable they appeared. He marched up the Zeravahan valley, burning and killing all in his path. Alexander established his frontier in Sogdiana with a series of forts based on Maracanda. He then married into the local aristocracy in order to find local friends and allies.

The perceptive local leaders understood that Alexander was not going to stay, and with a stake in the new regime, they settled for a precarious peace. Alexander left a large garrison of 10,000 foot and 3,500 horse, most probably older and less reliable men. This garrison would include, besides the soldiers, women, children, servants, slaves, craftsmen, horses and so forth. These people would be an important addition to the population of Bactria-Sogdiana. Equally important, Alexander took thousands of local people inducted into his forces for his march into India in spring 327 BC.

India

Alexander's army descended into the Indus valley like conquering Homeric warriors and collided with forces of Vedic warrior kings. The Indian rulers saw just another warrior community descending through the mountains to fight and loot. They did not really have to defeat the Macedonians, but simply make any victory more expensive than the Macedonians wanted to pay: stymie their efforts and soon the Macedonians would leave. Alexander won victories but his army would go no further. He marched down the Indus River and turned toward Babylon. He never came back.

India, however, began to change. A series of towns with irrigated agriculture, iron technology and ruled by a warrior aristocracy occupied the Indus River valley. The Achaemenid Persian Empire took control of the Indus lands and collected taxes and warriors for their armies. Their control was never very heavy and local powers continued to rule. Beyond, to the east, in the valley of the Ganges, a number of centralized states appeared. The primer state, Magadha, slowly expanded, starting in about 550 BC. The major city dominating the area, Rajagriha, was slowly being challenged by Pataliputra. There were many small clan and tribal organizations intermixed in the state structures. Alexander left India in 326 BC. By 321 BC, a new power rose out of Magadha. Chandragupta Maurya overthrew the old Magadha Dynasty, took over the rest of the states in the Ganges valley and marched west into the Indus valley.

While the Mauryan Empire expanded, the Macedonians began to fragment. Alexander died in 323 BC. By 311 BC, the eastern parts of Alexander's dominion fell to Seleucus the Victor. Seleucus took the Persian princess, Apama – daughter of Spitamenes, the Persian Bactrian magnate who had rebelled against Alexander – as mistress. He married her at the great marriage ceremony at Susa in 324 BC and she remained his consort and queen for the rest of her life. She had his son and heir, Antiochus, in 325 BC. So Seleucus was related by marriage to many of the Bactrian-Sogdianan nobles, and his heir, Antiochus I, by blood. The upper Satrapies, as Bactrian lands were called, had no difficulties recognizing King Seleucus' rule.

To the south, however, Chandragupta Maurya invaded the Indus valley. King Seleucus marched east to meet Chandragupta in battle (305-303 BC). The result was that Seleucus ceded his south-eastern satrapies of Carmania, Arachosia, Aria and Gandhara to Chandragupta. In return, Seleucus received 500 war elephants, fighting bulls and breeding stock. King Seleucus used his elephant corps to good effect, defeating and killing King Antigonus the One Eyed at the Battle of Ipsus (301 BC), and did the same to King Lysimachus at Coropedium (281 BC).

The Mauryan Empire unified lands from Kandahar through the Indus valley and on to the Ganges. The many local traditions and different religions merged together into a spiritual intellectual efflourescence that included, among many traditions, the growth of Buddhism. This empire flourished from 321-184 BC.

The Greco-Bactrian Kingdoms

King Seleucus' realm spread from Macedonia to the Upper Satrapies, and so included a large portion of Alexander's empire. But as he was about to take possession of Macedonia in Europe, an enemy struck him down (281 BC). His son by Apama, Antiochus the Saviour (reigned 281-261 BC), was often at war protecting his holdings, and kept the loyalty of the Upper Satrapies. In 278 BC, marauding Gauls invaded Asia Minor after plundering Macedonia. Antiochus, using his elephant corps, decisively defeated them, forcing them to settle, and so founded Galatia. He assume the title Saviour for this victory. All was not well in the east, however. Antiochus had appointed his eldest son, Seleucus, as viceroy of the east in 275 BC. This was the same position Antiochus had held under his father. But in 267 BC, King Antiochus ordered Seleucus' execution for rebellion. Evidently, some sort of intrigue was going on in the Upper Satrapies. When Antiochus the Saviour died in 261 BC, his son Antiochus the God succeeded him. This new King Antiochus was only distantly related to the Upper Satrapies families. The connection began to wear thin.

The Upper Satrapies were under the administration of Diodotus. With the upheavals following the death of Antiochus II (246 BC), Diodotus proclaimed himself king, severing Bactria from the Seleucid Empire. The new kingdom was very rich. The improved irrigation systems increased production of all sorts of crops. Later texts spoke of a 'thousand cities'. Archaeology has shown that there were no thousand cities in the Bactrian lands; however, if local magnates built walled compounds for their ranches, this might account for the tradition. The main forces of the Bactrian kingdom were cavalry, Scythian-style light cavalry backed up by Macedonian aggressive cavalry.

Diodotus II succeeded his father and made a strong alliance with Arsaces of Parthia. Together they defeated Seleucus the Triumphant and maintained their independence. Sometime after 230 BC, Euthydemus overthrew Diodotus II and expanded the Bactrian kingdom into the steppe beyond Sogdiana. Euthydemus faced an invasion by Antiochus the Great in around 210 BC. His 10,000-strong cavalry could not hold back Antiochus, and the Seleucid king put Bactria under siege for three years. Finally, the two kings made a deal: Euthydemus recognized King

Antiochus as overlord and Antiochus granted Euthydemus the Upper Satrapies. With his rule secure, the Bactrian king continued to expand the Bactrian realm's influence toward China. The Bactrians were the first to issue coins made from cupro–nickel (75/25 ratio). This alloy was only known in China, under the name 'white copper'. The Chinese exported metals for the goods they needed, and they needed many goods from Bactria. On the one hand, the Bactrians traded in India for goods shipped from China across the Indian Ocean; on the other, the main export from Bactria was their fine horses.

Demetrius I, son of Euthydemus, reigned from about 200-180 BC. He invaded India during the chaos at the end of the Mauryan Empire and the rise of the Shunga Dynasty. According to Buddhist tradition, Demetrius came to protect Buddhists from persecution by the Shungas. The invasion reached Pataliputra in eastern India. The result was the formation of an Indo-Greek Kingdom in north-western India which lasted from about 175-10 BC. In this kingdom, Buddhism flourished and developed new institutions. In Bactria, a military commander, Eucratides, overthrew the Euthydemid Dynasty. Up from India, Demetrius II marched to reclaim the Bactrian throne with a massive army of 60,000. Eucratides defeated and killed Demetrius II using his elite armoured aggressive cavalry unit of some 300 men. The Bactrian king then invaded north-west India, gaining lands in the Punjab. The Indo-Greek King Menander I repulsed him, and on the way back to Bactria, Eucratides' own son killed him and ran over the bloody body with his chariot, leaving it as carrion in the field. Bactria and Parthia were soon at war, the Parthian King Mithridates I invading Bactria. The game of kings continued.

Bactrian Cavalry and Horses

The military advantage that allowed the Bactrian and Indo-Greeks to prevail was their aggressive cavalry. The horses were a specially bred mixture of eastern Mediterranean strains with Central Asian varieties. We can see this on numerous coins. Two coins illustrate the character of this force. These are tetradrachm of King Eucratides. Both have the same reverse, of two horsemen. On the obverse of one is a portrait of King Eucratides in a Macedonian cavalry helmet and tunic. His face is older and determined. The second coin also has a portrait of Eucratides in a heroic pose, seen from behind, with his face turned toward the left, his right hand welding a cavalry *sarissa*. Both portraits picture Eucratides as a powerful cavalry commander. The key to his forces are the two cavalrymen on the reverse. Both are armoured and armed with the cavalry *sarissa*. Both horses are in collected stance and performing the *levade*. These two soldiers are trained and accomplished horsemen. Their horses are large muscular beasts, powerful and aggressive. The horsemen ride above 'of Great Eucratides' in Greek and Pali in the Kharoshthi script.

But even more, the two horsemen represent the *Dioskouroi*, the divine twin horsemen. These are an ancient pair, long accompanying horses. Originally deified charioteers, the Rigveda calls them the Asvins, Sons of the Sky. From the time of the Sintashta-Arkaim culture in the south Urals (2200-1800 BC), where chariots originated, charioteers were paired. One was the warrior, welder of weapons; the other was the driver, keeper of horses. The first recorded riding warriors in Near Eastern texts, in Assyria (800 BC), 'always go in pairs, translated from the chariot' (Asko Parpola, *The Roots of Hinduism*, p.109). Poludeukes was the fighter; Kastor was the horse tamer. So the two horsemen represent not two fighters, but a fighter and helper. The horses are a warhorse and a spare. The men are knight and squire. Here is the essence of the aggressive armoured cavalry, united in the bonds of training and the companionship of war, riding on carefully bred, powerful and drilled horses. This force was irresistible to all but its own kind.

References

Malcolm Errington, *A History of the Hellenistic World* (Malden, 2008).

Richard Gabriel, *Philip II of Macedonia* (Washington DC, 2010).

Peter Green, *Alexander of Macedon* (Berkeley, 1991).

Frank Holt, *Alexander the Great and Bactria* (Leiden, 1988).

Frank Holt, *Into the Land of Bones: Alexander the Great in Afghanistan* (Oakland, 2012).

Frank Holt, *Thundering Zeus: The Making of Hellenistic Bactria* (Berkeley, 1999).

Rachel Mairs, *The Hellenistic Far East, Archaeology, Language, and Identity in Greek Central Asia* (Oakland, 2014).

Asko Parpola, *The Roots of Hinduism* (Oxford, 2015).

W.W. Tarn, *The Greeks in Bactria and India*, 3rd edition (Chicago, 1997).

Peter Thonemann, *The Hellenistic World, Using Coins as Sources* (Cambridge UK, 2015).

Carolyn Willekes, 'Equine Aspects of Alexander the Great's Macedonian Cavalry', in Timothy Howe, Edward Garvin and Graham Wrightson (eds), *Greece, Macedon, and Persia* (Philadelphia, 2015). Very informative about horse breeding and training.

Ian Worthington, *By the Spear: Philip II Alexander the Great, and the Rise and Fall of the Macedonian Empire* (Oxford, 2014).

The Yuezhi

The Greco-Bactrians, Greco-Indian and other hybrid regimes fought and fragmented, but trade continued through the struggles. The towns became rich as goods came from the Near East, Africa, India, the Steppe and China. Wealth came from the shipping of many different goods, and added to that was Bactrian production of precious metals and horses, including powerful warhorses. Their horses went to the Iranians and the powers to the west. They also went east to China and the steppe peoples. Their main middle men to the east were the tribes of the Yuezhi. The Yuezhi were an Old Iranian Scythian-style nomadic people who tended flocks, engaged in intensive agriculture and maintained a merchant economy. Living just to the west of Gansu and in the Ordos, they sold horses and cattle to the Chinese for silk during the Warring States. Then they supplied the First Emperor of Qin (246-210 BC) with fine military horses, which we can speculate were Bactrian-trained war horses.

But the Yuezhi fell foul of the Xiongnu. In the Mongolian steppes, certain Scythian-style tribes began to coalesce into a massive confederation during the Qin Dynasty. The tribes consolidated in an organization the Chinese called the Xiongnu. In 209 BC, during the end of the Qin, a great leader, Modu, created the confederation. The Xiongnu threatened their neighbours, particularly the new Han Dynasty. As the Xiongnu expanded, they developed a deep dislike for the merchant-nomad Yuezhi. I suggest that the reason the Xiongnu suddenly became more powerful was their development of an armoured aggressive cavalry, along with their horse archers; they disliked the Yuezhi because of the Yuezhi's control of the horse trade with China. Whatever the reality, sometime around 175 BC, the Xiongnu invaded Yuezhi lands in Gansu and defeated Yuezhi forces. Rather than fight to extinction, the Yuezhi pulled up their tents, left their settlements and moved into the Tarim Basin.

The Yuezhi broke into two groups: the Greater Yuezhi (Da Yuezhi) and the Lesser Yuezhi (Xiao Yuezhi). The Greater Yuezhi moved out of the Tarim Basin about 165 BC and settled in the Ili River valley, pushing out the Scythian Sai. The Sai migrated south, through Kashmir and into India, where they founded an Indo-Scythian kingdom. The Greater Yuezhi stayed in the Ili valley for about thirty years, until another tribal group attacked. These were the Wusun, allies of the Xiongnu. The Greater Yuezhi moved again, this time south into and through the Ferghana valley, and settled on the north bank of the Oxus River (Amu Darya). Here they met the Bactrian Greeks.

The Dai Yuezhi were horsemen and merchants. Great feats of valour and fierce fighting were not to their taste. The Bactrians, also horsemen, overlords of merchant towns which produced valuable surpluses, were equally not interested in spreading death and destruction. There may have been violent confrontations at first (*c.* 135 BC), but the two groups merged together, intermarrying and finding solid common ground. The Yuezhi-Bactrians issued coins that imitated the old Greco-Bactrian kingdom, maintaining a continuum of administration.

The Chinese Empire and Central Asian Horses

While the Yuezhi were entering into Bactria, the Han Dynasty and the Xiongnu were at war. The Han Emperor Wu (156-187 BC) decided to stop paying tribute to the Xiongnu and attempted to defeat them in battle, but the Xiongnu easily outmanoeuvred the Han infantry armies and increased their raids on border areas. The emperor decided he needed strong cavalry to defeat the Xiongnu. He had heard about the 'Heavenly Horses' that were in the west, and sent expeditions to acquire some of this special breed. The horses came from Central Asia and were evidently called something like *hanxuema* by their breeders, or at least the Chinese transliterated the name into Chinese words meaning 'blood sweating horse'. The Middle Chinese pronunciation was *hanH* (sweet) *Xwet* (blood) *maeX* (horse), using the Baxter-Sagart system, but the Classical Chinese pronunciation is unclear. Besides bringing back breeding stock, the expedition also returned with alfalfa, a feed that excites and energizes horses. The Chinese imported large numbers of Central Asian horses. They exported to the Central Asian lands silk and high-grade steel. By about 100 BC, Emperor Wu had built strong, effective cavalry forces.

The Parthians and the Saka

Antiochus II, the Seleucid monarch, died in 246 BC. His administration then unravelled. The satrap of Hyrcania and Parthia was Andragoras, a long-time loyal officer of two Seleucid monarchs. With Ptolemy III's successful occupation of Antioch on the Orontes in the Third Syrian War, and a number of claimants to the Seleucid throne, Andragoras proclaimed his independence. Within ten years, a group of Dahae, living along the River Ochus south-east of the Caspian Sea, organized in the Parni tribe, elected a leader called Arsaces. This leader, seconded by six other noblemen, led a force against Andragoras, killing him and taking his realm. Arsaces' second-in-command was the head of the House of Suren, who placed the royal tiara on Arsaces' head. This became a hereditary office of the Suren. Biver suggests that the number of compatriots, seven, reflecting the rise of Darius the Achaemenid, was a reflection of the old Median cult of Mithras, part of the Zoroastrian religion.

The Parthian dominion faced a very serious challenge, beginning in 129 BC. King Phraates, involved with a war against the Seleucid Antiochus VII Sidetes in the west, found his eastern frontiers under attack by a major force of Sacae (Scythians) who were involved in the massive movement of peoples involved with the Yuezhi. Phraates defeated and killed Antiochus but found himself outmanoeuvred by his own mercenary armies. A joint force of mercenaries and Sacae killed Phraates. The Yuezhi defeated and killed the next Parthian king in 123 BC.

The dominion was in chaos when the powerful warrior king, Mithradates II the Great, seized power and repelled the western powers breaking into the Parthian lands. In the east, a forceful viceroy, head of the House of Suren, battled against the Sacae, pushing them into Arachosia and the Punjab, where they established a strong regime, Sakastan.

We need to see these people not as skin-clad barbarians, but rather as sophisticated pastoralists who lived in a literate environment. The Sacae King Azes I, about the turn of the epoch, issued coins with images of armoured horsemen holding lances. His kingdom's neighbours included Indo-Greeks, various Indian regimes, Buddhist monasteries, Hindu organizations of many types and all sorts of merchants and manufacturers. By AD 20, an Indo-Parthian king, Maharaja Guduvhara, known traditionally as Gondophares, gained power over the Indo-Sacae with a capital at Taxila. The Parthian dominion, ruled by a King of Kings in the west, was a series of sub-kingdoms, each local domain managing its own administration and coined money. The Indo-Parthian kings followed this general pattern. The Indo-Parthians of this time ran three mints in different areas. One was in Taxila, which produced coins similar to the Bactrian Greek issues. Another mint was in Kandahar and the third was in Sistan (Parthian Sakastan). These mints struck coins that were typical Parthian silver drachmas with a royal portrait crowned with jewelled tiara decorated with small deer. The reverse had the king enthroned, crowned by Victory, complete with name and title of an Indo-Parthian king. But a rising power threatened this realm.

Rise of the Yuezhi Kushan Empire

In the second half of the first century AD, the Kushans had gained power in the Punjab and the Indo-Parthian kingdom recognized the Kushan great king. There were five tribes in the Bactrian Yuezhi confederation. The Chinese called them the Xiumi, Shuangmi, Xidun, Dumi and Guishuang. The Guishuang, the most important tribe, transliterates to Kushan. The first Kushan ruler who left a name was Heraios, who called himself a tyrant and produced Greek-style coins. While the rising Kushans absorbed Bactria and neighbouring areas, Bactrian Greeks descended into the Punjab and established new dominions. This age of the Kushans is very murky. A little of this fog cleared with the discovery in the late twentieth century of the Rabatak Inscription. The great Kushan king, Kanishka, installed a dedication inscription for a temple. The best guess is that Kanishka ruled about AD 127-163. The inscription names three predecessors, the Great King's father, grandfather and great grandfather. Heraios may be the founder of the line. This indicates that the Kushan Empire began to coalesce about the start of the era. Kanishka informs the reader that he is the king who decreed that the Arya language replace the Ionian language for official affairs. Modern commentators take this to mean that the Bactrian Iranian tongue replaced Greek. The inscription also lists the empire's extent: from Pataliputra in the Ganges through the Indus valley, north through the Khyber Pass and on to Bactria, Sogdiana and north-east to the Tarim Basin. The Kushan Empire had four capitals: Begram, Peshawar, Taxila and Mathura.

This was a very large area with a myriad of cultural traditions and religions. A princely burial at Tillya Tepe from about mid-first century AD contained artefacts which showed influences from the Far East, Mediterranean and Indian lands. Iranian and Greek motifs predominated, but in a highly original and competent way. Gold, precious stones and a Chinese mirror demonstrate a rich and vibrant culture. Jewellery found in Taxila has Greek, Persian and Indian motifs. Among the many traditions that swirled through the Kushan cities, Greek practices of individualism, rationalism and athletic prowess spread throughout Central Asia with their horses and sports. Iranian concepts of integrity and honour, revolving around the worship of Mithras, garnered the respect integrity evokes. Equally important, Buddhist ideas and monasteries had spread in India. Massive Buddhist establishments slowly grew in cities and the countryside, such as the monumental structures at Sanchi. Normally connected with lay settlements, the *sangha* (monks etc.) interconnected with neighbouring populations. In the first century AD, a new interpretation of Buddhism developed, Mahayana Buddhism. In these establishments, the *sangha* separated from the general laity and lived in separate compounds, often distant from urban settlements. During the Kushan Empire, many Buddhist congregations founded fortified *Viharas* (monasteries) in distant but strategic sites. One of the main objectives of the Buddhist understanding is developing discipline in which body function is put under the control of personal will. This is also recommended in older Indian traditions and spread into other traditions, but remains a main Buddhist objective.

The Coming of the Horse Lords

The Third Wave: the *Chevalier*

Central Asia was a unique land during the turn of the epoch. The ancient cities of the BMAC civilization still existed and held mixed populations of craftsmen, manufacturers and merchants from far and wide. Languages clashed in a chaos of sounds and cultures. But those used to such human environments had little problem speaking different tongues. The rulers were pastoral tribesmen who managed sophisticated literary bureaucracies and complex financial institutions. Between the cities and the rulers sat a group of merchant-warriors, the fighting men who lived on their ranches. They bred, trained and sold horses, all the while training their families and dependants as riders. The pastoralists also raised horses and they all knew how to ride well. But they were horse archers, light cavalry with spear or arrow, who manoeuvred like flocks of birds, twisting and turning, shooting and throwing at their enemies. Hand-to-hand combat was not to their taste.

Such combat took large, aggressive horses, ridden by powerful, disciplined men, proficient with the bow, of course, but also able with lance and sword. These were the horses and men that held the Central Asian complex together. Dynasties could change and new tribes could come; the ranchers sold them their horses so long as the coins were good, while at the same time the ranchers looked to their own interests, their ranching and farming estates. Here, developed the *Chevalier*, the heavy cavalry of the knights in armour. This was not a swift development but took generations, as the large Macedonian–Bactrian horses joined with strict riding and training methods to result in an ever more aggressive and dynamic horseman.

First, there had to be the horse, specially bred, trained by experts, handled delicately and with great care. Then there were fields of crops for horse feed. Grains that could feed whole households went to the horses. The warhorses needed alfalfa for energy and boldness, so fields grew alfalfa instead of food. All of this in terms of valuable land and labour was very expensive. The horse lord was rich and the horses' price had to cover these costs. If the horses were unusual, the men had to be extraordinary. Physically, they were big men, tall, muscular, hardy, fearless. These men wore expensive fitted armour of steel, leather and cloth, all of the best quality, to flash and dazzle in the sun. The introduction of Chinese high-grade steel meant that weapons were sharp and armour effective. The Central Asia mix of ideologies, customs, religions and ethnic characteristics allowed a broad spectrum of qualities that made a proper *Chevalier*.

The men were big and strong, but that was not enough. The Hellenic concept of athletic training and individual purpose gave direction to strength and agility. Each armoured man on his warhorse was a powerful figure, but such power brought responsibility. He had to act in accord with others, and together exercise authority. If they were not just fighting for fighting's sake, they needed direction. Here, in Central Asia, the divine Mithra, an Iranian and Indian figure of justice, was the focus of many *Chevaliers'* worship. Each *Chevalier* was seen to represent justice and righteousness. Another influence came from Buddhism. While Buddhism emphasizes peace and harmony, combat trainers have often found Buddhist discipline useful. The 'yoking' of personal physical activity to strict mental exercise produces extraordinary kinetic abilities. The *Chevalier*, practising the physical discipline of Indian spiritual tradition, became not simply another fighting man but a separate order of skilled and masterful warriors.

The *Chevalier* crystalized sometime after the beginning of the first century BC, after the Roman defeat of Mithridates VI and before the Parthian defeat of Crassus.

Indeed, it is the defeat of Crassus at Carrhae in which the *Chevalier* first appears in Classical sources. Our main source is probably Titus Livy, whose account is lost but was used by Dio Cassius and Plutarch. This battle demonstrates the new methods of combat tactics that made the *Chevalier* so effective. This is the great battle of Roman legions against Parthian cavalry in 53 BC. The Roman Triumvir, Marcus Crassus, led an army of some seven legions with auxiliary troops and allied cavalry to conquer the Parthian Empire. Trying to better Julius Caesar's conquest of Gaul, Crassus looked for vast wealth, many slaves and great power. The Parthian Empire, however, was not Gaul. The narrative:

> The Roman commander Crassus was unaware that the Parthians were nearby. Led by the grandee commander Suren, the Parthian force was entirely cavalry, some ten thousand light horse archers with a core of a thousand armoured aggressive cataphracts. As support, a caravan [of] thousands of camels carried supplies including large numbers of arrows for Suren's forces. When Crassus saw the position in which he suddenly found himself, he panicked. Instead of deploying in battle formation, infantry in centre, cavalry on wings which would allow manoeuvre in any direction, Crassus ordered the infantry to form a square, twelve cohorts to a side, providing cover for the rest of the legions and cavalry. This provided good protection but could move only slowly.
>
> Suren, seeing the enemies' army of nearly forty thousand men, infantry, cavalry, auxiliaries and supply troops while [himself] commanding some eleven thousand cavalry, decided to attempt to frighten the Romans. As the Parthians approached, the vanguard carried large kettle drums and played them loudly, sounding an ominous beat. The cataphracts had wraps covering their armour. When they closed to the Roman lines, they dropped the wraps and their armour suddenly gleamed in the sunlight. But the Romans did not flinch. The cataphracts wheeled about and rode back through the mass of horse archers. The horse archers split into smaller units and began to ride around the Roman square, shooting at vulnerable targets. Crassus sent out skirmishers to push the archers back but with the horsemen turning and riding to and fro, the skirmishers suffered more casualties than they dealt. The arrow storms rained against shields and armour doing little damage but hit enough arms and legs to discomfort the Romans. The Roman cohorts often charged out against the enemy horse but the Parthians eluded these attacks and continued shooting arrows.
>
> To protect his soldiers from the rain of arrows, Crassus ordered the cohorts making up the defensive square to form *testudo*, the cohorts

interlocking their shields in front, to the sides and on top, to protect against the constant missiles. While effective for such defence, the *testudo* allowed the armoured cavalry free access to attack and break up the formation. But when the cohorts reformed to counter the armoured cavalry, the horse archers started their arrow storms again, catching the Roman soldiers at an even greater disadvantage.

Scouts brought word about the camel caravan, so waiting for the archers to use up their arrows was not going to happen. Crassus organized an offensive force to drive off the horse archers but be strong enough to repel the armoured cavalry. Using an infantry corps of eight cohorts backed up by 500 foot archers and supported by 1,300 Gallic cavalry, Crassus sent out his son, Publius, to break the armoured cavalry and drive away the horse archers, destroying the caravan in the process. The horse archers withdrew from the Roman advance, still launching arrow storms, drawing Publius' force out into the countryside. Then, the armoured horsemen closed with the Gallic cavalry while the horse archers swarmed toward the Roman rear. The Parthian armoured cavalry crushed the Gallic cavalry, leaving the Roman foot isolated and vulnerable. The Romans attempted to rally on a hill top but the Parthians continued to slaughter them. Publius, it is said, managed to kill himself. The rest fell.

That his effort at breaking the Parthian hold had failed became obvious to Crassus. He ordered his army into battle formation and launched forward against the enemy. Surena was unimpressed. He ordered his horse archers into the Roman rear to continue the arrow storms while his armoured cavalry paraded to the front, following a standard made from a spear bearing Publius' head. Crassus lost heart. The Roman army panicked. The masses of men and animals fled toward the fortified town of Carrhae, leaving many thousands of wounded behind.

With the fall of night, many Roman soldiers, their officers, and Crassus reached Carrhae. The next day, Surena offered a truce in order to negotiate an evacuation of Parthian territory. Crassus was in no position to reject such negotiation, although he probably guessed what they would be like. Sure enough, at the meeting, the terms were simple: surrender or die. The Parthians cut down any member of Crassus' entourage who resisted and seized the rest. Seeing what was happening, many Romans tried to escape from Carrhae but it was hard to out-run the Parthian horsemen. Some 20,000 Romans died in the battle. Some 10,000 became Parthian slaves. Crassus was given a drink of molten gold so he could have his fill of Parthian treasure.

Significant points of this engagement include the spectacular armour of the cat-aphract horsemen and their disciplined manoeuvring, along with their ability to charge into the attack yet draw rein and pull back. Suren's *Chevalier* demonstrated a virtuosity of cavalry warfare not seen in the west since Philip and Alexander. Even more, Suren introduced the Mediterranean world to a method of warfare not seen before.

The Battle of Carrhae took place in northern Syria in 53 BC; just a few years later, in 36 BC, large armies fought another battle far to the east, near Lake Balkhash, at the western frontiers of the Chinese Central Asian protectorate. Here, we see the *Chevalier* in a much weaker stance, few in number and without strong support. Yet there is the same disciplined operation and thoughtful manoeuvre. The narrative is from the *Hanshu* and *Zizhi Tongjian*, probably based on Governor Gan Yanshou's official report:

The Imperial Han Protector of the Western Regions, Gan Yanshou, faced a rebellious Xiongnu prince, Zhizhi. This prince withdrew from his brother's dominion in 56 BC and led his followers westward. He united his force with the local Iranian Kangju people near Lake Balkhash but soon ruled them with a despotic hand. Zhizhi built a fortress capital near the Talas River, now Taraz. The Protector, stationed near the Jade Gate, saw Zhizhi's efforts as a mere distant distraction. But Gan's sub-ordinate commander, Chen Tang, claimed that Zhizhi wanted to seize all the Western Lands. Chen forced Gan's hand by taking on himself all responsibility with a forged imperial edict. Chen mobilized some 40,000 troops around a core unit of Chinese crossbowmen. Supporting troops consisted of local light cavalry and many supply troops, lightly armed but carrying heavy loads. Commander Chen divided his force for the long march from Gansu to the Talas River.

Marching along both sides of the Tarim Basin, Chen reunited his troops at Kashgar. From there, Chen continued on to the western shore of Lake Balkhash. While Chen's forces began to settle in, several thou-sand Kangju cavalry struck, scattering the supply troops and grabbing large amounts of food and many weapons. When the Kangju attacked again, Chen was ready. His crossbowmen suddenly shot barrages of bolts, bringing down over 400 Kangju and sending the rest away with a new lesson in tactics. Some 400 Wusun slaves of the Kangju joined Chen. A large contingent of Sogdians arrived to support the Chinese and fight the Xiongnu. Commander Chen then sent his supply troops back, having a strong enough force to maintain his supplies in the Balkhash region.

Some local Kangju nobles joined the Chinese forces, having had enough of the Xiongnu. With their advice, Chen advanced on Zhizhi's fortress and built a camp about a mile from the fortifications. Large flags bearing coloured figures waved over the fortress walls and armoured soldiers stood at the ready along those ramparts. The gates of the fort opened and an armoured cavalry force several hundred strong emerged, backed up by an infantry force in hedgehog formation with armour looking like fish scales. They marched toward the camp ramparts. The walls were lined with people shouting 'Fight! Fight!' The Han crossbowmen lined up in order, brought their crossbows to the ready and waited for the armoured cavalry and hedgehog infantry to approach. The horsemen stopped in their tracks when they saw the Han troops. The Chinese crossbows shot, hitting some horsemen and infantry, piercing their armour. The armoured horse and foot turned and entered the fort's gate. The Chinese followed, attempting to seize the palisade covering the entrance. They succeeded in setting the wood on fire but got no further.

That night, the cavalry force attempted to escape the fortress but the crossbowmen shot many of them down. The next morning Chinese soldiers attacked the gate. Advancing behind large shields, crossbowmen and spear throwers protected engineers who attempted to burn the doors of the gate. The attempt failed. Then Chen ordered a full siege of the fortress. The Chinese built a siege wall palisade around the fortress, facing both inward and outward. Archers on the wall top shot at the fort's defenders. The defenders attempted to throw flaming combustibles on to the siege walls but the archers killed many in this attempt.

The Chinese started to build a dirt siege ramp to top the walls. Zhizhi and his forces lined the walls, everyone, even his concubines, attempting to shoot arrows at the construction crew. But the crossbowmen on the siege walls swept the fortress walls clear, killing many and wounding Zhizhi in the nose. Zhizhi decided that the time to leave had come. At night with a force of his armoured cavalry, he managed to pass the siege wall palisade but the Sogdian soldiers, divided into dozens of units posted about the siege lines, intercepted Zhizhi and his companions and started to raise the alarm. Seeing forces collecting to attack him, Zhizhi turned around and re-entered the city.

In the morning, the Chinese began to shoot fire arrows into the fort, starting large fires. The Chinese and their Sogdian allies began to cheer. The beat of the war drums started and the attackers surged up the siege ramp, breaking into the fortress. Zhizhi and his remaining forces retreated into the citadel. While the Chinese began to construct a ramp against the citadel's walls, a force of Kangju cavalry attacked the Chinese.

The crossbowmen again repelled them with loss. Soon the ramp reached the top of the citadel walls and the infantry battered their way to the palace. Already burning, the palace provided little protection for Zhizhi and his men. The Han soldiers battered the door and set fire on it. A Han soldier killed Zhizhi with a spear and beheaded him. The Chinese beheaded 1,518 people including Zhizhi's concubines, his child and his officers. One hundred and forty-five men were taken prisoner and more than 1,000 made their submission and were parcelled out to the cities of the Tarim Basin as slaves. Gan Yanshou and Chen Tang returned to Chang'an the following spring with Zhizhi's head as a trophy.

Some Chinese commanders saw logistics as more important than subtle operations. Such was Chen Tang. Yet this allowed him to bring overwhelming force to his battle front. Horses were sparse in the Former Han armies, but their crossbow infantry were crack troops. So long as they had flank protection and a ready supply of bolts, they were invincible. Zhizhi simply did not have enough troops. Logistics and firepower defeated him. If there had been more armoured horsemen supported by mounted archers, they would have given the Chinese a very hard time.

We can see the *Chevalier* on the peripheries of the Central Asian land in the west and east. We have very little information about the constant battles within Central Asia. There was certainly constant friction and regime changes, but the towns and farmlands remained in business. Trade and manufacturing continued. Religious sacred places and institutions maintained themselves. But there is a source that seems to tell us about the *Chevalier*'s development.

An enduring feature of the emerging *Chevalier* was a surrounding aura of romanticism. Even as the aggressive armoured heavy cavalry emerged, we can see the birth of whole cycles of epic poetry celebrating the *Chevalier*. The epic narratives brought out the dilemmas caused by the mixture of power, justice, love and passion. Centred on the character of the *Chevalier*, parading the contradictions of ends and means, love and hate, the epics were a heady mixture of triumph and tragedy. The first great epic eventually grew into Ferdowsi's *Shahnameh*. Ferdowsi wrote his work about AD 1000. The series of tales runs from the Creation to the Arab conquest. This is not history but is based on a strong historical substructure. The text is often described as consisting of three main sections: the mythical age, the heroic age and the historical age. The heroic age is the longest section. It runs from the reign of King Manuchehr to the conquests of Eskander. Ferdowsi clearly sees Eskander as the Great Alexander. He draws much of his description of the conqueror from versions of the *Alexander Romance*. However, if we can see the figure of the conqueror in the sources behind Ferdowsi as the great Kushan King Kanishka, then the historical setting of the Heroic Age becomes much clearer.

The Age of Heroes takes place for the most part in Sistan, that is Sakastan. After about 150 BC, a group of Scythians invaded the Greek-Bactrian Kingdom. These became the Indo-Scythians or Saka, spread from this heartland of eastern Iran into Gandhara. But with the revival of the Parthian Empire under Mithradates II, about 100 BC, the House of Suren assumed command of the eastern marches. The ruler of the Parthians was King of Kings, the commander of the east was a king. While the storyline is complex, the kings in the east battled against evil forces in the area of the old Bactrian and Indian kingdoms. Their union under noble warriors seems to represent old traditions of the House of Suren. The scholar of Iranian traditions, Ernest Herzfeld, suggested that the great Suren, who defeated the Romans, is the historical basis for the hero Rostam. These are the beginnings of the *Chevalier*. The first time we can actually see *Chevalier* are those portrayed in the rock sculptures of the Tang-Ab gorge near Firuzabad in Fas. Here the Sassanid ruler, Ardashir I, killed the Arsacid Ardavan, and Ardashir's son, Shapur, killed the Parthian vizier in the Battle of Hormozgan in AD 226. The rising Sassanid Empire is a *Chevalier* state: a tempestuous federation of noble horse lords dominating merchant towns under a 'holy' royal ruler who is either a figurehead or a master soldier.

This epic tradition followed the *Chevalier* across the Mediterranean world and north into the west. With the reign of Constantine I, the *Chevalier* merged into the Christian traditions such as St George and others. In the north, with the emerging Germanic kingdoms came the *Songs of the Nibelung*, and beyond there are the tales of Arthur and his knights. In Gaul, which becomes France, there are the *chanson de geste*. The final compositions of all these epics are centuries from their settings, but they appear to begin with the arrival of the *Chevalier*. In the east, the *Chevalier* arrived at the end of the Later Han Dynasty. Rather than an epic poem or cycle of songs, there is a series of adventure stories finalized in Luo Guanzhong's *Three Kingdoms*.

References

Erich Anderson, *Cataphracts Knights of the Ancient Eastern Empires* (Barnsley, 2016).

D. Bivar, 'The Political History of Iran under the Arsacids', in *Cambridge History of Iran*, vol. 3 part 1 (Cambridge, 1983).

John Boardman, *The Greeks in Asia* (London, 2015).

Rai Govind Chandra, *Indo-Greek Jewellery* (New Delhi, 1979).

Vesta Sarkhosh Curtis (chief ed.), *The Parthian and Early Sasanian Empires: Adaptation and Expansion* (Oxford, 2016).

Vesta Sarkhosh Curtis and Sarah Stewart (eds), *The Age of the Parthians* (New York, 2010).

Vesta Sarkhosh Curtis and Sarah Stewart (eds), *The Sasanian Era* (New York, 2010).

Touraj Daryaee, *Sasanian Persia* (New York, 2009).

Kaveh Farrokh, *Sassanian Elite Cavalry AD 224-642* (Osprey, 2005).

Heleamor Feltham, 'Lions, Silks, and Silver: The Influence of Sasanian Persia', *Sino-Platonic Papers*, 2010.

Lars Fogelin, *An Archaeological History of Indian Buddhism* (Oxford, 2015).

Lars Fogelin, *Archaeology of Early Buddhism* (New York, 2006).

Richard Frye, 'The Political History of Iran under the Sasanians', in *Cambridge History of Iran*, vol. 3 part 1 (Cambridge, 1983).

John Grainger, *Rome, Parthia and India: The Violent Emergence of a New World Order 150-140 BC* (Barnsley, 2013).

Janos Harmatta (chief ed.), *History of Civilizations of Central Asia*, vol. II, *The Development of Sedentary and Nomadic Civilizations: 700 BC to AD 250* (UNESCO, Paris, 1994).

Hyun Jin Kim, *The Huns* (New York, 2016).

Raoul McLaughlin, *The Roman Empire and the Indian Ocean: The Ancient World Economy and the Kingdoms of Africa, Arabia and India* (Barnsley, 2014).

Raoul McLaughlin, *The Roman Empire and the Silk Routes: The Ancient World Economy and the Empires of Parthia, Central Asia and Han China* (Barnsley, 2016).

Daniel Michon, *Archaeology and Religion in early Northwest India* (New Delhi, 2015).

Gareth Sampson, *The Defeat of Rome: Crassus, Carrhae and the Invasion of the East* (Barnsley, 2008).

Vincent Smith, 'The Kushan or Indo-Scythian Period of Indian History, BC 165 to AD 320', *Journal of the Royal Asiatic Society*, 14 January 1925.

Li Shimin's Horses

'Horses are the military preparedness of the state; if Heaven takes this preparedness away, the state will totter to a fall.'

Tangshu, 36, 3718d

The House of Li claimed descent from noble Han families. In part, that may well be true, but they also came from steppe antecedents. This was no secret. Anyone at the time of Li Yuan and Li Shimin who might be interested in such things would know all about the House of Tang. The Later Han commentators said the Xianbei weapons were sharper and their horses stronger than the Xiongnu, whom they defeated and pushed out of power. The Xianbei's powerful tribes fought for supremacy, but rather than forming a united polity, the tribal confederation fragmented in about AD 235. By 317, Xianbei tribes, led by the Tuoba, overthrew the Jin Dynasty's dominions along the Yellow River (the Western Jin, 265-316), pushing the Chinese court south to the Yangzi (the Eastern Jin, 317-420). The Tuoba Xianbei continued to fight among themselves, forming a series of ephemeral dynasties until they established the Northern Wei (386-535).

The Northern Wei horsemen held their empire together, but fractious as ever, the horsemen continued to fight among themselves. The Northern Wei tried to turn themselves into Chinese, but administrative disruption and crop failures hit hard. In 534-535, the Northern Wei collapsed into the Western and Eastern Wei, and then became the Northern Zhou and Northern Qi (550-557). With the rise of the Sui, the northern horse lord family, the House of Li, became governors in Shensi, under Li Yuan.

The House of Li's main source of power was its capacity to mobilize and manoeuvre large formations of horses. Their family members were raised with horses and appreciated fine horse flesh. After he became emperor, Li Shimin did not forget the valiant steeds which carried him into battle. As part of his imperial tomb, Emperor Shimin commissioned sculptures of six of these beasts. Along with these sculptures, Li Shimin wrote accompanying poetic verses describing these horses. Li Shimin wrote the following: 'When I engaged in military campaigns, these war chargers carried me, rushing against the enemy. They broke the enemy's lines and rescued me from perils. Their accurate images are to be portrayed on stone and be placed left and right on my tomb demonstrating the beauty of "'curtain and cover".' (The old chariot masters used to save their chariot curtains and covers for the burial of their horses to show affection and respect.)

The emperor commissioned Yan Lide to direct the construction of his mausoleum. Yan Lide's brother, Yan Liben, a famous court painter, made coloured drawings of the six horses chosen by the emperor. Imperial artists carved the reliefs following the drawings. Both the sculptures and a copy of the original drawing exist.

The six horses in chronological order were:

1. Baidiwu, a black horse with four white feet, called the 'white hoofed crow'. In one night, the horse carried Li Shimin for 65 miles during the war with Xue Renguo (AD 618).

'With a sword long enough to touch the sky,
This swift steed could run with the wind;
On one gallop, I recovered Gansu.
I returned after bringing peace to Shu with one look from the saddle.'

2. Telebiao, a yellow and white horse with a slight black snout. Li Shimin rode him against Song Jingang. The horse is pictured walking on an icy road full of confidence (AD 619).

'When whipped the horse reared into the air.
The noise of the horse's neighing reached half the land.
Rushing toward danger the horse bore down on the enemy.
The horse appeared at the critical moment and saved the day.'

3. Saluzi, Autumn Dew the Whirlwind Victory, a large bay horse. At the siege of Luoyang, the horse was hit by an arrow in battle. Qiu Xinggong gave his horse to Li Shimin and walked the horse back to Tang lines. The sculpture shows Qiu Xinggong pulling out the arrow (AD 612).

'The horse was as restless as a purple swallow,
The horse pranced with high spirits;
The horse was feared in the region of Three Rivers,
The horse struck awe into the enemy on all battlefields.'

4. Qingzhui, a piebald coloured horse. In the battles with Dou Jiande, the animal survived five arrow wounds to his front (AD 621).

'Light footed, a streak of lightening,
This horse was full of energizing spirits.
I whipped up this flying steed,
And so I was able to lay down my armour.'

5. Shifachi, a brick red horse. Fought in wars with Dou Jiande and Wang Shichong, defeating two enemies in one battle (AD 621).

'There was trouble in the lands of the Chan and Jian Rivers,
With poleaxes and battleaxes, I showed my power;
In red sweat, this horse dashed forward,
Under the green flag, our army returned,
Singing the song, Victory.'

6. Quanmaogua, a saffron yellow coloured horse with a curly coat. Fought in battle against Liu Heida. The horse is pictured walking briskly forward despite severe arrow wounds, six in front, three in back (AD 622).

'The moon rabbit grabbed the bridle,
The stars of Scorpio crossed the heaven in their course,
The Dog Star announced the halt,
The dusty mist brought the end.'

There is a discussion about Eurasian influences in the depiction of Li Shimin's horses. The horses are shown made up with crenellated manes, tied-up tails, round stirrups and five striped saddles. A very similar make-up for warhorses is found in the great Sassanian reliefs near Persepolis. Of course, the decoration of horses may be similar without a direct influence. Most probably, although speculative at this time, both Sassanian and Tang styles reflect the milieu of some centrally located tradition in Central Asia.

Besides his six chargers, late in his reign Li Shimin chose ten horses to exhibit excellence in horses. The Turks had sent 100 choice beasts to the emperor as personal tribute. Out of the 100, Shimin choose ten as particularly excellent for his own use. He named them Frost Prancing White, Shining Snow Grizzle, Frozen Dew Grizzle, Suspended Light Grizzle, Wave Plunging Bay, Sunset Flying Roan, Lighting Darting Red, Flowing Gold Yellow, Soaring Unicorn Purple and Running Rainbow Red.

The Tang Dynasty's quest for power started from the back of a horse.

References

Edward Schafer, *The Golden Peaches of Samarkand: A Study of T'ang Exotics* (University of California, 1963) ('Horses' chapter).

Xiuqin Zhou, *Zhaoling:* 'The Mausoleum of Emperor Tang Taizong', *Sino-Platonic Papers*, No. 187, April 2009.

Appendix 9

Chinese Imperial Armies

The First Armies: Nobles and Chariots

The large agrarian settlements along the Yellow River and its tributaries fought with each other in the third millennium BC. They built walls and battled with hand weapons of wood, stone and copper. Sometime in the second millennium, chariot warfare entered the lands. Lords of chariot armies centralized administrations and began building strong kingdoms. About 1100 BC, Chinese civilization began crystalizing when Zhou chariot lords defeated the older Shang chariot armies. The new Zhou Empire spread along the Yellow River to the ocean. On the steppe border with northern China, nomadic tribes developed light cavalry with composite bows. In 771 BC, such horsemen ended the Western Zhou Dynasty by plundering their capital in Guanzhong. The succeeding Eastern Zhou Dynasty disintegrated into a series of successor states. These states still used chariots but were developing strong infantry armies. The large infantry armies, built around units of heavy armoured infantry, easily defended themselves against chariots. Even more importantly, the rise of the peasant soldiers displaced the foundations of the horse-drawn war wagons. The reasons for this development have to do with economics and social class.

Each chariot needs two horses to operate and another two or three as replacements. For a force of 500 chariots, commanders need somewhere around 3,000 horses. Some of those carried supplies for the rest, but pack animals do not do well as war horses. These horses needed many thousand acres of suitable pasture. Warhorses need grain feed besides pasture. Total food for a 1,000lb horse per day is some 25lb of forage and some grain. Further, each horse needs some ten gallons of water per day. To raise horses meant that land that could support a peasant family was needed to support a horse. By raising large infantry armies from farmer-soldiers, the states of the Spring and Autumn Age utilized their resources to increase their military force while breaking up the large aristocratic estates needed to support chariot warfare.

Chinese Infantry Armies

From the Age of the Warring States, Chinese rulers deployed large infantry armies, made up of armoured heavy infantry, crossbowmen, archers and light skirmishers.

These massive armies replaced the older chariot forces of the Shang and Western Zhou dynasties as part of the social developments which saw the patrimonial systems of aristocratic lineages replaced by autocratic monarchs who depended on an appointed bureaucracy. Chinese metallurgists, working in bronze, extended their expertise to iron during the Early Zhou Dynasty. Quench-hardened steel appeared by the early Han Dynasty and was soon mass produced. Used in weapons and armour, the armies of major states were better armed than the smaller states which could not mass-produce high quality steel.

The monarchies rested their support on settlements (*yi*) of monogamous nuclear families. These settlements divided their agricultural lands into equal shares, based on marking fields with balks (a raised strip of ground that separates fields into plough routes which are assigned to individual families living in the village that holds the land; balks are ploughed under after harvest and constructed anew before sowing) that were long and narrow, and assigning these sections to individual families. When sons reached adulthood, the state required them to establish their own households. Officials oversaw these settlements and used them as the base of taxation and conscription. Each district had a main fortified town that was the seat of administration and held storehouses for commodities collected as tax.

To defend against nomad raiders, many states fortified their frontiers. They constructed long walls, manned by infantry. Certain northern states found the idea of light cavalry very useful, both to track raiders as scouts, and as skirmishers in the wars with their neighbours. According to tradition, King Wuling of Zhao formed the first official cavalry unit in 307 BC when he decreed that soldiers should wear 'nomadic dress and learn horse archery'. But such forces remained small.

Imperial Forces

Holding the 'Land within the Passes', the state of Qin adopted a policy of emphasizing agricultural development, based on peasant smallholdings, and powerful infantry armies. The peasant soldiers were disciplined and drilled. Qin metallurgists supplied the soldiers with excellent steel weapons and armour. The great infantry armies of Qin ended the Age of Warring States by establishing the First Emperor's dominion (221 BC). To deal with the steppe nomads, the First Emperor rebuilt the long walls and connected them together. As the Chinese state prospered under the Qin and Han (founded 206 BC), steppe nomads also consolidated under the dominion of the Xiongnu. The Xiongnu dominion extended from Korea to the oasis of Central Asia. Large masses of light cavalry archers swept across the frontiers of China, challenging the infantry armies and plundering the northern commanderies. The Qin and early Han dynasties maintained equal conscript infantry forces, but after the reign of the Han Emperor Wu (180-157 BC), the Han regime slowly allowed the growth of large holdings. The Han emperors awarded *mingtian-zhai* allotments to deserving individuals. These awards did not give ownership of the land but allowed the recipient to receive the revenue. The income produced the wherewithal for the recipients to acquire farmland as property. As the Han Dynasty continued (71 BC–AD 13), the power of the administration weakened. The great landholders, *Haozu*, were powerful magnates. The operative factor that caused this change was the introduction of warhorses by Emperor Wu (reigned 141-87 BC).

Wu believed that he needed to improve his horse stock and sent expeditions to Central Asia to bring back a special breed of horse known as the Ferghana horse, or the Horses that Sweat Blood (汗血馬), pinyin, *hànxuèmǎ*. This is not an indication of some infection but is an attempt to write the sound of the horse's name in Chinese. Of course, as a battle mount, after exertion in fighting the horse would end up with blood on its coat, hopefully that of the enemy, and so sweat blood, which fitted the sound. Part of the effort to secure breeding stock was the equally important import of alfalfa, a rich ground growth that is useful in energizing horses to be more active and aggressive. Feeding riding or work horses alfalfa is never a good idea because these animals need calmness to do their job, but it makes forceful and dynamic warhorses. Representations in Chinese pictures and statues, as well as Bactrian coins, show horses with powerful chests, short thick legs and heavy rounded rumps. Some suggest the modern Chinese sub-breed, *Guoxia* (under the Fruit [tree]), is the Ferghana steed, but the breed is not recognized by Western horse breed registries, which consider the Ferghana horse extinct.

A cavalry unit, using arrows and shock tactics, could easily defeat an unprepared infantry force, with the result that cavalry commanders were in demand at court. Even more important, the cavalry commander was closely connected to horse ranches. The equal field system was not going to raise horses, because raising horses is very different from the small single household farming. To keep a horse is not easy, and is expensive in terms of time, feed and land for pasture. A horse takes constant care and attention. While the animals look strong, they are actually fragile. They can live, barring disease and accidents, for a little more than thirty-five years. The horse can pull a plough or wagon, or carry a rider. But that horse is no warhorse. Horse ranchers need good pasture lands to raise warhorses, and must have large herds. Selective breeding is necessary to get the best animals, and only experienced people who know and are good with horses can break them to the saddle and train them for war. Moreover, their warrior riders need to grow up with the beasts, riding before they walk.

The horse ranches needed to raise three types of horses: heavy warhorses for armoured riders, light fast horses for mounted archers and pack horses for everyday transport. That way, the animals are familiar with the animals around them.

Each armoured rider needs four or five backup horses on the ranch, and has to take at least two with him on expeditions. His entourage – assistant in training, armourer, cook-washer and perhaps others – each need two transport animals, one to ride and a pack animal. In all, such a ranch raises thousands of horses, with farmlands to grow horse feed and the food necessary to feed the staff, which may approach 1,000 people. This is a large estate. The economy of the early Han Dynasty changed after the reign of Emperor Wu. The single household redistributed farms remained, but a new economic–social class arose, the magnates. These people controlled large estates, and we may presume many of these estates raised warhorses. The imperial Han found the cavalry soldiers useful on the northern frontiers and the western regions, but saw the growth of powerful magnate houses a threat to imperial unity and Ruist thought. From one decade to the next after Emperor Wu, the emperors tried to squeeze out the great houses in favour of the peasantry. However, their need for military might often force the emperors to call upon the help that only the great houses could supply. Ultimately, this conflict of interests brought down the Former Han regime.

The New Dynasty (AD 9-23)

An imperial relative, Wang Mang, took over and founded the Xin (New) Dynasty (AD 9-23). He tried to make massive reforms, abolishing the Han nobility, redistributing land and not allowing private land ownership or slavery. The reforms upset economic processes, famine came, and corrupt, incompetent officials were unable to relieve the distress. Massive revolts broke out, which sputtered for years until they united under the leadership of cadet branches of the House of Liu. The Battle of Kunyang on 7 July AD 23 ended the Xin Dynasty and so marks the beginning of the Later Han Dynasty. The new Han Emperor Gengshi mobilized a small but powerful army based on an armoured cavalry force. Wang Mang raised a million men, of whom some 420,000 were trained infantry; the rest were supply troops. Wang Mang issued orders for scholars, who mastered the books of military strategy to form the military staff. Nevertheless, the Han force cut up and decimated Wang Mang's large infantry army, which could not stand up to the Han heavy cavalry.

Later Han Dynasty (AD 23-220)

Emperor Gengshi (23-25) was soon deposed and replaced by Emperor Guangwu (25-57). Unlike the Former Han Dynasty, the Later Han emperors were never very strong. The realm often remained in the hands of the magnates managing child or inept emperors. The magnates held the northern frontiers, raiding the nomads just as often as the nomads raided the Chinese settlements. Different factions struggled for control of the imperial administration and the imperial army. The army consisted of three main organizations: first, there were the frontier garrisons, backed up by magnate cavalry, ostensibly commanded by imperial appointees; second, the Northern Army, a powerful cavalry force with an infantry component, guarded the capital, Luoyang; and third, in the south, along the Yangzi, units of the Southern army guarded the land. This was a conscript infantry force with a river-borne naval component.

The inability of factions in the capital to agree on consistent and effective policies, added to natural flood disasters, created widespread unrest along the Yellow River. A vast peasant uprising, the Yellow Turbans, swept across China. Local leaders rose in the towns, mobilized cavalry forces and broke the rebellion over a number of years. Commanders of frontier armies, units of the Northern Army and forces of local potentates struggled for control. Armies fought with each other in large, wide-ranging battles. Light and aggressive armoured cavalry, light and heavy infantry, along with river-borne water forces struggled for years. In 207, Cao Cao defeated the horse nomads, the Wuhuan, at the Battle of White Wolf Mountain. The Wuhuan horsemen then joined with Cao Cao, giving him a powerful cavalry force.

By 220, Cao Cao's Kingdom of Wei held the Yellow River valley; Sun Quan's Kingdom of Wu held the Yangzi River to the sea; and Liu Bei's Kingdom of Shu held Sichuan. Wei's cavalry could not overcome Wu and Shu's river forces. So began the age of the Three Kingdoms.

The Three Kingdoms fought each other in devastating wars: the Wei with their cavalry; the Wu behind their river defences; and the Shu huddled in their mountain fastness. Wei accepted many tribes of nomad horsemen to settle in their lands. The head of the Wei armies overthrew the dynasty and founded the Western Jin (265). The Jin Dynasty united both the Yellow River valley and the Yangzi valley, along with Sichuan, restoring unity to China. Reorganizing river and flood management, restoring irrigation in many places, the Jin brought prosperity to the land. To maintain their predominance, the Jin allowed evermore nomad immigration into the Yellow River area, so in some places there were more nomads than Han peoples. To solidify his power, the founding Jin emperor appointed his brothers and sons as local princes, thus decentralizing military control. This worked well for him, but in the hands of his weak successor lead to the War of the Eight Princes (301–305), a violent and destructive series of events.

Nomadic Invasions and Chaos

Different Jin princes depended on nomad cavalry for support. Moreover, just at this time, stirrups become common. The force of aggressive cavalry manoeuvres was multiplied and the horsemen became even stronger. The nomad cavalry simply took over and began fighting among themselves, overthrowing Jin rule in the north. Later Chinese historians called this event 'the Uprising of the Wu Hu', Wu Hu being the 'Five Barbarians'. These were the Xiongnu, who had fought the Han Dynasty, their allies the Jie, the Xianbei – a Mongolian peoples who fought the Xiongnu – the Di and the Qiang, Tibetan-Burmese peoples to the west and south. Equally, there is the possibility that many of these people in these groups were Turkic. The devastating warfare caused the hydraulic control systems along the Yellow River to collapse. The result was plague, famine, even cannibalism.

Many Chinese officials, landowners and merchants fled to the Yangzi valley in a development called 'Garments and headdresses move south'. The north shattered into the Sixteen Kingdoms and constant war. The refugees in the south set up the Eastern Jin Dynasty (316-420), always hoping to return north. The wars in the north were destructive, killing tens of thousands of people at a time, sacking cities and forcing hundreds of thousands of people to migrate hundreds of miles. The land was desolate, except for fortified manor houses protecting sheltered farms. Different northern warlords tried to conquer the south, but trained infantry armies successfully defended the water crossings. Southern Jin commanders launched large forces north, but cavalry armies stymied their efforts.

The Tuoba clan, part of the Xianbei people, founded the Northern Wei Dynasty in 386. Their heavy cavalry had swept away numerous small regimes. The establishment of the Northern Wei marks the beginning of the end of the Sixteen Kingdoms and the start of the Northern and Southern Dynasties. The Northern Wei maintained strong Xianbei traditions and manners. Slowly they became Chinese, requiring their notables to speak and dress as Chinese. From initially a Shamanistic-Daoist formal religion, the Wei became strong supporters and patrons of Buddhist practices. They united northern China by 439, but strong opposition grew in their own ranks because the tribesmen of the Tuoba forces opposed the Chinese orientation of their rulers. The Wei Dynasty moved their capital to Luoyang in 494. They had encouraged intermarriage of noble Wei families with the older noble Chinese families. Taking the Eight Noble Names, the highest Wei nobility all changed their names to Chinese. The Wei cavalry, originally tribal units, slowly became noble *Chevalier*, based on Iranian and Central Asian architypes, as we see in contemporary pictures and statues.

Peace and order was not the *Chevalier* way. In 523, great rebellions broke out and after much struggle, the empire split into Eastern and Western Wei in 534-535. In this series of conflicts, a warlord *Chevalier*, Yuwen Tai (507-556), emerged. His line, Xianbei-Chinese, founded the Northern Zhou (557-581). Among his many horse lord supporters we find the families of Puliuru Jian, who as Emperor Wen founded the Sui Dynasty, and Li Hu, who became the first Lord of Tang.

Tang Armed Forces Organization

Armed Forces

Li Yuan, Lord of Tang, took over the existing military structures and organized them to fit his needs.

The Northern Zhou, during the chaos of the Northern Dynasties period, established military colonies of Chinese farmer warriors called the *fubing* system. The men were well-trained soldiers who settled in special villages and received generous 'equal field' allotments. Near a group of these villages, there was a military headquarters which commanded all the men in the villages. These settlements were part of the administrative structure of the northern commanderies. Along with the infantry units in many commanderies, the Tang organized 'loose rein' or 'bridle' commanderies. These, only on the northern frontier, supplied the horses and horsemen who were such an important factor in the early Tang Dynasty.

The *fubing* headquarters drew men from the village and organized them into provisional units. The *dui* was the basic unit building block. A *dui* consisted of fifty men, either foot or horse, and stood five ranks deep. Five officers commanded, headed by the *duitou*, assisted by a *fu duitou*, with a standard bearer, *qitou zhiqi* and two colour guards, *qianqi*. A minimum of six *dui* made a *tong*. Five *dui* stood in the *tong* and one *dui* protected the baggage. Once called and accepted, the men marched to their appointed field army.

Once the men reached the field army, the field commanders reshuffled the *dui* and presumably individual personnel. Men were swordsmen, crossbowmen, archers and cavalry. They were either assault troops or manoeuvre troops. They were joined together in *dui* that matched their classification. The *dui* were grouped as spearheads, combat experts and support troops. Within the *tong*, there was one *dui* spearhead, two *dui* combat, two *dui* support and one *dui* baggage guard. Commanders collected *tongs* together to build a unit of about 1,000 soldiers, called a *ying*. A number of *yings* together was a *jun*, or army. Commanders added to their professional soldiers conscripts from the general populace. These people were given spears and shields and a little training, but for the most part conscripts carried loads and dug ditches.

Chinese commanders gave a great deal of attention to logistics. Standard texts said that each fighting man should receive 2 *sheng* (1.2kg) a day of hulled grain or millet. We should note that this is some 4,000 calories, enough for at least three people. This would indicate that each fighting man had at least two assistants, perhaps picked up from the conscripts. Each group of ten fighting men carried a foot-driven pestle. Even more important than the men were the horses. Men who are overworked and starved generally recover with rest and recuperation. This is not so with horses. The cavalry masters must keep the animals fit. Once over-used, the horses become useless for military purposes. Each day, a horse needs 1 *dou* (5kg) of unhulled grain, plus two bundles of hay. In summer, in the right places, horses can be left to pasture, but pastured horses are not as strong as feed beasts. Besides cavalry mounts, Tang armies allotted six pack animals to each group of ten fighting men. When animals were not available or for extra supplies, the Chinese wheelbarrow allowed one man to push, over fairly level ground, some 120kg. Water for man and beast was always necessary and often determined where armies marched to get to their destinations.

Weapons

Chinese society was armed. Most men trained in hand-to-hand martial arts as boys. Civilians could have certain weapons, particularly swords, bows and short spears. Training in the use of these weapons was a normal part of their upbringing. Weapons classed as military were outlawed to civilians. These included crossbows, long-bladed pikes and armour, particularly horse armour.

Soldiers used many of the same weapons. The old Han Dynasty straight two-edged sword (*jian*) went out of style and was replaced by the sabre (*dao*). While the sabre is most useful from horseback, even foot soldiers carried them. The sabres' length varied from waist-worn swords to long swords carried horizontally on horseback. Soldiers often carried both sword and shield. Both horse and foot carried a long pole tipped with a sabre called a *chang dao*, or poll sabre. Lines of infantry carried pikes, but instead of the older long leaf-shaped blade, the Sui and Tang armies carried pikes with short thick steel spearheads. Cavalry carried lances with similar heads. Heavy cavalry used *qiang shuo*, 18ft-long lances. Both horse and foot were trained archers. Each *fubing* soldier carried a bow with thirty arrows. These bows were of mulberry wood (*sangzhe*). Horse archers carried composite reversed bows made of horn. Sometimes these archers dismounted to shoot, with a range of some 280ft. Entrenched and wall-defending armoured infantry used crossbows, high-powered but with short range.

Protection

Chinese armies had armoured infantry since the Age of Warring States. By the Sui Dynasty, armoured infantry had suits of 'plaque and cord' armour. These were made of front and back plates made of iron connected by laminar bound together with strong cords. Below the hips, broad skirts protected the legs. The soldier had an iron helmet and a large shield. Besides units of heavy infantry, there were many other units with lesser amounts of armour. The supply troops had none.

There were two types of cavalry. *Yue Ji* were light cavalry, mounted archers, with little armour and small circular shields. *Wu Ji* were heavy cavalry, riders armoured in a cuirassier with an enclosed iron helmet. Their horses were also armoured. This armour consisted of bardings covering the horse's neck and front, draped across the rump, and extended down to cover the legs. We must note that bardings were heavy; commanders only ordered their units barded when close combat faced them. For normal service, the horse had a body harness which could hold bardings but allowed the animal normal movement. The rider still wore armour and participated in raids and skirmishes, so there are not two types of heavy cavalry as some contend, but different war dress for close battle and open actions.

Command and Control

Chinese commanders communicated their orders by sound and visual signals. Drums were the main method of signalling, along with horns and gongs. Drums sounded the advance; horns gave specific orders. Each *tong* had twelve drums, twelve horns and five different colours of flags. Horn blasts, by the numbers, told the direction of march. When drums sounded, soldiers were to look at the yellow flags at the tong commander's position. When the yellow flag dropped forward and the drums rolled in unison, the soldiers shouted, 'Wuhu! Wuhu!' together, moving forward. When the drums rolled very fast, the soldiers charged the enemy lines, shouting, 'Kill! Kill!' From the march, when the first horn call sounded, the soldiers stopped and raised spears. At the second horn call, soldiers planted spears pointing front, furled banners, strung bows and drew sabres. The third horn call commanded soldiers to raise points of spears to make a spear wall. At the fourth horn call, soldiers braced spears and knelt. At the sound of the gong, soldiers stopped shouting, shouldered spears and fell back. To execute tactical manoeuvres successfully, each unit needed to drill until such actions became automatic.

The key to a successful army is the quality of its officers. In medieval China, an officer had to demonstrate that he could lead his men by being in the front of the battle line. This demanded strength, guile and a commanding presence. However, good officers also had to read documents. Organization requires lists: lists of men, equipment, supplies, units and officers. It may be that some officers had educated assistants who read such documents to them but would hand to others the authority, which was the officer's alone. A good officer, especially a high commander, needed to read. While many direct, demanding people find intellectual speculation and discussion a waste of good time, few of them pass up a useful *How to Do It* book. The Chinese military handbook is exceedingly useful. The main text, often presented under the name of a Spring and Autumn sage, Sun the Master, is a brilliant discussion of how to manage warfare. Concise but explicit, we can see its influence through Chinese history.

Conclusion

The great wars of conquest that swept across the Chinese lands in the early seventh century were not the only such wars at that time. The clans of horse lords slowly spread through Eurasia, in the service of different states and tribal confederations. The Turks, experts in horse breeding and iron metal working, conquered Central Asia, overthrowing the Hephthalite Empire and establishing a number of nomadic states in Inner Asia. The Gupta Empire in India lost control, only to be succeeded by a series of warring states. The Sassanid Empire fought a long and bitter war with the Byzantines, who were already involved in terrible civil strife. Italy, Gaul and Britain were the site of a myriad of chaotic small wars. An explosive growth of Arab tribes and towns had begun to create unrest in the Arabian Peninsula. From small specialized groups of soldiers, the horse lords grew into dominating clans, their influence spreading with their horse-raising manors and fortified houses.

China's journey from chaos to order led Li Shimin, Emperor Taizong, to work toward settling his realm into peaceful patterns of life. The emperor's armies defeated the Eastern Turks in 629, after which he assumed the title of Tian Kehan, Divine Khan of the Eastern Turks, who recognized him as their khagan. Taizong, at the same time, established Buddhist monasteries at the sites of his major battles with the charge to pray for the souls of the fallen from both sides. His realm prospered; his people did well. Emperor Taizong died in 649. His son, Gaozong, succeeded Taizong and ruled until 683. One of Taizong's concubines became Gaozong's empress, and after his death became regent for child emperors, but then assumed the throne as emperor of the Zhou Dynasty. She became seriously ill and her regime collapsed in confusing court intrigue in 705. Her son by Gaozong became Emperor Zhongzong of the Tang Dynasty (ruled 705-710). While the court intrigues never stopped, the empire remained peaceful in the Chinese lands and waged successful wars on the frontiers.

As the decades passed, the *fubing* settlements and the imperial heavy cavalry connected to them disappeared, replaced by professional infantry soldiers and nomadic cavalry. The imperial government abolished all the remaining *fubing* settlements by 750. The imperial administration saw these developments as cost-effective while still providing security. The men who held the swords and shields did not agree. By 756, a great rebellion began ripping through the empire under An Lushan. The men on horseback despised the men in robes. The rebellions finally ended, but the problem remained: how could a civilian farming state accommodate the military power that cavalry provided without coming under the horse lords' domination? The recurrent theme played itself out many times, the most significant being the Song succumbing to the northern tribes and then the Mongols, and the Ming succumbing to the Qing.

References

Nicola Di Cosmo, *Ancient China and Its Enemies* (Cambridge UK, 2002).

Albert Dien, *Six Dynasties Civilization* (New Haven, 2007).

Albert Dien, 'The Stirrup and its Effect on Chinese Military History', available online, *Silk Road Foundation*.

Richard von Glahn, *The Economic History of China* (Cambridge UK, 2016).

David Graff, *Medieval Chinese Warfare* (London, 2002).

Mark Edward Lewis, *China between Empires* (Cambridge MA, 2009).

Mark Edward Lewis, *The Early Chinese Empires, Qin and Han* (Cambridge MA, 2007).

Xiaobing Li, *China at War* (Santa Barbara, 2012).

Chris Peers, *Battles of Ancient China* (Barnsley, 2013).

Arthur Waldron, *The Great Wall of China* (Cambridge UK, 1990).

Bibliography

Chinese Sources

Suishu, Weishu; Zhoushu; Jiu Tangshu (*Old Book of Tang*); *Xin Tangshu* (*New Book of Tang*); Wen Daya, *Da Tang Chuangye Qiju Zhu* (*Court Diary of the Founding of the Great Tang*); *Zizhi Tongjian.*

The Chronicle of Fu Chien, a Case of Exemplar History, translated and anointed with prolegomena, Michael C. Rogers (Berkeley, 1985).

Language Reference Books:

Harbaugh, Rick, *Chinese Characters: A Genealogy and Dictionary* (Yale, 2009).

Huang, Quanyu, *et al*, *McGraw-Hill's Chinese Dictionary and Guide* (New York, 2010).

Kroll, Paul, *A Student's Dictionary of Classical and Medieval Chinese* (Leiden, 2015).

Multi-volume sets:

Cambridge History of China, Denis Twitchett and John Fairbanks (eds) (Cambridge UK, 1979). Specifically vol. 3, Denis C. Twitchett (ed.), *Sui and Tang China, 589-906 AD, part 1, Political History.*

History of Chinese Civilization, Yuan Xingrei, Yan Wenming, Zhang Chuanxi, Lou Yulie (eds), (Chinese original, Peking University Press, Beijing). English translation (Cambridge UK, 2012). Specifically vol. III, Yuan Xingpei (ed.), *Sui and Tang to mid-Ming Dynasties.*

History of Civilizations of Central Asia, H. Dani (ed.), vol. I; Janos Harmatta (ed.), vol. II; B.A. Litvinsky (ed.), vol. III; M.S. Asimov (ed.), vol. IV (Paris, 1996-98).

History of Imperial China, Timothy Brook (ed.) (Cambridge US, 2009-10);

vol. 2, Mark Lewis, *China between Empires: The Northern and Southern Dynasties*; vol. 3, Mark Lewis, *China's Cosmopolitan Empire: The Tang Dynasty.*

Modern Works:

Anderson, Erich, *Cataphracts: Knights of the Ancient Eastern Empires* (Barnsley, 2016).

Anthony, David, *The Horse, the Wheel, and Language: How Bronze-Age Riders from the Eurasian Steppe Shaped the Modern World* (Princeton, 2007).

Barnes, Gina, *Archaeology of East Asia: The Rise of Civilization in China, Korea, and Japan* (Havertown PA, 2015).

Baumer, Christopher, *The History of Central Asia: The Age of the Silk Road* (London, 2014).

Beckwith, Christopher, *Empires of the Silk Road* (Princeton NJ, 2009).

Benjamin, Craig, *The Yuezhi Migration and Sogdia* (online, Creative Commons, 2003).

Bielenstein, Hans, *The Restoration of the Han Dynasty* (Stockholm, 1953).

Bingham, Woodbridge, *The Founding of the T'ang Dynasty: The Fall of Sui and the Rise of T'ang, a Preliminary Survey* (Baltimore, 1941).

Bivar, D., 'The Political History of Iran under the Arsacids', in *Cambridge History of Iran*, vol. 3 part 1 (Cambridge, 1983).

Boardman, John, *The Greeks in Asia* (London, 2015).

Bueno, Andre, 'Roman Views of the Chinese in Antiquity', *Sino-Platonic Papers*, No. 261 May 2016.

Cernenko, E.V., *The Scythians* (Oxford, 1983). Translated from Russian. E.V. Cernenko was Head of the Scythian Department of the Archaeological Institute of the Ukrainian SSR Academy of Science.

Chandra, Rai Govind, *Indo-Greek Jewellery* (New Delhi, 1979).

Craig, Benjamin, *The Yuezhi Migration and Sogdia* (online, Creative Commons).

Cunliffe, Barry, *By Steppe, Desert, and Ocean: The Birth of Eurasia* (Oxford, 2015).

Curtis, Vesta Sarkhosh (chief ed.), *The Parthian and Early Sasanian Empires: Adaptation and Expansion* (Oxford, 2016).

Curtis, Vesta Sarkhosh and Stewart Sarah (eds), *The Age of the Parthians* (New York, 2010).

Curtis, Vesta Sarkhosh, and Stewart, Sarah (eds), *The Sasanian Era* (New York, 2010).

Daryaee, Touraj, *Sasanian Persia* (New York, 2009).

Dien, Albert, *Six Dynasties Civilization* (New Haven, 2007).

Dien, Albert, 'The Stirrup and its Effect on Chinese Military History' (available online, Silk Road Foundation).

Errington, Malcolm, *A History of the Hellenistic World* (Malden, 2008).

Fa-Hsien, *A Record of Buddhist Kingdoms*, translated by James Legge.

Fairbanks, John, and Reischauer, Edwin, *China: Tradition and Transformation* (New York, 1978).

Farrokh, Kaveh, *Sassanian Elite Cavalry AD 224-642* (Osprey, 2005).

Feltham, Heleanor, 'Lions, Silks and Silver: The Influence of Sasanian Persia', *Sino-Platonic Papers*, 2010.

Findley, Carter, *The Turks in World History* (Oxford, 2005).

Fitzgerald, C.P., *China, a Short Cultural History* (New York, 1954).

Fitzgerald, C.P., *Son of Heaven: A Biography of Li Shih-Min, Founder of the T'ang Dynasty* (Cambridge, 1933).

Fogelin, Lars, *An Archaeological History of Indian Buddhism* (Oxford, 2015).

Fogelin, Lars, *Archaeology of Early Buddhism* (New York, 2006).

Frye, Richard, 'The Political History of Iran under the Sasanians', in *Cambridge History of Iran*, vol. 3 part 1 (Cambridge, 1983).

Gabriel, Richard, *Philip II of Macedonia* (Washington DC, 2010).

Gernet, Jacques, *History of Chinese Civilization* (Cambridge UK, 1982).

Glahn, Richard von, *The Economic History of China* (Cambridge UK, 2016).

Graff, David, *Eurasian Way of War* (London, 2016).

Graff, David, *Medieval Chinese Warfare* (London, 2002).

Graff, David, and Higham, Robin (eds), *A Military History of China* (Lexington, 2012).

Grainger, John, *Rome, Parthia and India: The Violent Emergence of a New World Order 150-140 BC* (Barnsley, 2013).

Green, Peter, *Alexander of Macedon* (Berkeley, 1991).

Grousset, Rene, *The Empire of the Steppes* (New Brunswick NJ, 1970).

Hill, John, *Through the Jade Gate to Rome: A Study of the Silk Routes* during the *Later Han Dynasty 1st to 2nd Centuries CE* (privately printed by John E. Hill, 2015).

Holt, Frank, *Alexander the Great and Bactria* (Leiden, 1988).

Holt, Frank, *Into the Land of Bones: Alexander the Great in Afghanistan* (Oakland, 2012).

Holt, Frank, *Thundering Zeus: The Making of Hellenistic Bactria* (Berkeley, 1999).

Kim, Hyun Jin, *The Huns* (New York, 2016).

Lewis, Mark, *China Between Empires* (Cambridge MA, 2009).

Liang Ssu-ch'eng, *Chinese Architecture* (Cambridge MA, 1985).

Lorge, Peter, *The Asian Military Revolution* (Cambridge UK, 2008).

Lorge, Peter, *The Reunification of China* (Cambridge UK, 2015).

Lorge, Peter, *War, Politics and Society in Early Modern China* (London, 2005).

Mairs, Rachel, *The Hellenistic Far East: Archaeology, Language, and Identity in Greek Central Asia* (Oakland, 2014).

McGovern, William, *Early Empires of Central Asia* (Chapel Hill, 1939).

McLaughlin, Raoul, *The Roman Empire and the Indian Ocean* (Barnsley, 2014).

McLaughlin, Raoul, *The Roman Empire and the Silk Routes: The Ancient World Economy and the Empires of Parthia, Central Asia and Han China* (Barnsley, 2016).

Michon, Daniel, *Archaeology and Religion in early Northwest India* (New Delhi, 2015).

Parpola, Asko, *The Roots of Hinduism* (Oxford, 2015).

Pulleyblank, Edwin, *The Background of the Rebellion of An Lu-Shan* (London, 1955).

Rossabi, Morris, *A History of China* (Wiley Blackwell, 2014).

Sampson, Gareth, The *Defeat of Rome: Crassus, Carrhae and the Invasion of the East* (Barnsley, 2008).

Schafer, Edward, *The Golden Peaches of Samarkand: A Study of T'ang Exotics* (University of California, 1963).

Sinor, Denis, *The Cambridge History of Early Inner Asia* (Cambridge UK, 1990).

Sinor, Denis, 'The First Turk Empire (553-682)', in Litvinsky (ed), *History of Civilizations of Central Asia, Crossroads of Civilizations: AD 250 to 750*, vol. III.

Skaff, Jonathan, *Sui-Tang China and its Turkish Mongol Neighbors* (Oxford, 2012).

Smith, Vincent, 'The Kushan or Indo-Scythian Period of Indian History, BC 165 to AD 320', *Journal of the Royal Asiatic Society*, 14 January 1925).

Stein, M. Aurel, *Ruins of Desert Cathay* (London, 1913), vols 1 and 2, both text and pictures (available as eBook, *Internet Archive*).

Stein, M. Aurel, *Sand-Buried Khotan* (London, 1903), two volumes, text and plates (available as eBook, *Internet Archive*).

Tarn, W.W., *The Greeks in Bactria and India*, 3rd edition (Chicago, 1997).

Thonemann, Peter, *The Hellenistic World: Using Coins as Sources* (Cambridge UK, 2015).

Twitchett, Denis, *The Writing of Official History under the T'ang* (Cambridge UK, 1992).

Walter, Mariko Namba, 'Sogdians and Buddhism', *Sino-Platonic Papers*, No. 174, November 2006.

Wheatley, Paul, *The Pivot of the Four Quarters: A Preliminary Enquiry into the Origins and Character of the Ancient Chinese City* (Chicago, 1971).

Willekes, Carolyn, 'Equine Aspects of Alexander the Great's Macedonian Cavalry', in Timothy Howe, Edward Garvin and Graham Wrightson, *Greece, Macedonia, and Persia* (Philadelphia, 2015).

Worthington, Ian, *By the Spear: Philip II, Alexander the Great, and the Rise and Fall of the Macedonian Empire* (Oxford, 2014).

Wright, Arthur, 'Sixth Century China', in *Cambridge History of China*, vol. III.

Wright, Arthur, *The Sui Dynasty* (New York, 1978).

Xiong, Victor Cunrui, *Capital Cities and Urban Form in Pre-modern China, Luoyang 1038 BCE to 938 CE* (Abingdon, 2017).

Xiong, Victor Cunrui, *Emperor Yang of the Sui Dynasty* (Suny, 2006).

Yu, Taishan, 'A History of the Relationship between the Western and Eastern Han, Wei, Jin, Northern and Southern Dynasties and the Western Regions', *Sino-Platonic Papers*, No. 131, March 2004.

Yu, Taishan, 'A Study of the History of the Relationship between the Western and Eastern Han, Wei, Jin, Northern and Southern Dynasties and the Western Regions', *Sino-Platonic Papers*, No. 173, October 2006.

Yu, Taishan, 'The Origins of the Kushans', Sino-Platonic Papers, No. 212, July 2011.

Yule, Henry, *Cathay and the Way Thither*, numerous editions, final edited by Henri Cordier (1915), (available as eBook, *Internet Archive*).

Yule, Henry, *The Book of Ser Marco Polo the Venetian, Concerning the Kingdoms and Marvels of the East*, translated and annotated by Henry Yule, 3rd edition revised by Henri Cordier (London, 1903).

Zhou, Xiuqin, 'Zhaoling: The Mausoleum of Emperor Tang Taizong', *Sino-Platonic Papers*, No. 187, April 2009.

Index